WAGGING TONGUES
and
TITTLE TATTLE

© 2025 by the University of Georgia Press
Athens, Georgia 30602
www.ugapress.org
All rights reserved
Designed by Mary McKeon
Set in Minion Pro by Mary McKeon

Most University of Georgia Press titles are
available from popular e-book vendors.

Printed digitally

EU Authorized Representative
Easy Access System Europe—Mustamäe tee 50, 10621
Tallinn, Estonia, gpsr.requests@easproject.com

Library of Congress Cataloging-in-Publication Data

Names: Hoffert, Sylvia D. author
Title: Wagging tongues and tittle tattle : gossip, rumor, and reputation in a small Southern town / Sylvia D. Hoffert.
Description: Athens : University of Georgia Press, [2025] | Includes bibliographical references and index.
Identifiers: LCCN 2025025571 (print) | LCCN 2025025572 (ebook) | ISBN 9780820374987 hardback | ISBN 9780820374970 paperback | ISBN 9780820374994 epub | ISBN 9780820375007 pdf
Subjects: LCSH: Small cities—North Carolina—Hillsborough—Social life and customs—19th century | Gossip—North Carolina—Hillsborough | Rumor—North Carolina—Hillsborough | Slavery—Social aspects—North Carolina—Hillsborough | Hillsborough (N.C.)—Social life and customs—19th century | Hillsborough (N.C.—Social conditions—19th century | Hillsborough (N.C.)—Race relations
Classification: LCC F264.H7 H64 2025 (print) | LCC F264.H7 (ebook) | DDC 305.8009756/56509034—dc23/eng/20250827
LC record available at https://lccn.loc.gov/2025025571
LC ebook record available at https://lccn.loc.gov/2025025572

WAGGING TONGUES
and
TITTLE TATTLE

Gossip, Rumor, and Reputation
in a Small Southern Town

Sylvia D. Hoffert

The University of Georgia Press
Athens

CONTENTS

Introduction / 1

CHAPTER 1. More Than Idle Chatter / 15

CHAPTER 2. Almost (But Not Quite) Free / 37

CHAPTER 3. School Days, Rule Days / 63

CHAPTER 4. To Work the Livelong Day / 93

CHAPTER 5. The Plague of Madness in Our Midst / 123

Conclusion / 147

Acknowledgments / 157

A Note on Sources / 159

Notes / 163

Bibliography / 197

Index / 215

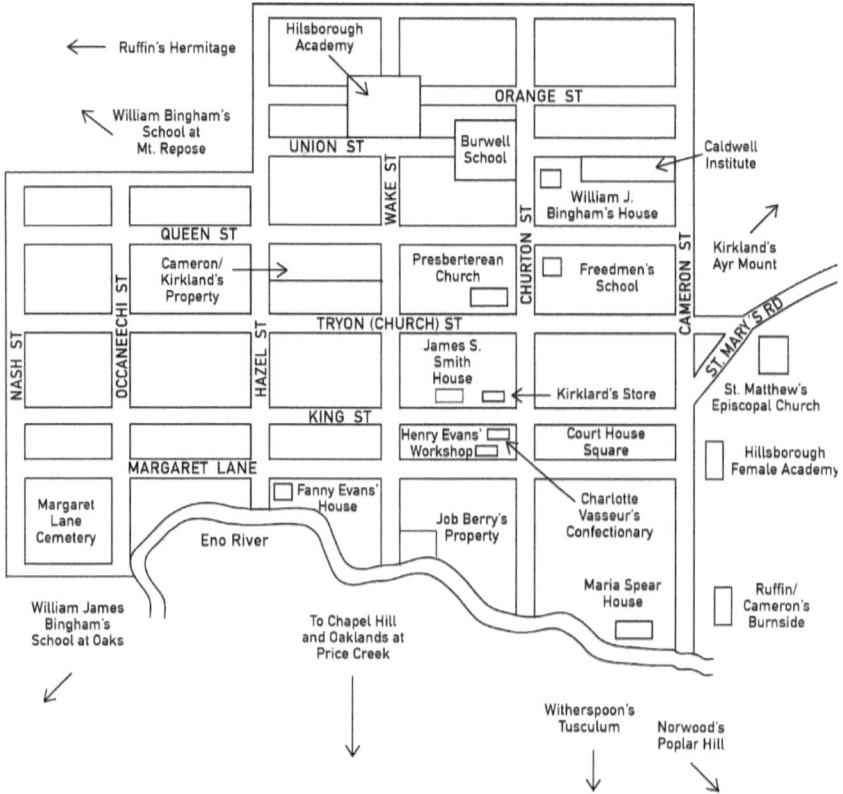

Antebellum Hillsborough, North Carolina.

INTRODUCTION

If it hadn't been for the Eno River and the Great Indian Trading path that crossed it, there might never have been a Hillsborough, North Carolina. The Occaneechi were the last of the Indigenous population to settle where the river, flanked by ridges and bluffs, curves in a U-shape around the flood plain as if cradling it in its arms. Its headwaters begin to the north and west of town. Fed by the creeks and springs along its path, it snakes its way east for forty miles past Hillsborough until it joins the Flat River to form the Neuse. Its flow and appearance depend on the season and weather. Its water turns brown with silt in the spring as it catches the melting snow and rain. In the heat of the summer, the tree canopy along its banks filters out the light and dapples the landscape. The river becomes a mere trickle in those places where it must make its way around boulders, debris, and fallen tree limbs. In the autumn, speckled leaves swirl together like dancing partners as they float along its surface. Gray skies turn it murky. But in the winter sunshine, it flows crisp and clear toward the sea.

Before they arrived in North Carolina, the Occaneechi made their mark in Virginia as traders and guides. Caught up in an intra–Native American struggle between the Susquehannock people, the Piscataway people, and the Five Nations, and competing with both their Indigenous neighbors and the English to control the land and trade along the Roanoke River, they were defeated by white settlers under the command of Nathaniel Bacon in 1676. Their response was to pack up their belongings, abandon their settlement, and make their way south to a ford on the Eno, a site well suited for farming, trading in furs and deerskins, and monitoring traffic along the Great Trading Path that connected Virginia with the Georgia backcountry. There they built a palisade to protect themselves from their enemies. Inside their fortress was a central plaza surrounded by bark-covered roundhouses, storage sheds, and a sweat lodge for ritual purification, cleansing, and healing. According to archeological studies, they buried their dead just outside the entrance to the stockade. Theirs was a subsistence economy based on hunting deer, small animals, and wild turkeys; gathering acorns, hickory nuts, wild fruits, and berries; and raising corn, beans, and squash. They did their best to control commerce along the trading paths in the area by serving as guides, establishing their own trade networks, and offering hospitality to explorers and the traders whose pack trains could include as many as one hundred horses each carrying 150 to 200 pounds of salable goods across the Eno into territory to the south.

It was there on the Eno that John Lawson, sent by royal authorities in New Bern to explore the colony's backcountry, found them. In 1709 he published *A New Voyage to Carolina*, which served as promotional literature for white settlement by describing the area as a wilderness paradise. Extolling the virtues of Piedmont land with its virgin timber, fertile soil, and abundant wildlife, he assured future settlers that the area was full of promise.

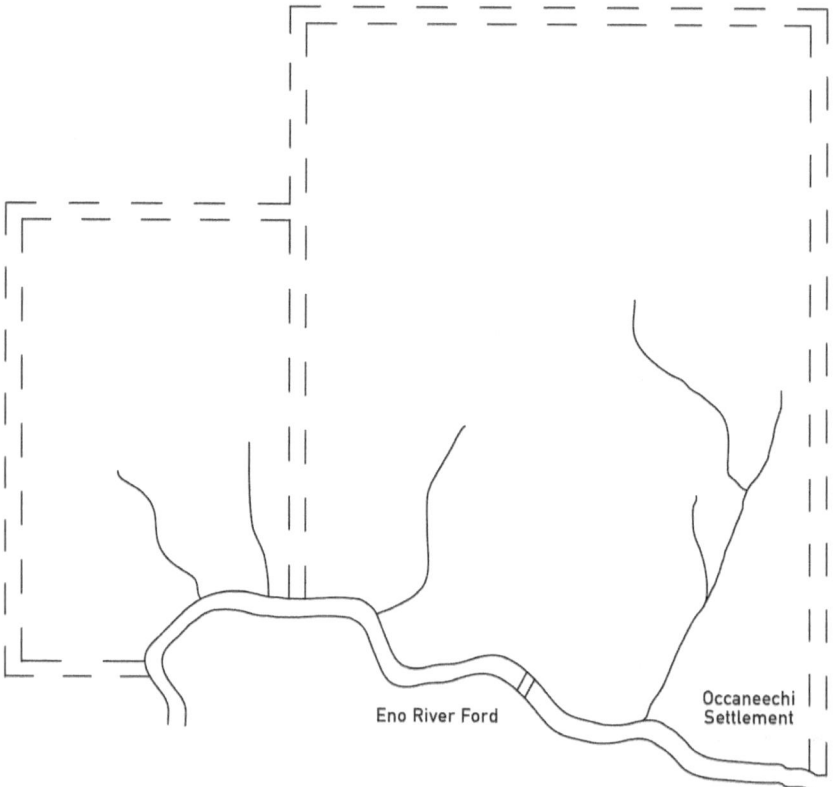

Site of Hillsborough, 1700.

By the time of Lawson's visit, smallpox, measles, and influenza—diseases that accompanied settlers and traders along the trading paths—had begun to decimate the Native population. The remains of young adults found by archeologists in the Occaneechi cemetery in Hillsborough suggest that those most susceptible to such diseases were the very people the community depended on for economic production and political leadership. Military losses resulting from the Occaneechi's attempts to maintain their dominance over trade also contributed to the depopulation of their settlement. When it became impossible for them to continue as a community, the Occaneechi deserted their village. Some of them returned to Virginia and settled around Fort Christiana in Brunswick County. Other remnants migrated up the trading path and settled in existing Saponi communities in Orange County. A few families remained.[1] It was on their land on the banks of the Eno that the small town of Hillsborough was built.

Despite the fact that the South was sprinkled with villages serving the needs of a largely rural population, it was not until 1994 with the publication of Darrett and Anita H. Rutman's essay "The Village South" that those interested in the history of the American South began to recognize the important role that small towns played in the development of the region and the symbiotic relationship that existed between those who lived in towns and the people who lived in the countryside that surrounded them.[2] More than mere crossroads marked by the presence of a general store, a mill, a blacksmith shop, or an isolated church, small towns provided critical services for a largely rural population—a courthouse where they could register their deeds, lawyers who could help them settle their disputes, doctors willing to treat their broken bones and fevers, ministers who tended to their spiritual needs, teachers who could educate some of their children, and shopkeepers who could sell them what they could not produce for themselves. It was in small towns that farmers and entrepreneurs could access public and private sources of credit that allowed them to buy land, purchase or hire a work force, and invest in manufacturing equipment to set up mills, tanneries, and distilleries. Small towns served as cultural centers providing entertainment that broke up the tedium of everyday life and schools where the affluent could educate their children. It was from towns like Hillsborough that farmers and businessmen sent raw materials, agricultural products, and manufactured goods to larger markets, first by wagon and eventually by railroad. It was from small towns that former students, who had studied at their academies, spread out across the state to become leaders in the economic, political, and religious lives of their communities. Throughout the nineteenth century, small towns provided homes and employment in agriculture, commerce, manufacturing, and service industries for their white, Black, and mixed-race inhabitants. Together, free and enslaved, they formed communities and networks of face-to-face human relationships that gave each town its character.[3]

Prompted by the Rutmans' call to broaden the focus of southern history beyond county and regional studies, the region's major cities, and plantation life, scholars such as Christopher Hedricks, Warren Hofstra, and Craig Friend began to explore the factors that led to the early development of southern small towns.[4] Others wrote longitudinal histories of such places employing a fairly narrow, often antiquarian and celebratory narrative pattern focusing on prominent citizens and the economic, civic, and cultural institutions they helped develop.[5] As a whole, such studies provide little more than glimpses of the ordinary people, free and enslaved, who populated towns and their environs, supplied the labor for their development, made use of the services they offered, and sometimes disrupted the peace and tranquility of their households. Apart from Lisa Tolbert, they have little to say about the human dimension of small-town life, the interpersonal relationships of those who lived there, and the factors that influenced those relationships.[6] Ignoring such matters obscures the power struggles and tensions that a town's inhabitants dealt with on a daily basis.

Using a particularly rich collection of primary sources including diaries, letters, memoirs, newspapers, census data, public records, and church records relating to Hillsborough, I employ a biographical approach in this microhistory to argue that gossip and rumor were central to the formation of interpersonal relationships and an integral part of small-town life.[7] They exposed the insecurities and anxieties of the town's inhabitants. They served as an important weapon in the power struggle between whites and their slaveholding elite and the Black and mixed-race men and women, free and enslaved, who did their best to challenge white claims to social, political, and economic dominance. They fed upon an underlying culture of racial violence that permeated everyday life. And they exposed fissures in the social fabric that discretion, good manners, and historical amnesia could not obscure.

Gossip in a place like Hillsborough was ubiquitous.[8] Repeated in parlor, church, and tavern, and on the streets as well in the living quarters of the enslaved and their work environments, it often distorted the facts but nevertheless served a variety of functions from trying to establish and enforce commonly accepted standards of behavior and negotiating racial and gender conventions to managing information and providing entertainment.[9] Oral communication in the form of gossip and rumor had enormous implications in places such as Hillsborough where only the white elite were likely to be literate, where people lived in close proximity to each other, and where lack of privacy made it easy to monitor each other's behavior. It took on a particular urgency in the slaveholding South where the white population was hypersensitive to anything that portended a challenge to white supremacy and where the personal security of the town's Black and mixed-race inhabitants depended on access to information that had implications for their well-being and future.

Gossip oiled Hillsborough's news network and helped determine the way its inhabitants, whatever their station in life, related to each other, how they ran their households, how they conducted business, and the way they approached mental health issues. Whether benign or malicious, judgmental talk between two or more acquaintances about the private affairs of absent third parties moved fast through the town's neighborhoods. Typically considered the purview of women, gossip served men's interests as well since "intelligence" regarding their neighbors helped them manage their business affairs and influenced their political opinions.[10] As might have been expected, those who heard and repeated it did not dwell on its unreliability.

The topics included in town gossip were endless. It was through the grapevine that people learned who among them drank too much, who beat their wives and abused their enslaved workers, who was a reliable laborer, who was about to be given away or sold, what employment opportunities might exist, who was a soft touch for a loan, who couldn't be relied on to pay their bills, and who had trouble controlling their temper. Household servants, whether free or enslaved, were a gold mine of information about the intimate lives of those they served. A laundress might be the first to know who was pregnant. Housemaids could tell you who did or did not sleep in which bedroom. Gossip played a critical role in local politics and helped determine who won or lost elections.

Closely associated with gossip is rumor. The two terms are commonly used interchangeably, but, for purposes of this study, I argue that there is a subtle difference between the two. Both can be true or false, and both express anxieties that pervade people's lives. But while gossip tends to focus on a judgmental assessment of an absent individual, is typically spread among a small group of people who know each other, and more often than not concerns past behavior, rumor spreads among people who do not necessarily have an interpersonal relationship. Speculative and anticipatory in nature, rumor usually concerns something that is about to happen, seeks to clarify the ambiguities found in everyday life, and is intended to provoke a response or defense mechanism to avoid some perceived potential threat. Gossip and rumors sometimes work in tandem in the sense that what may have started as gossip about an individual could transition into a rumor regarding something of concern to the larger community, such as a threat to public safety or the stability of the town's credit market.[11] Both had a profound influence on the social politics of a small town like Hillsborough.

The influence of gossip and rumor was grounded in the fact that many of Hillsborough's residents were concerned with establishing and maintaining their reputations for respectability based on their self-presentation and known history. In the South as in the rest of the country, the opinion of others not only determined one's place in the ordered ranks of society but also could not be separated from a person's sense of inner worth no matter their race or social class.[12] Concern about reputation had real impact on how white, Black, and mixed-race men, women, and children presented themselves to each other, judged the behavior of their friends and neighbors, and tried to hold them to account. It held white men honor bound to take care of dependent relatives. An oral pledge from a gentleman was thought to be the equivalent of a signed oath. Men considered drinking and gambling excusable if a man fulfilled his civic responsibilities and financial obligations to his family. Fear of insulting a friend made it extremely difficult to refuse to guarantee his debts. And reverence for ancestry and male bloodlines meant that when someone asked, "Who are your people?" they were not just making conversation.[13]

Gossip, rumor, and concern for reputation also had implications for white women and their children. They gave a woman the power to uphold or undermine a man's reputation while society demanded that she be outwardly submissive to male authority, chaste before marriage, and self-sacrificing after it in order to protect her own. They put immense pressure on sons to match the character and exceed the accomplishments of their fathers and grandfathers on one hand, or to make up for their failures on the other. Their sisters learned early on that their marriage prospects hinged on avoiding any action that might result in talk of possible youthful sexual impropriety.[14]

Gossip and the reputations that it helped form influenced the Black and mixed-race community somewhat differently. It had tremendous influence on the ability of a free Black or mixed-race man or woman to support his or her family. And it could be used to either preserve or undermine their freedom. Among the enslaved, it could provide information crucial to their physical and mental well-being. It made a reputation for obedience, loyalty, and industriousness the price to be paid in order to avoid the constant surveillance of white owners and neighbors.[15] It could exacerbate already tense relationships between the enslaved and their enslavers and be used to justify both physical and mental mistreatment. And it could threaten the integrity and stability of enslaved families and communities.

Hillsborough, the place where all this gossip and the spread of rumors took place, had only 474 inhabitants living in sixty-five households in 1800.[16] At the time, it had a market house and a few taverns. But there was not a school in sight, and its Anglican church had been abandoned as a house of worship after the revolution when it lost its funding from the state.[17] Its streets were a sea of red mud when it rained, a condition that would plague its residents for many years.[18] In dry weather, plumes of dust the color of bricks rose from behind passing wagons and settled on laundry left hanging out to dry. Weeds, sometimes waist high, impeded the progress of pedestrians on Hillsborough's side streets in the summer when the odor of horse manure and rotting garbage added an extra degree of unpleasantness to the heat and humidity.[19]

By the 1830s Hillsborough had begun to grow. According to historian Robert Kenzer, it would reach a population of 942 by 1860.[20] Clapboard-sided houses slowly replaced the one-room cabins of the early settlers. Entrepreneurs such as Duncan Cameron, William Kirkland, Thomas Ruffin, and James Webb, who had accumulated wealth in real and enslaved property, built their houses on town lots or large farms not far from town. With their wives and children, they formed the core of the town's social and economic elite.[21] They and their friends dominated political affairs at local, state, and national levels and provided the financial resources and

One of Hillsborough's early buildings, the Faddis Tavern provided travelers with lodging, food, and drink while serving as a community center for social and political activities. Courtesy of the Mary Claire Engstrom Photographic Collection, Wilson Special Collections Library, UNC–Chapel Hill.

enslaved labor to help build the white infrastructure that allowed Hillsborough to flourish. As the nineteenth century progressed, multigenerational slave-owning families consolidated their social, economic, and political power. The town still had its courthouse, the site of quarterly court sessions, which brought judges, witnesses, lawyers, and their clients to town and offered nearby farmers the opportunity to take a holiday from their chores. They and their families converged on the town, temporarily swelling its population and disrupting the rhythms of daily life with public auctions, militia drills, horse racing, and politicking. Its streets were still a quagmire when it rained. But it also had raised flagstone sidewalks, a post office, a newspaper, four churches, highly successful schools for white girls and boys, and a commercial center along Churton Street with specialty shops and general stores. Old King Street Tavern and the Colonial Inn stood on side streets, and a whole range of businesses from tanneries and saddleries to brickyards and lumberyards stood along the river. Through the years, community leaders created voluntary organizations that played an important role in tying the white citizens of Hillsborough to each other regardless of social class. A Masonic lodge, a Sunday school union, a lyceum and literary club, and a temperance union provided outlets for white philanthropic, intellectual, and communal impulses.[22]

Hillsborough's inhabitants saw each other regularly at the market house or making their way down the streets. The town's white population congregated at the courthouse, at church, or in the taverns. They attended election rallies, concerts, school examinations, Bible study, Masonic lodge meetings, Sunday school classes, and private social occasions. Familiarity did not impinge on the hierarchical nature of their association, however. As one of the Webb descendants put it many years later, "Here in this small village lived 'the people' and 'the other people,' attending the same churches, doing business together, exchanging friendly greetings when they met abroad, but in their homes living an entirely separate existence, never exchanging visits or intermarrying."[23] She, of course, was referring to white people. The invisibility of the Black, mixed-race, and enslaved populations in her formulation of who counted in Hillsborough and the historical amnesia that virtually erased their contributions to community life underscores the degree to which Hillsborough was a community divided against itself by race as well as class.

The text that follows chronicles the lives of an ensemble of white, Black,

Raised sidewalks helped protect the ladies' petticoats from being soiled by the red mud that filled the streets when it rained. Courtesy of the Mary Claire Engstrom Photographic Collection, Wilson Special Collections Library, UNC–Chapel Hill.

and mixed-race men, women, and children, free and enslaved, who inhabited Hillsborough and the land surrounding it in the early nineteenth century and into the post–Civil War period. It demonstrates how gossip, rumor, and concern for reputation worked together to determine the quality of their relationships with each other, negotiate racial boundaries, reflect the collective anxieties of the population, and expose the tensions that plagued their lives.

A word should be said about the way the materials for this book have been gathered together. Building on the efforts of history professor J. G. de Roulhac Hamilton to create a southern history archive at the University of North Carolina, some of Hillsborough's most prominent families donated their papers to the Southern Historical Collection as well as other repositories. Mary Claire Engstrom, a Hillsborough resident, spent the 1960s collecting not only images of Hillsborough and its people (now in the

Southern Historical Collection) but also the letters and diaries of schoolmistress Margaret Anna Burwell, known as Anna. She also began a project intended to profile her students and collect letters and artifacts related to their sojourn at the Burwell School. The Historic Hillsborough Commission, which now owns the buildings that once made up the Burwell School for young ladies, and its research committee have built on her work over the years by continuing to collect documents relating to the history of the school and the Burwell family as well as their students, domestic workers, friends, and neighbors, which they have carefully stored away in acid-free boxes located in one of the upstairs rooms where boarding students once slept. Stewart Dunaway has compiled and published a two-volume history of town lots that traces ownership of the land within the town's boundaries back to the eighteenth century and provides a picture of how Hillsborough's inhabitants related to each other spatially. Historian Jean Bradley Anderson published biographical profiles of the Kirklands and the Camerons, two of the area's most notable families. Peter H. Wood wrote a small pamphlet chronicling the contributions that Hillsborough's Black and mixed-race inhabitants made to the town. And local historian Betty Eidenier not only generously shared her own research with me but also, along with Janie Morris, coordinated the publication of materials related to the lives of enslaved and free people of color in early nineteenth-century Hillsborough, including a useful compilation of census data, profiles of those who worked at the Burwell School, and a list of those associated with the white-dominated Episcopal church. Those church records were easily accessible because in the many years he served as rector of St. Matthew's Episcopal Church, Rev. Brooks Graebner carefully preserved materials documenting the role that the church members played in the history of the town. The Presbyterians were equally conscientious about keeping records of the activities of their congregation. Mark Chilton, the register of deeds in Orange County, digitized apprenticeship records as well as material relating to the transfer of estate and enslaved property to be found in county records, thus making them easily accessible to the general public. And access to Ancestry.com and digitized newspaper collections was critical to recreating the world inhabited by Hillsborough's residents.

As is the case in every small town, the historical record that its inhabitants left behind and the collective stories they told about themselves are replete with sometimes complementary, sometimes competing narratives.

One kind of storyline has been documented and interpreted by researchers willing to spend solitary days in darkened rooms reading microfilm, checking Ancestry.com on their computers, or bending their heads over impossible-to-decipher letters and diaries in the quiet chamber of an archive. That narrative is in a constant state of flux as information from new documents comes to light and adds nuance to our understanding of a people and their past. What seemed a valid interpretation based on the evidence available one day can be rendered less reliable based on new information discovered the next.

A second kind of narrative comes from outside academia. In small towns where people gossip and have long memories, those stories are the ones passed down orally through generations of families and their neighbors.[24] Oral history and its cousin, historical gossip, may or may not be verifiable in the documents available; but for the people who understand their place in the world partly because of their memories and oral tradition, such stories have a validity that transcends anything a scholar might have to say. Their crucial role in constructing a sense of community explains why belief in their legitimacy persists in the face of contradictory evidence or no evidence at all.

Finally, there are the stories that have been forgotten or ignored, sometimes unintentionally, but more often quite deliberately in order to protect reputations, retain social and political power, or bury shame. For Hillsborough's white elite, pride of place and family allowed them to belie the evils of slavery and their role in perpetuating a labor system that was anything but benign. Such blindness to the realities of slavery encouraged them to convince themselves, for example, that it was "poor whites who could scrape up enough to buy only one or two slaves, who treated them with indifference to their welfare. None of the 'Best people' were cruel to their slaves."[25]

By its very nature, the process of selecting, collecting, and archiving the papers of prominent families privileges their stories over others. The reluctance of the formerly enslaved to pass down to their grandchildren and great-grandchildren stories of the undeserved humiliations and indignities imposed on them while in bondage allowed them to focus on their resilience in facing the challenges inherent in adjusting to freedom. Collective amnesia served as a balm to soothe memories of a painful past and helped expedite the process of forging new identities as a free people. Such forgetting helps mask the tensions and power struggles that continue to prevail among Hillsborough's inhabitants.

It is impossible to explore what neighbors meant to and how they related to each other without taking these factors into account and without being aware that the passing of time brings shifting changes in sensibilities and perspectives that affect the way they tell their stories and the way we interpret what they said. Respecting these sometimes disparate and contradictory narratives allows us to see how history and memory intersect to help the people in a small-town frame their understanding of who they are and where they have come from.[26]

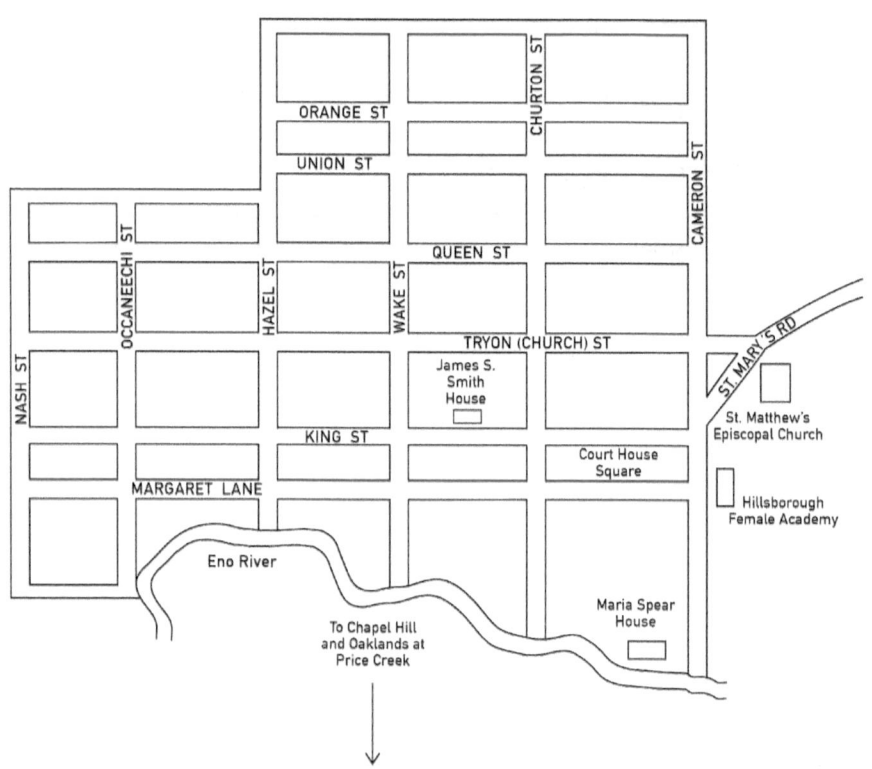

1
MORE THAN IDLE CHATTER

In May 1831 an outraged Maria Spear wrote to her friend Catharine Ruffin, the daughter of North Carolina Supreme Court justice Thomas Ruffin then living in Raleigh, regarding slanderous gossip concerning Mary Ruffin Smith, Maria's former student, protégé, and best friend. Mary had been unjustly accused, Maria said, of whipping one of the enslaved servants in her parents' household and then pouring "boiling peas" down her throat, cutting another with a knife and then whipping her for letting her wounds be seen, and beating a third with a pair of tongs.[1] The accusations against Mary reveal where the fault lines in Hillsborough's white society lay in its treatment of the enslaved and provide an example of what sort of person was most vulnerable to the kind of small talk that could threaten their reputation and place in the community.

Mary was the seventeen-year-old daughter of Dr. James Strudwick Smith, the head of a family who turned out to be particularly vulnerable to defamation.[2] Her father's origins are obscure. He was born in Orange County in 1787 and may have been the illegitimate child of the then eighteen-year-old William F. Strudwick against whom bastardy charges were issued in 1788.[3] Whatever the case, James grew up near Hillsborough, and as he approached adulthood he began to study medicine with local doctor James Webb. In 1811, with the help of his mentor and the immensely wealthy and influential planter Duncan Cameron, he was able to enroll in the medical program at the University of Pennsylvania. Insufficient funds forced him to return to Hillsborough to set up his practice after two years without completing his course of study. Without a social pedigree or an academic degree to smooth his way, James was determined to distinguish himself through the practice of medicine, public service, and business.

When he wasn't tending the sick, he volunteered to fill municipal offices—town trustee, justice of the peace, and police commissioner—presumably with the hope that the town fathers would note his willingness to serve, listen when he spoke, and elevate him to more important and prestigious positions of leadership even when they disagreed with him. Eventually elected to the state legislature and the U.S. Congress, he also served as a delegate to the 1835 North Carolina constitutional convention. He joined

Physician, civic leader, politician, and business entrepreneur, James Strudwick Smith was the patriarch of one of the most gossiped-about families in Hillsborough. Courtesy of the State Archives of North Carolina, Raleigh.

the Masons, served St. Matthew's Episcopal Church as a vestryman, and sat on the board of the Hillsborough Female Academy, a local school for young ladies.⁴

In the nineteenth century, southern doctors had difficulty maintaining a steady income, and what they received for services rendered was more likely to have been in the form of goods such as firewood, fresh eggs, or free labor rather than cash.⁵ In Hillsborough, the problem was exacerbated by an overabundance of doctors all competing for a finite number of patients.⁶ In order to solve this problem, James turned elsewhere to supplement his meager income and borrowed money guaranteed by his friends and associates to invest in land and a wide variety of business enterprises as well as the enslaved labor needed to run them. His propensity to thrust himself forward made him the focus of many public and private conversations, not all of them flattering. It was to be expected that the increasingly venomous partisanship that was emerging in the early nineteenth century would influence the way his neighbors talked about him. But his brash self-promotion and reckless business practices caused people who counted in Hillsborough to conclude that he was pursuing his ambitions with unseemly enthusiasm. Willie P. Mangum, a fellow Orange County politician, referred to him as a "puffing" doctor. And when asked to give a deposition in a lawsuit involving James, his mentor Dr. James Webb remarked that he was not to be trusted when his interests were at stake.⁷

James's marriage to Delia Jones in 1813 improved his economic prospects but did nothing to enhance his personal reputation or social standing. Delia's father, Francis Jones, owned some three thousand acres of land south of Chapel Hill on the Orange-Chatham county line and had provided for her inheritance, but he was more interested in accumulating land and an enslaved workforce than he was in guaranteeing his daughter's intellectual development or social position. Despite the fact that she was an heiress, Delia came to her marriage without the education or social graces that would have helped her carve out a place for herself, her husband, and her children among Hillsborough's social elite. In her letter to Catharine Ruffin, Maria described Mary's mother as an unrefined, "ignorant woman" who spoke in "ungrammatical language." James did not place much importance on buying her the clothes or providing her with the household amenities that would have enabled her to socialize comfortably with the other ladies of Hillsborough. And at a time when religious affiliation was a prerequisite for female respectability, she did not seek church membership even though her husband served on the Episcopalian vestry.[8] Given those circumstances, it is not surprising that while James frequently hobnobbed with men of great wealth, impeccable social credentials, and impressive power and influence, Delia did not move easily among their wives, who, according to Maria, made her the focus of a great deal of hurtful gossip.[9]

The Smiths were social climbers trying to make their way in Hillsborough society, not really one of "the people." Instead, James and his family found themselves in the "other people" category. Given those circumstances, seventeen-year-old Mary was fair game for the town's rumormongers. There was little risk for them in gossiping about her. "Tall, angular, dark-haired, sallow-skinned," Mary was no beauty.[10] She was a bookish, introverted, awkward teenager with no social capital of her own. And she belonged to a family whose social position was tentative at best. There was little she could do on her own to refute the allegations made against her.

Mary lived in a community where the social and economic elite depended on enslaved labor to ensure their comfort and financial well-being. Hillsborough's early white settlers either brought enslaved workers with them when they moved to town or purchased them after they arrived. By the 1830s, one-third of the population in Orange County was enslaved.[11] There is no evidence to indicate that even the most religious of Hillsborough's slave owners questioned the morality of slaveholding.[12] Most enslavers had been reared in a culture where slavery was believed to have been sanctioned by God and where a slaveholding ethic held that masters were obliged to take care of those they enslaved in return for their labor.[13] They considered slaveholding to be a good investment in that it provided them with the labor to run their households and various enterprises, collateral for loans, rental income when they needed ready cash, or assets that could be sold in the event of a financial emergency.[14]

Mary grew up watching her parents trying to manage enslaved workers. By the time she was six, her father owned or rented nine enslaved laborers, some of whom worked in the house while others provided the labor necessary to run his various business enterprises.[15] When she was ten, her grandfather Jones deeded her a six-year-old enslaved child named Patsy (or Betsy).[16] And by the time she was in her teens and was accused of abusing the family's enslaved servants, her father owned or employed a total of seventeen enslaved workers.[17]

Maintaining discipline in the slaveholding South was crucial for sustaining both its economic system and its hierarchical, class-based society. There were at least two competing narratives about how to best ensure the obedience of enslaved workers. The first sanctioned whipping as a form of discipline when it was used as a correction rather than a punishment and administered immediately without anger or malice in a manner consistent with the offense.[18] The second, directed at southern housewives, warned that such severe disciplinary measures would only make the management of enslaved workers more difficult.[19]

As historian Thavolia Glymph has pointed out, the inhumane behavior that Hillsborough's gossips attributed to Mary was pervasive if not condoned in slaveholding households throughout the South. Judged on their skills as domestic managers, white housekeepers who enslaved their domestic staff created exploitative working conditions that often resulted in attempts on the part of those who were forced to do their bidding to thwart their power and ignore their instructions. Glymph has described the domestic environment in slaveholding households in terms of "a kind of warring intimacy" where enslaved domestic workers resisted the demands made on them and their owners responded to that resistance with both psychological and physical violence.[20]

The treatment of enslaved workers needs to be understood within a context where white women often struggled to assert their autonomy in a deeply masculine world. They benefited from their place as white. But racial hierarchies created unbalanced power relations that often led to the use of unjustified violence to maintain what little power they had. The result was that when frustrations overwhelmed good sense and Christian charity, tempers flared, and it was all too easy for the mistress of the house to resort to abusive language or reach for the nearest weapon.

As gossip about Mary made its way through the local grapevine, Maria Spear was quick to dispute it. Ten years Mary's senior, Maria had been born in London and immigrated to New York with her parents. They sent her to school in Philadelphia, where an Englishman, Thomas P. Jones, supervised her education.[21] In 1818 he and his father-in-law, Joseph Andrews, purchased the highly regarded Warrenton Female Academy in Warrenton, North Carolina, and moved south to continue their work, taking Maria with them.[22] After Maria finished her education, she taught at the Wadesborough Female Academy in Anson County, North Carolina, until 1826 when she accepted a position to teach at the newly established Hillsborough Female Academy on Margaret Lane run by Rev. William Mercer Green, the Episcopalian rector.[23]

Described as "a prim" young woman "with cork screw curls," hazel eyes, and a notably fine complexion, Maria was a single, twenty-two-year-old when she arrived in Hillsborough, accompanied by her mother, also named Maria; her aunt, Susan Esther Baker; her sisters, Mary Ann and Elizabeth; and her brothers, William and Charles. Her father's conspicuous absence suggests that she was forced by circumstances to trade on her parents' investment in her education to become the breadwinner of the family. Her aunt bought a house near the school and the Episcopal church and employed enslaved domestic servants. As members of a family of intense piety and evangelical sensibilities, Maria and her mother, sister, and aunt joined Green's congregation shortly after their arrival.[24]

Maria's friendship with Mary began when Mary's father enrolled her in Maria's class and placed her under Maria's "particular care."[25] Like any socially ambitious father, James intended to provide Mary with the opportunity to associate with the daughters of Hillsborough's social and economic elite while she absorbed those intellectual and social refinements that had apparently eluded his wife. Mary was a serious and intelligent young woman of twelve when she started school. She was eager to embrace the intellectual rigor of the classroom, did exceptionally well in her studies, and earned high marks in every subject.[26] After she finished the school's curriculum, she convinced her father to allow her to continue her studies privately with Maria, allowing the two of them to spend as much time as possible together. By May 1831 the two young women had known each other for five years and had developed a friendship that, according to Maria, was characterized by "the closest, confidential intimacy."[27] In short, they were devoted to each other.[28]

Given their regard for each other, it is not surprising that Maria defended Mary with striking emotional intensity. The stories about Mary were "cruel," Maria said, and "the most unaccountable piece of malice that I have ever heard of." She reported that Mary was distraught at the thought that she could be accused of such things. Maria assured Catharine that such rumors were "utterly false" and argued that there were two reasons why the rumors could not be true. First, she said, Mary could not have abused the workers enslaved by her family because she was temperamentally incapable of such cruelty. She had, Maria wrote, never exhibited the sort of "dreadful, ungovernable temper" that would have prompted such action. Rather, Maria had always been impressed with Mary's "forgiving disposition in instances where I know she was very ill-treated." Even in this instance, she said, Mary had solemnly declared that she did not bear "the least malice towards those who are the inventors of these reports although she is grieving herself to death about them." Moreover, Maria claimed that Mary was physically unable to have abused her family's enslaved servants because she was only just recovering from a long illness.[29]

From the distance of almost two hundred years, there is no way to determine if Maria's defense was justified. On one hand, the gossip may have been completely fabricated by someone who had a grudge against Mary. In particular, the charge that she was able to pour boiling peas down another woman's throat all by herself seems implausible. On the other hand, it is possible that Mary, who had been ill and may have been feeling out of sorts and short-tempered, did in some way abuse one or more of the Smiths' domestic workers. Maria admitted that Mary did not know how to effectively manage her family's household staff. "I have often observed," she wrote, "that she [Mary] was a great deal more submissive than I thought proper, and I know very well that she cannot get one of them, even the little ones, to do a thing for her, unless they choose." Maria had advised Mary to complain about the situation to her parents, but Mary, apparently unwilling to expose her administrative inadequacies to them, refused.[30] That being the case, there is no reason to believe that Mary was immune from the frustrations associated with having to deal with what she perceived to be persistently disobedient or disrespectful enslaved household workers.

The nature and function of this particular piece of gossip must be understood within the context in which it was initiated and spread. Spreading hearsay was not just a random activity or a source of entertainment for people with too much time on their hands. Neither frivolous nor trivial, it was one among a number of mechanisms designed to establish and sustain relationships in small groups, monitor public and private conduct, judge whether an individual was conforming to social conventions, and sanction those whose behavior was deemed unacceptable.[31] Local ordinances, for example, identified disturbing the peace or public drunkenness as unacceptable and provided punishment for such breaches of proper behavior. Governing bodies of some of the local churches held their members to high standards of conduct. The Session of the Hillsborough Presbyterian Church passed judgment on its members for all kinds of unchristian behavior ranging from slave trading and gambling to using profanity, threatening the unrepentant with suspension of membership or dismissal from the congregation.[32] Gossip provided yet another way to identify, judge, and censure those whose behavior did not reflect community values and conventions. It was an important component in the oil that smoothed the wheels of social, economic, and political intercourse in the town. And by identifying those moral and behavioral values that most of Hillsborough's inhabitants held in common and wanted to enforce, it helped build a sense of solidarity and community among them.[33]

In this case, the issue at stake was treatment of the enslaved. An ever-present, haunting fear of being unable to control one-third of the population terrified slave- and non-slave-owning families alike in Orange County, leaving them hypersensitive to any evidence of insubordination among those they held in bondage. Their anxiety was exacerbated by the appearance of David Walker's pamphlet, *Appeal to the Colored Citizens of the World*, which denounced southern slavery and called on the enslaved to rise up and kill their masters. Printed in Boston in 1829, Walker's appeal did not attract the attention of North Carolina authorities until August 1830, when a magistrate of police in Wilmington reported to the governor that a copy of the pamphlet was being distributed in his jurisdiction.[34]

Unsubstantiated rumors of conspiracies fed the fears of the state's white population and left them alert to any sign of resistance on the part of their enslaved workers.[35] In late December 1830 Charles Pettigrew, then a student in Hillsborough, wrote to his father that a rumor about a slave insurrection had begun to circulate in town. The town's enslaved population, the rumormongers said, had been implicated in a plot initiated by their counterparts in Chatham County and Chapel Hill to kill their masters and then "assemble at the place of rendezvous and march directly to Hillsborough where they might have plenty of arms and ammunition and kill all the people there."[36] It is unclear how the plot was discovered. One version asserted that two lady's maids told their mistresses about the plot and its timing. Another claimed it was a Black woman who told some children of the plot, reporting that the plan was to kill all the white men but spare "some of the handsomest of the white women" so that the leaders of the revolt could marry them. And yet another maintained that a preacher had stirred up the "negroes" in Chapel Hill and Hillsborough.[37]

Whatever the rumor's origins, the white citizens of Hillsborough took it seriously. They armed themselves, sent to Raleigh for more weapons, and formed a temporary militia of twelve companies with about ten men in each company to patrol the streets of the town and surrounding area at night. And they designated the Masonic hall, next door to the Smith house, as the place of rendezvous for women and children in event of attack.[38] There was no Christmas insurrection, but the rumor had long-term consequences. It fueled white fear of their Black and mixed-race neighbors, which was only exacerbated in January 1831 by William Lloyd Garrison's publication of *The Liberator*, which called for the immediate end of slavery in the United States.[39]

The discovery of Walker's pamphlet in their midst, rumors about a slave insurrection in Hillsborough, and the publication of *The Liberator* coming within months of one another would have done little to calm the nerves of Hillsborough's white citizens. It was in this climate of hypersensitivity about keeping the potentially rebellious enslaved in check that Hillsborough's gossips began talking about Mary's treatment of her family's enslaved domestics. The specificity of the description of real or imagined violence that Mary was alleged to have inflicted on defenseless servants held in bondage not only exposed the gossips' appreciation of the brutality of slavery but also laid bare their unarticulated fear that there was a direct connection between the way enslaved servants were treated and their own personal safety. Neither of these concerns could have been straightforwardly articulated in public by southerners complicit in defending and perpetuating such a labor system. But gossip—accompanied by an appropriate degree of self-righteous anger, indignation, and outrage—provided a way to address such issues, directed attention away from others in the community who were known to lose their tempers when dealing with enslaved servants, and reassured anyone who was listening that white citizens of Hillsborough had a collective abhorrence about using corporal punishment to discipline enslaved servants.[40]

How or whether the controversy over the charges leveled against Mary was resolved is unclear. But the damage had been done. Those responsible for spreading the gossip had separated themselves from the Smiths by making a social pariah of Mary. The Smiths might have been able to survive this social setback had the gossips left them alone. But circumstances conspired to keep them in the crosshairs of neighbors who continued to closely monitor their behavior.

Three years after Mary suffered the mortification of being singled out by her neighbors as a cruel and heartless mistress, she turned twenty, and to serve as her lady's maid, her father purchased fifteen-year-old Harriet from William Kell for $450.[41] Doing so stood as testimony to James's growing affluence and his willingness to recognize the social cachet of being able to provide one's family with the trappings of gentility.

We know nothing of Harriet's origins. She was probably one of the six enslaved workers living in the Kell household in 1830. Kell's need to raise capital to finance his move to Marion County, Tennessee, may have prompted her sale.[42] What we do know about her, we know because her great-granddaughter, the civil rights advocate and Episcopal priest Pauli Murray, told what she knew of Harriet's story in a family history called Proud Shoes, originally published in the 1950s. According to Murray, the arrival of this extremely attractive, light-skinned young woman with "flashing dark eyes and luxuriant wavy black hair" had explosive consequences for the Smith family.[43]

Harriet was reputed to have been quiet, well mannered, and accommodating. She slept on a pallet outside Mary's bedroom door and accompanied her when she went out in public. In about 1839 Harriet and Reuben Day, a freeborn mulatto farmworker whose family lived nearby, began courting. Because of Harriet's enslavement, their courtship was fraught with complications. Reuben owned his own time, but Harriet did not. Unlike enslaved field workers who lived and played according to an agricultural calendar and often enjoyed authorized free time after the harvest and at Christmas, Harriet was pretty much confined to the Smith home and at their beck and call. Somehow, however, the couple managed to forge a romantic relationship, and eventually Harriet got permission from Mary's father to marry. As Harriet's owner, James, no doubt in collaboration with Mary and her mother, would have determined what sort of wedding it was—whether it would involve jumping the broom or saying wedding vows, who among Reuben's relatives would be allowed to witness the ceremony, what Harriet wore, and whether any sort of celebration reception would follow the ceremony. Given the seriousness with which Mary took her religious commitments and the fact that James served as an Episcopalian vestryman, it seems likely that the ceremony had some sort of Episcopal component.[44]

Harriet's marriage had no validity under North Carolina law, but it did bring about a change in the Smiths' domestic arrangements. When she pledged herself to Reuben, she became part of what was called an "abroad marriage." James refused to allow Harriet to live with her husband. Instead, he assigned her a cabin on the Smith property, which meant she would no longer be immediately available to wait on Mary at any hour of the day or night.[45] At the same time, however, he asserted control over both Harriet's body and her time by demanding that Reuben ask permission whenever he wanted to visit his wife.

In about 1842 Harriet bestowed on her master another piece of property by bearing a little boy named Julius. Midwives typically delivered the babies of enslaved women on plantations, but since Harriet was a member of a small-town doctor's household in an age in which doctors were increasingly entering the field of obstetrics, James may have attended her if only to practice his technique.[46] Whatever the case, Harriet now had responsibility for rearing a child while she remained at the beck and call of her enslaver and his family. Reuben may have been Julius's biological father and a free man, but he had neither the social influence nor the legal power to protect his son from the degradation of bondage.[47]

When James purchased Harriet in 1834, Mary's two brothers, Frank and Sid, were in their teens and students at the University of North Carolina in Chapel Hill. It is unclear where they received their preparatory education. Frank, a "tall, dark, brooding" young man, attended the University of North Carolina from 1832 to 1836. There is no record indicating that he graduated, but, like his father, he enrolled at the University of Pennsylvania to study medicine. He left after one year and returned to Hillsborough in 1838 to join his father's practice.[48] His return may have been prompted by his father's ill health. A notice appeared in the *Hillsborough Recorder* in November 1840, announcing: "Dr. James S. Smith's health is so far restored as to enable him to resume the practice of his profession. He cannot promise to ride in the night, as his eyesight has so far failed him to render night travel dangerous." The notice continued that his son was available to attend patients at night and in bad weather.[49]

Frank's high-strung, impetuous brother Sid enrolled in the university in 1833 at the age of fourteen, and they lived together on campus. Like

Frank, Sid did not graduate. Instead, he returned to Hillsborough to study law.[50] By 1838 both of Mary's bachelor brothers were living at home. One can only imagine the tittle-tattle that ensued when it became clear to the mothers of the town's marriageable daughters that Sid was more interested in pursuing his sister's enslaved lady's maid than in getting engaged.

His infatuation was impossible to miss. In Murray's version of family lore, "His eyes followed her everywhere when she was in the room. He seemed to be always behind her when she went out the door or standing in the shadows when she went to her cabin at night." Such attention must have been as startling as it was terrifying for someone in Harriet's position. She was a married woman with a small child and had no way to fend off his advances. Her mistress Delia seems to have ignored the situation. Frank tried to warn his brother off. Mary, who understood perfectly what was going on, begged her father to intervene, but he dismissed what was happening as a case of sowing wild oats. Matters came to a head when Sid confronted Harriet's husband Reuben and forbade him to set foot on Smith property. When Reuben tried to see Harriet one more time, both brothers beat him "with the butt end of a carriage whip" and warned that they would kill him if he ever returned. With Reuben gone, Sid had free rein. After beating down Harriet's barricaded cabin door and stuffing "rags in the door and window cracks" to "muffle" her shrieks, he raped her, presumably in the presence of her son.[51]

It should be noted that Sid's rape of Harriet was an outrage neither recognized nor punishable by law. The law assumed that because an enslaved woman was property, she was not an autonomous agent with a will of her own and therefore could not give or deny consent to sexual advances. She was assumed to always be willing and could do nothing to try to prevent them or protect herself from injury because of them. Thus, it was legally impossible to be charged with and convicted for raping an enslaved woman. Moreover, the law held that ravishing such a woman did not damage her value as property and indeed might increase it if she proved to be a good "breeder."[52] To make matters worse, cultural assumptions about the nature of men and the sexualized character of Black women held that white men were by definition sexually aggressive and lacking in self-control.[53] At the same time, Black women lived and worked under conditions that contributed to the belief that they were uncommonly sensuous, sexually promiscuous, and lacking in virtue. Their bodies were exposed and handled when they stood on the auction block. They were often inadequately clothed and sometimes found it necessary to expose their legs and arms as they went about their work. And it was common to strip their clothes from their bodies before laying on the lash. As historian Deborah Gray White has pointed out, the idea that Black women were Jezebels dominated the imaginations of white southerners. The result was that white men did not take seriously Black female resistance to coupling with them.[54]

Sid did not confine himself to a single night of debauchery. His assaults continued night after night until Frank decided to put a stop to them. One night Frank attacked his brother as he was leaving Harriet's cabin, leaving him unconscious and bleeding in the yard. Sid's recovery was long and painful. According to Murray, the Smiths were not willing to discuss what happened that night even among themselves; they tried to hush up the talk that began to circulate by laughingly referring to it "as ignorant slave gossip" and attempted to explain Sid's injuries by saying that he had fallen from his horse. Sid never touched Harriet again, but in early 1844 she bore his daughter and named her Cornelia. "She was indistinguishable from a white child" and looked just like her father, Murray wrote. Fathering a mixed-race child was common in the antebellum South and not in and of itself enough to stain a southern gentleman's reputation as long as he didn't flaunt what he had done. But Sid made no effort to hide his paternity, showing off his daughter to whoever came to the house. His lack of circumspection sent Hillsborough's gossips into a feeding frenzy.[55]

Mary was outraged by her brother's behavior. Because Harriet was her maid and the baby was her niece, she insisted on bringing the child into the house and kept a nurse to tend her for six years.[56] It took both moral courage and a disdain for the opinion of others to have done so. In her mind, she was doing the right thing knowing that this particular right thing was not the "done" thing.

The situation went from bad to worse after Cornelia's birth when Frank began to visit Harriet's cabin. Apparently, she did not resist his advances and became his concubine, combining her labor in the Smith house with the added burden of providing sex on demand.[57] "Perhaps she was resigned," Murray wrote, or lonely, or flattered. Perhaps she was afraid that if she refused, she would suffer a punishment too painful to bear such as the abuse or sale of her child. Perhaps she understood that no Black or mixed-race man in Hillsborough or its vicinity would have anything to do with her as long as she belonged to the Smiths. Perhaps she depended on Frank to protect her from Sid. Whatever the case, Harriet bore Frank's daughter Emma in about 1847.[58]

The gossips had a field day, according to Murray. "First Sid, then Frank laying up with a slave wench and refusing to marry their own kind like decent people. And the Smiths . . . bringing their little bastards right into the home and raising them up as if they were part of the family." James could have sold Harriet and her children, but "the talk would have been worse. Then folks would have said the Smiths sold their own blood into slavery."[59] It is impossible to determine exactly what the larger community of Black and mixed-race inhabitants of Hillsborough had to say about the situation. They almost certainly knew what was going on and no doubt expressed their opinions about it among themselves, but Murray says nothing specifically about them in her memoir. Whatever they said or did not say, there was nothing they could have done to protect Harriet or to influence the situation in any meaningful way.

As a matter of fact, "talk" about the Smiths did get worse when James's fortunes began to deteriorate. He had begun dabbling in real estate in 1807 when, at the age of twenty, he purchased almost five hundred acres in western Orange County from his alleged father, William Francis Strudwick. Where James got the five hundred dollars to pay for it is unclear. Selling land on credit was common in the South, a cash-poor region whose banking system was underdeveloped. Real estate transactions and business deals frequently involved one man borrowing money from another and getting friends to guarantee loans, which may or may not have been guaranteed by collateral.

After he returned from Philadelphia in 1812, James purchased another tract of land for $3,500. That same year he began to buy up lots in town, including the one on King Street that became the site of his residence. After James married Delia in 1813, his father-in-law deeded Price Creek plantation in southern Orange County to him with the understanding that it was to be held in trust for Delia until she died and then transferred to her children. James's neighbors would not have been privy to the details of the arrangement, but the idea that James had access to more than a thousand acres south of Chapel Hill may have played a role in the ease with which he gained access to credit. Whatever the case, by 1825 James had accumulated more than 3,300 acres of land in and around Hillsborough. When land prices plummeted in the 1830s, James went on a buying spree, acquiring yet another 1,300 acres.

At the same time, he formed partnerships with a number of local entrepreneurs. In 1819 he joined with Thomas Jefferson Faddis to open a general store. In the 1820s he and Josiah Turner Sr. opened a copper shop together and advertised the manufacture of stills. And in the 1830s he and Thomas D. Crain were operating mills, a distillery, and a tanyard on the Eno River. During this time he also purchased a number of enslaved workers as investments to be used as labor in his various businesses.[60]

James's thirst for investment opportunities meant that by 1845 he was overextended and owed a great deal of money to a great many creditors. They only had to read the local newspaper to realize that James was desperate for ready cash. One advertisement published in August under the title "Bacon and Leather" offered both for very low prices if payment was made in cash, or in the case of leather, on credit "for ninety days to those he knows to be punctual." In an effort to drum up business for his medical practice, he advertised his willingness to "accept any call."[61] And he hired John W. Norwood, whose mother Robina had loaned him five hundred dollars, to collect debts owed to him by his patients.[62]

A reputation for creditworthiness was critical for businessmen such as James, who lived in a cash-poor environment. The loss of it meant that his creditors would try to recoup their money while they still could. With his property at risk, he began conveying it to his children. He tried to transfer ownership of his mill to Frank. He sold Harriet, Julius, and Cornelia to Mary and a number of other enslaved workers to Delia and Frank. And he tried to shield Mary's ultimate claim to Price Creek by deeding it to her, even though her mother, who had a life claim on it, was still alive.[63]

His efforts were futile. In September 1845 he found it necessary to hold an auction in front of his leather shop to sell his mill tract, tanyard, home, and unimproved land including bounty lands in Illinois as well as his personal property and his wife's household goods to pay off his debts. He was still trying to sell his mills and tanyard in November.[64]

In the process, former business associates and loan guarantors such as Josiah Turner Sr. and James Turrentine turned into enemies. Lawsuits, countersuits, and private agreements eventually resolved the situation, but not until 1849.[65] In the end James was financially ruined, his reputation, such as it was, in tatters. He had subscribed to the nineteenth-century ideology of self-making that held that men could start from humble origins and rise in the world through their own efforts. There was no way for him to appreciate or anticipate the precariousness of his good fortune. He was a bit player in a market revolution characterized by rapid economic expansionism, excessive speculation, instability in the credit and banking system, and periodic financial crises that left him and those like him subject to economic forces they barely understood and had no way to control.[66]

James would have found little comfort in the knowledge that having to declare bankruptcy was common—so common, in fact, that historians estimate that one in three businesses during the antebellum period failed.[67] The fact that he had a great deal of company in his misery did not make his failure less painful. He left no record of his feelings about the matter, but he could not have been under any illusions about the state of his reputation. He had proved himself untrustworthy and no longer commanded the respect of his former associates. And in a culture that equated manhood with economic autonomy, he was forced to become dependent on his wife and her assets to support his household.[68]

After almost thirty-five years in business, James retreated to Price Creek with his family and enslaved workers in a cloud of humiliation. Faced with the prospect of having to liquidate all of his property in Hillsborough, he had had the foresight to set aside building materials and prepare for his imminent exile by constructing a substantial farmhouse called Oaklands on the property.[69]

When Mary moved to Oaklands, Maria was bereft. In December 1846 she ended the school session at Hillsborough Female Academy and immediately left for Price Creek to join Mary there. As the day approached for her to return, she decided she was willing to sacrifice her income, at least temporarily, to avoid another separation. Her departure caused Anna Burwell, whose school in Hillsborough was in competition with Maria's academy, to comment: "Miss Maria Spear spent Christmas with Miss Mary Smith & I hear she will return here to open school in June. It seems she can't live separated from Miss Mary."[70] The fact that the Smiths had left Hillsborough did not diminish their former neighbors' interest in their affairs and their propensity to talk about them and those who associated with them.

Away from the wagging tongues of the Hillsborough gossips, the Smiths lived quietly. Their new neighbors lived too far away to monitor their everyday life, although the birth of two more biracial babies must have caused comment. Annette was born to Harriet and Frank in 1848, Laura in 1851. James died in 1852. Delia followed him in 1854. Upon Delia's death, the land and enslaved laborers her father had bequeathed to her during her lifetime went to her children. Mary became the undisputed owner of Price Creek plantation, Frank inherited Jones Grove plantation, and Sid became the owner of Flowers Place plantation. The enslaved workers they inherited were valued at more than $11,500, the equivalent of almost $4 million in 2023.[71]

Six weeks after her mother died, Mary caused a stir by taking Harriet's son and four daughters into Chapel Hill to have them baptized at the Episcopal church. She made sure they received religious instruction and had them confirmed ten years later during the Civil War.[72] The gossip that ensued became part of the oral history passed down in Pauli Murray's family. "Every Sunday morning the four attractive girls were seen riding along with Miss Mary Ruffin Smith in her beautiful white family carriage on their way to the Chapel of the Cross," Murray wrote. "People seeing them pass nudged one another and said, 'There goes Miss Mary Smith and her girls.' To keep up appearances, Miss Mary sent them upstairs to the balcony in church while she sat alone or with Miss Maria Spear downstairs in the Smith pew. This only heightened the curiosity of the congregation." Cornelia is said to have remembered the commotion their presence made as she and her sisters sat primly upstairs, visible but inaccessible. When the young white men sitting below craned their necks to catch a glimpse of them, she remembered flirtatiously tossing her sixteen long, black "curls from side to side" to acknowledge their attention.[73]

Mary was sensitive to the sensation she was causing but refused to be cowed. She had been subjected to the sting of gossip since she was a teenager. She was now fifty-four, a wealthy woman, and a devout Christian. Without social ambition, she spent most of her time on her plantation and held herself aloof from Chapel Hill "society" other than to worship with them on Sunday. When anyone unfamiliar with her situation and curious about her circumstances asked her who she had brought to church, she defiantly replied that they were her maid's daughters. "As far as Miss Mary was concerned that ended it," Murray wrote. "Her lips snapped shut as if she'd bite their heads off if they asked anything further. She never let remarks touch her. When church was out, she looked straight ahead as if she heard nothing, gathered up her girls, piled them into the carriage and drove off."[74]

Mary spent the war years running her plantation as well as Frank's Jones Grove. Her brothers did not serve in the Confederate army, and federal troops did not destroy their property. After building bonfires to camouflage the places where her valuables were hidden, she and the rest of her household waited for the Yankees to arrive. Frank remained with her, but, according to a gossipy family friend, Sid "took to the woods, and with a long beard and mean apparel, passed himself off as the uncle of some poor family in the neighborhood."[75] Mary sent her niece Laura out to greet the troops holding a white flag in one hand and a Union flag in the other. There was no violence, but she was forced to watch as some members of her household helped the federals dig up what had been buried and to turn over all of her bed linens and towels to the invaders, presumably to be used as bandages. She escaped with her house still standing and her crops still in the fields, although one of her newly freed workers took her laundry into town and never returned.[76]

When the war ended, she stabilized her workforce by coming to an agreement with those of her former enslaved laborers who remained to provide them with food, clothes, and shelter in return for their labor.[77] Her life had purpose, and she kept herself busy, but the reality was that she lived and worked in relative isolation as a childless spinster on a plantation.[78] She had neighbors and had become friends with the Chapel Hill Malletts, the Mickles, and the Battles. But the only people she could count on for white, adult company on a day-to-day basis were her two dissolute brothers, who had been a constant source of embarrassment over the years.

Through correspondence she maintained her relationship with Maria, who had spent the war years working as a governess for the Fayetteville branch of the Mallett family. When Sid died in April 1867, Mary convinced Maria to come live with her at Price Creek.[79] While Mary supervised the work on her plantations, Maria taught school on the property.[80]

The Civil War freed those whom the Smiths held in bondage, including Harriet and her children. Harriet remained at Price Creek and continued to serve her former mistress as long as she was able. She died in 1873, having been struck by lightning during a particularly violent summer storm the year before.[81] By that time her four daughters had married: Annette to Chatham County preacher Ned Kirby, Emma to Henry Morphis of Chapel Hill, Laura to Grey Toole, a Charlotte barber, and Pauli Murray's great-grandmother Cornelia to Robert George Fitzgerald, a teacher and bricklayer from Durham.[82]

In 1875 Mary's elder brother, Frank, fell ill, suffered a stroke, and slowly sank into insanity.[83] He died on April 17, 1877.[84] By the time of Frank's death, Maria had developed a cataract in her right eye and could barely see. "The fact is," she wrote to Carrie Mallett, "my eyes have failed me so rapidly in the last year or two, that I cannot do anything at night and even now, I do not see the lines, just catch the glimpse of one now and then."[85] Perhaps because of her own ill health, Mary became increasingly concerned about Maria's economic future. Accordingly, she signed a will ten days after Frank's death leaving all of Price Creek plantation's fifteen hundred acres plus its stock, farming implements, and household goods to Maria for life.[86] Maria never inherited the property. In 1880 she wrote to one of the Mallett girls that she had been thinking of her friends, "many of who lie in their graves where I must soon join them."[87] Realizing that her health was failing, she quietly made arrangements for her death, preparing her own burial clothes and storing them away in an old trunk.[88] She died during the night of January 4–5, 1881, at the age of seventy-six. "She retired to her bed that night in her usual health and spirits. . . . In the morning she was found just as she had laid herself to sleep, placid and easy, with no trace of a pang or a movement."[89]

Mary was understandably distraught. "I feel so unhappy I do not know what to do with myself," she wrote to the Malletts in Fayetteville two weeks after Maria's death. "You and Maggie can understand how I feel for I know you loved my dearest best friend. I am alone in the world. . . . She is buried in our graveyard. And when my time comes I shall be beside her. . . . Oh! My heart is broken. Pray for me."[90] Mary died four years later on November 13, 1885. Her executor, Kemp Plummer Battle, buried her next to Maria in the little Smith family cemetery at Jones Grove, six miles south of Price Creek.[91]

There is no evidence to indicate that the fact that they were both buried in the same cemetery caused any gossip among their friends and neighbors. It was an age before close female relationships were considered suspect. Mary and Maria had been associated for many years. Anyone who knew them understood their devotion to each other. Both women were devout Christians, and except for the fact that neither of them married, they conformed in every way to the code of respectability that women were expected to follow. And Maria, who had no family in the area, had made herself a part of the Smith family by the time she died. So together they remain under moss-covered tombstones in the little Smith cemetery surrounded by a crumbling wall covered with trailing ivy and Virginia creeper.

It is hard to imagine a household more predisposed to attract the attention and censure of their neighbors than the Smiths. Mary's alleged treatment of those enslaved in her household fueled a whole range of anxieties and insecurities among Hillsborough's white inhabitants about social mobility with regard to what it took to be accepted as equals by the town's elite, fear that trying to uphold standards of discipline that included corporal punishment could lead to slave insurrections, and the legitimacy of social conventions that theoretically precluded interracial liaisons. The men in the Smith family pushed the boundaries of acceptable behavior and reaped the benefit of their neighbors' disdain. We have no record of Delia's response to her sons' fornication aside from Murray saying that Delia took to wringing her hands when she thought about it.[92] Nor do we know what she thought of the circumstances surrounding her husband's bankruptcy, which put so much of her property at risk. She lives in the shadows of the historical record, a woman who was there but had no voice. We cannot know the depth of her isolation or humiliation at the social rejection that her Hillsborough neighbors subjected her to, and we have no idea what the ladies of Chapel Hill made of her.

Talk among the enslaved and free people of color about her long ordeal isolated Harriet as well because it forced those who either knew what was going on or heard about it through the grapevine to reconsider their relationship to her. The way she remembered it, the other enslaved servants in the Smith household felt sorry for her but kept their distance as a form of self-protection. And the Black and mixed-race men of Hillsborough were afraid to have anything to do with her.[93] So talk about her situation cut her off from the very people whom she should have been able to count on for sympathy, comfort, and companionship.

Mary never got over the sting of her neighbors' scorn. An introvert to begin with, she seems to have turned even further inward, finding comfort in her faith, the belief that her actions were sufficient to stand as testimony to her moral integrity, and Maria's enduring loyalty and friendship. "Quiet in manner, reserved in speech, and with an air half timid, and a smile half deprecatory, she passed on her way unnoticed, and very few even of those who knew her best gave her credit for the close observation, the intelligence, or the discriminating judgement with which she took note of men and manners," a friend wrote in 1886.[94] It is not that Mary did not care what people thought, but through the years she developed an armor of indifference to those who she felt were likely to pass judgment on her and went about her business selectively choosing her friends from among those who were willing to overlook the transgressions of the men in her family.

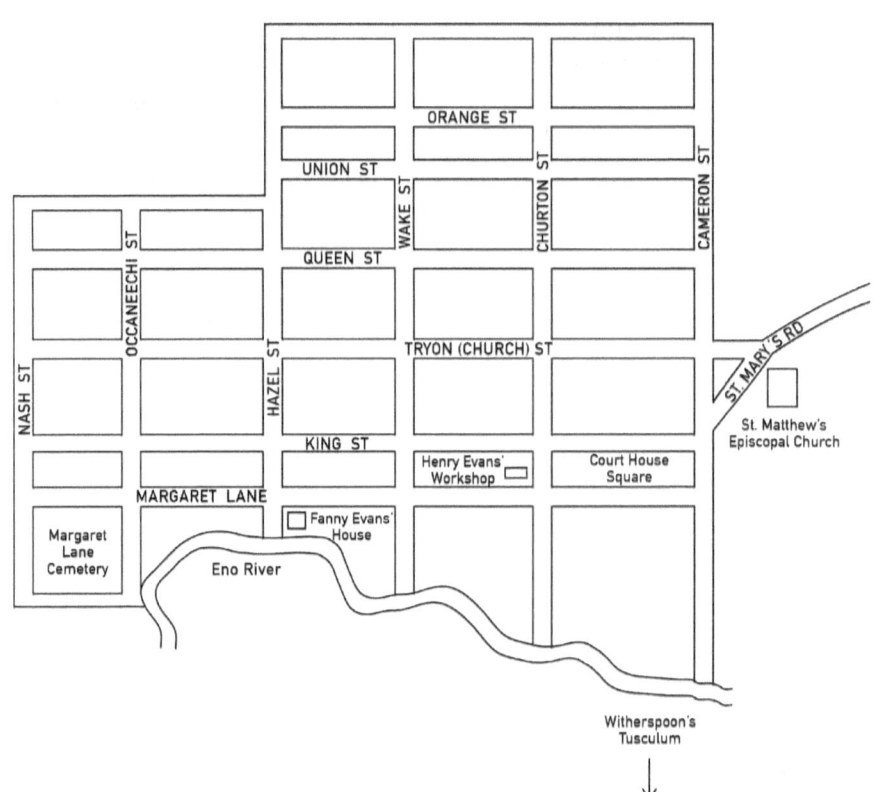

2
ALMOST (BUT NOT QUITE) FREE

Because their claim to freedom was so fragile, Hillsborough's free people of color had to be concerned about their reputations and the damage that unfavorable gossip could do to them. Most of them worked hard, nurtured reputations as respectable and honorable, obeyed the law, and went about their daily lives without attracting much attention. They stayed in their homes after the curfew bell rang at ten o'clock.[1] And they did not cause public disturbances. Others, however, did not. The cases of Henry Evans, Anderson Mayo, and Anderson's son James illustrate how gossip and reputation could impact their ability to derive whatever benefits were to be had by living in a community where racism and slavery impacted almost every aspect of their everyday lives.

It was not until they grew to manhood that they had to worry about such matters. As young, free men of color, they were as anonymous as it was possible to be in a town that small. Even the designation of their race obscured their backgrounds. As historian Warren Milteer and others have pointed out, racial categories in North Carolina were fluid and complex during the early nineteenth century. White people in charge of documenting racial distinctions in the census or court documents were inconsistent in categorizing free people of color at one time or another as "colored," "negro," "black," "mulatto," "mustee," or "Indian," obscuring ancestral distinctions, conflating those of African descent with East Indians and Native people, and allowing free people of color to negotiate the boundaries of racial difference to their advantage through social networks.[2] The two characteristics that people so designated had in common were that they were free and they were not considered white.

Henry, Anderson, James, and those like them never comprised a large segment of the South's population.[3] In 1800 there were a little more than a hundred free people of color in the whole of Orange County. By 1830 the number had grown to more than five hundred, but it did not reach a thousand by 1860.[4] These were individuals who had been born free, had been freed by their owners, had purchased their freedom, or believed themselves to be free and behaved as if they were.

Hillsborough had its fair share of free people of color.[5] Some, like the Jeffryses (Jefferies) and the Chavoises (Chavis or Chaves), both mixed-race families with Native American roots, lived in and around the town for decades. Others were more transient, staying for a few years and then moving on. In 1850, for example, Green Caudle and Richard Mayo were making furniture, Mornell Valentine and Henry Freeman worked as shoemakers, and James Valentine made his living as a barber. By 1860 they were all gone, replaced by Slit Cameron, a cabinetmaker; Cuoni Chavois, a shoemaker; and Henry Martin, a barber. Living among them as members of the forty or so free nonwhite households were skilled craftsmen who provided a wide variety of services for the county's residents, serving as blacksmiths, carpenters, masons, painters, plasterers, and wheelwrights. Other free people of color were engaged in agriculture or domestic service.[6]

Despite their small numbers, they were a thorn in the side of white southerners who assumed that their existence undermined the very foundations of slave society. The presence of free people of color served as living proof that obtaining one's freedom was possible, an eventuality that gave Hillsborough's white slaveholders and nonslaveholders alike pause as they assessed the degree to which the town's free people of color posed a security threat to the white community by fomenting dissatisfaction among the enslaved, assisting their efforts to make their way to freedom, and plotting to rebel. Rumors about them and their alleged attempts to destabilize the racial and economic status quo resulted in a wide variety of laws and social customs designed to keep them under white control or be rid of them entirely.[7] At the same time, Hillsborough's white population depended on their labor, and as Kirt von Daacke has convincingly argued, daily face-to-face interactions served to mitigate some of the impact of the hostility whites may have borne toward their Black neighbors.[8]

Because their claim to self-sovereignty was razor thin, day-to-day life for Hillsborough's free people of color was a constant struggle to preserve their status and reputations in the face of white suspicion and hostility. Their security as individuals was dependent on establishing and maintaining the goodwill and patronage of their white neighbors, whom they counted on to stand up for them in court, sell them property, rent them a place to live, or provide them employment. Face-to-face interactions on a daily basis created bonds that were critical for the conduct of everyday life in a community that was dependent on their labor.[9] Their actions were always constrained by constant surveillance by white people, contested rules of racial etiquette, and the possibility of being the object of their white neighbors' idle talk.

The color of their skin made a difference in a society where their labor was valued but their presence was not. Those of mixed race with fair skin, like Henry Evans, found themselves in an advantaged position vis-à-vis their relationship with white people, who were prone to find them more attractive and assume them more intelligent and more law-abiding than those with darker complexions.[10] At the same time, their very existence as people of mixed race blurred the difference between Black and white while it exposed the prevalence of miscegenation, a practice that many white southerners were desperate to ignore. The diarist Mary Boykin Chesnut summed it up nicely when she wrote, "God forgive us, but ours is a monstrous system, a wrong and iniquity! Like the patriarchs of old, our men live all in one house with their wives and concubines; and the mulattoes one sees in every family partly resemble the white children. Any lady is ready to tell you who is the father of all the mulatto children in everybody's household but her own. Those, she seems to think, drop from the clouds."[11]

Henry did not drop from the clouds. His mother, Fanny Evans, was a free, mixed-race woman who arrived in Hillsborough sometime between 1810 and 1820.[12] By 1825 she was living there with her four children: Delilah Evans born in 1809, Henry Evans born in 1817, Jane Evans born sometime before 1822, and another son, Wilson Bruce Evans, born in 1824.[13]

Fanny never married. As Suzanne Lebsock and others have argued, a number of factors combined to discourage marriage among free women of color in small southern towns, including an unfavorable sex ratio among the free nonwhite population, a prohibition against marrying across the color line, a predisposition not to marry the enslaved whose marriages had no legal standing and from whom one could easily be separated, a desire for personal autonomy, and the ability to support themselves.[14] While she remained single, Fanny apparently cohabited with at least two men during her childbearing years. It is impossible to determine who Delilah's father was, but Henry and Jane were almost certainly the children of John Wilson, a slave-owning planter who lived in Caswell County, North Carolina.

On May 1, 1822, he registered a deed transferring one-half of a town lot in Hillsborough on the corner of Hazel Street and Margaret Lane to Jane and Henry Evans "for and in consideration of the natural love and affection" he felt for them and provided that Fanny should have use of the property during her lifetime.[15] It seems likely that Wilson Bruce Evans, who was born two years later, was named for his father. The space of eight years between the birth of Delilah and Henry and John Wilson's lack of provision for Fanny's eldest child in his deed suggest that her father was someone other than Wilson.

It is unclear how Fanny supported herself. As a free, single woman, she had the legal right to sign contracts and could therefore hire herself out to do laundry, cook, or perform housekeeping duties. Since Wilson had provided her with a home, she could also have run a boardinghouse for mechanics and laborers. However she earned the money to support herself and her children, she managed to provide them with a basic education, despite the fact that she was illiterate and there were no schools for them to attend.[16]

Equally important to Henry's future was the fact that she apprenticed him to a cabinetmaker. Historians disagree about the impact of apprenticeship on the lives of free nonwhite workers in the South. John Hope Franklin characterized it as the primary educational institution for freeborn children of color in the early nineteenth century. In 1826, almost ten years after Henry's birth, the North Carolina state legislature authorized county courts "to bind out the children of free Negroes or mulattoes, where the parent, with whom such children live, does not or shall not habitually employ his or her time in some honest industrious occupation." Under such court orders, apprentices were bound for a specific period of time, were required to obey their masters, and had no freedom of movement. In return for their unpaid labor, their master was supposed to teach them a trade, provide them with shelter, food, and clothing, and, before the 1830s, teach them to read, write, and cipher.[17]

The problem was that while the apprenticeship system supplied farmers, master craftsmen, and householders with free labor, there was little if any supervision of apprentices' circumstances, leaving masters free to treat their apprentices any way they liked. This sort of reality prompted Ira Berlin to look on such apprenticeships as "labor extortion," simply "another means of locking free Negroes into virtual slavery."[18] In fact, it could actually lead to slavery. In November 1826 Judge Thomas Ruffin of Hillsborough heard a case involving Susan Revels (Revill, Suck Revel, Suky), a free young woman of color from Orange County, who alleged that she had never been legally indentured and was being held in slavery in Guilford County. Ruffin found in favor of Susan, but by the end of the month she was legally indentured to Moses S. Pratt of Orange County.[19] Such records stand as testimony to the vulnerability of apprentices when no one provided oversight into the conditions of their servitude.

There is no evidence in the Orange County records that Henry Evans's apprenticeship was arranged through the court. Nor is there any reason to assume that his mother could not support him. What she did have was the power to arrange an apprenticeship for her son informally. That sort of arrangement would have allowed her oversight over her son's training while she ensured his economic future.

It is unclear where and under whose supervision Henry learned to be a cabinetmaker. The U.S. manuscript censuses of 1820, 1830, and 1840 do not list the specific occupations of heads of households, so it is impossible to tell from the census who was making furniture in Hillsborough during that time. Thomas Day had done so between 1821 and 1823. Fanny would have known Day, but Henry was too young to have served as his apprentice during those years.[20] According to an ad in the *Hillsborough Recorder*, Uriah Jeffreys was making furniture in Hillsborough until he left in 1828.[21] By September 1829 Joseph Marshall had taken his place. Henry could have apprenticed under him, although it is not clear how long Marshall remained in town.[22] It is also possible that when Henry was old enough, Fanny arranged for him to go to study with Day, who by then had set up his business in Milton in Caswell County, North Carolina. Given her association with John Wilson, who was still living in that vicinity, she would have been familiar with the area and may have been able to count on him to monitor the progress of his son.[23]

Whoever assumed the responsibility for training Henry in the mysteries of furniture making had to teach him a wide variety of skills. A good furniture maker had to be able to identify the difference between elegant and imported wood such as mahogany and the more widely available cherry, walnut, poplar, or maple. He had to learn to use hand tools such as planes, lathes, and chisels and to master the art of veneering, painting, and staining the secretaries, sideboards, bedsteads, tables, and chairs commissioned by his customers.[24] In order to be a successful businessman, he had to know how to estimate costs, keep a set of books, draw up invoices, and keep track of the money his customers owed him. His interaction with his master's clients allowed him to observe and master the rules of racial etiquette that required him to carefully monitor his deportment and speech in order to balance confidence in his abilities with the humility and deference those in the white community expected of him. In his world, a disrespectful word or careless gesture could earn him the reputation for being "too uppity" and doom his prospects.[25]

Henry was in his early twenties by the time he was ready to go into business for himself.[26] It was at this point in his life that gossip and its impact on his reputation began to matter. On August 24, 1838, he purchased a piece of prime real estate from William E. Anderson for $265 with the intention of setting up a cabinetmaking shop on Churton Street across from the courthouse.[27] His next challenge was to acquire tools and a supply of wood. Where he got the money to do all of this is unclear. His mother Fanny was still alive in 1840, so he could mortgage but not sell the land given to him and his sister by John Wilson. The other option was to borrow the money from his father or some other man of means willing to take a chance on a young, mixed-race man with a marketable skill and a great deal of promise.[28] In order to do so, he had to present himself as a trustworthy and ambitious man of character who would be able to attract the patronage necessary to establish and maintain a successful business.

As a free artisan of color working in Hillsborough in the 1820s, Thomas Day had established a business model useful for attracting white customers, filling their custom orders, and collecting his fees. Henry was in the position of building on Day's reputation and the goodwill he left behind. But he was on his own when it came to working through the awkwardness of negotiating a fair price for his work. Implicit in this process was his right to refuse to sell except on his own terms. When he quoted a price, he subtly asserted his power and thereby undermined prevailing white assumptions about Black dependence and subordination. When his customers found it necessary to bargain with him, they found themselves in the uncomfortable position of tacitly acknowledging that power. Considerations of race and class would have infused the whole process, making his ability to negotiate contracts and collect payment from his white customers a potential challenge.

Since he lived in a place where most of the white inhabitants found his presence undesirable and were predisposed to distrust anyone with dark skin, he had to work doubly hard to establish a reputation as a respectable, law-abiding, hardworking, churchgoing family man in order to integrate himself into the business community. Church membership was one of the most important markers of respectability. There were no established Black churches in Hillsborough, so Henry had to join a white church in order to publicly express his religious sensibilities. He had three to choose from: Presbyterians formally organized their church in 1816. Early Methodists depended on ministers willing to ride a circuit to care for the spiritual needs of believers. It was not until after a camp meeting revival in 1821 that those in Hillsborough raised the money to build a church. And with the Anglican Church having been disestablished following the American Revolution, Hillsborough's Episcopalians reorganized themselves in 1824.[29]

As historian John Boles has pointed out, during the antebellum period Christians, both free and enslaved, typically worshipped in biracial churches.[30] Hillsborough's Presbyterians and Episcopalians both left records of having tended to the spiritual needs of the town's people of color during the first part of the nineteenth century. Beginning in 1816, the names of about two dozen people of color, most of them associated with prominent white people, began to appear in the Presbyterian session records as having been baptized, accepted into membership, or disciplined.[31] The Episcopalians took an equally active approach in their ministry to the town's nonwhite population. In July 1829 alone the Rev. William Mercer Green baptized ten enslaved workers belonging to William Kirkland of Ayr Mount, a plantation just outside of town. Dozens of such baptisms followed. Also scattered among the parish records are the names of those who were married in the church and confirmed as members.[32]

We have no way of knowing why Henry chose to join St. Matthew's Episcopal Church. He may have sensed some ambivalence about the South's racial hierarchy in its rector, Moses Ashley Curtis. Born in Massachusetts as the son of a Congregational clergyman, Curtis was educated at Williams College, came south to tutor the children of former Governor Edward Bishop Dudley, and married into the prominent, slave-owning DeRossett family of Wilmington, North Carolina.[33] Given his background, it seems safe to assume that Curtis did not come south with a predisposition to support slavery and that his willingness to accept it evolved over time. There are hints in his diary and letters that his conscience was uneasy about his complicity in supporting an institution that condoned abuse of power and callous cruelty.

His lessons in mastery began shortly after his arrival in North Carolina when his employer left him in charge of his enslaved workers. "Revolting as the idea of master and slave is, the relation was unwillingly forced upon me & I have submitted," he wrote in his diary in the fall of 1831. "At first they [the slaves] were disposed to run all lengths, perhaps doubting my authority to check them," he said. He wanted to prove he was up to fulfilling his new responsibilities but was somewhat at a loss as to how to proceed, so he bought a "cow skin" hoping that his possession of it would intimidate them. That strategy apparently did not do the trick. "Alas," he wrote, "the time came. In accordance with my creed, never threaten without executing, I stripped a black boy's coat off intending to give him a dozen as I promised." Curtis only managed four lashes before he stopped. Afraid that his restraint might be interpreted as weakness, he felt compelled to use the excuse that it was the victim's "first offense" to explain his failure to carry out the sentence he had imposed.[34]

Negotiating the principles of mastery followed him into marriage and his career as a slave-owning clergyman when he was forced to deal with circumstances that made clear the degree to which slavery complicated the ability of both the enslaved and their masters to uphold the moral standards expected of practicing Christians. In 1845 his wife's enslaved maid Mary asked permission to marry a laborer owned by a local Presbyterian minister, John Knox Witherspoon. Curtis hesitated to approve the marriage, perhaps because he was planning to leave the area and understood that his family's departure with their enslaved workers would separate the newly married couple. The alternative to sanctioning their marriage was to forbid them to see each other or allow them to cohabit. Forbidding their association was impractical. And as an Episcopalian rector, it would have been unacceptable to allow them to live together in his household without the benefit of the church's blessing. So he wrote to his father-in-law (and Mary's legal owner) for advice. Armand DeRossett's solution was pragmatic. He offered to buy Mary's suitor so that the couple could marry and accompany Curtis anywhere he chose to go.[35]

Whatever internal conflicts Curtis may have had about slavery, he indulged his evangelical impulses by taking responsibility for the moral uplift of Hillsborough's people of color. Toward that end, he baptized Henry on August 28, 1842. On the same day, Bishop Levi Silliman Ives confirmed him as a member of St. Matthew's.[36] Formal affiliation with St. Matthew's provided Henry with a spiritual home, confirmation of his spiritual equality in the eyes of God, testimony to his moral responsibility, and an opportunity to associate with some of Hillsborough's most prominent families and potential customers.

Acceptance into membership in a white church may have masked white hostility toward Hillsborough's free people of color, but Henry's sister's situation in Raleigh served as a painful reminder of the tenuousness of his position. In 1831 Delilah had married a formerly enslaved carpenter

Henry Evans joined the biracial congregation of St. Matthew's Episcopal Church in 1842. Courtesy of the Mary Claire Engstrom Photographic Collection, Wilson Special Collections Library, UNC–Chapel Hill.

named John Copeland.[37] They settled in Raleigh just at a time when race relations in North Carolina were becoming more and more unsettled.[38] First, the Nat Turner Rebellion in Virginia that year had left the state's white residents increasingly anxious about what they perceived to be the subversive presence of free people of color in their midst. Then, in 1835, the new state constitution deprived free nonwhite men of the right to vote. The Panic of 1837 disrupted the conduct of business and access to credit. And the city of Raleigh passed an ordinance forcing its free nonwhite inhabitants to apply for residency permits.[39]

Matters came to a head just as Henry was preparing himself for church membership. In April 1842 a large mob in Raleigh tarred and feathered a free man of color named Lunsford Lane who had come to the city to purchase his family. Rumor had it that Lane was an abolitionist speaker who had attended antislavery meetings in Massachusetts to raise the money he needed to liberate his wife and children. Declaring themselves the "Raleigh Regulators," mob leaders subsequently papered the town with a "Bulletin" threatening anyone who condemned their act of violence. A few days later, they tore down a log schoolhouse about 1.5 miles from town where Baily Smith and Allen Jones, a free man of color, had organized classes for Black children.[40]

Nothing is known of Baily Smith, but Allen Jones, a mixed-race blacksmith, was a good friend of Delilah and John. Born into bondage in 1794, Jones bought his freedom, purchased his wife and several of their children, and in 1842 was trying to free two slaves who resided in his household, a difficult enterprise since, by that time, the state legislature had passed a law declaring that anyone who wanted to emancipate a slave had to pay at least one thousand dollars to do so. Starting a Black school and attempting to free slaves was apparently enough to bring him to the attention of both the authorities and Raleigh's rabble-rousers. In April he was charged with forgery and, with the help of five defense attorneys, was tried and acquitted. Less than two months after Henry joined St. Matthew's, on a mid-October evening, a mob dragged him from his home and brutally whipped him. The editor of the *Raleigh Register* reported the attack and condemned the outrage, but not because he believed that Jones deserved sympathy. Dismissing Allen Jones as "obnoxious" and a "rascal," he objected to the incident because he believed that the use of vigilante justice tarnished the town's reputation as a peaceful, law-abiding community.[41]

Such atrocities combined with everyday reminders of the tenuousness of their freedom prompted the Copelands and the Joneses, along with a free man of color named John Lane, a Fayetteville blacksmith, to pack up and head north to find a new home. The group drove by wagon toward Ohio, crossed the Ohio River at Cincinnati, and made their way a few miles south and east to New Richmond, a terminal for steamboat traffic where abolitionist sentiment was strong.[42]

Delilah, her family, and her friends were about to settle permanently in Russia Township in the Oberlin area when Henry married Henrietta Leary on April 10, 1843. Henrietta was the daughter of Matthew Leary, a free, mixed-race saddler who lived in Fayetteville.[43] A year later, Henry became a father, another step in his road to respectability. The couple's first child, Lizzy, was born in 1844; Julia followed two years later. Matthew was born in 1848 and Sarah in 1849.[44]

As time passed, Henry's business grew. Henry's brother Wilson Bruce worked as his assistant amid the sweet smell of sawdust and the sight of curly wood shavings lying beneath the furniture parts that rested on wood trestles in his shop. Advertisements in the *Hillsborough Recorder* indicate that the brothers repaired and revarnished old furniture and produced new sofas, sideboards, bureaus, and tables of the finest quality.[45] Individual orders to build and repair furniture showcased their skills as craftsmen and led to a demand for their services by community institutions. The St. Matthew's vestry asked Henry to provide chairs and balcony panels for the church's sanctuary.[46] And in 1851 he was paid $3.50 to construct a jury box and fit carpeting in the Orange County Courthouse.[47]

Henry's reputation as a fine craftsman spread beyond Hillsborough. In September 1847 David Swain, the president of the University of North Carolina, sought the advice of Governor William Graham, who had practiced law in Hillsborough, about hiring a furniture maker to furnish two dormitories on campus. "[William] Thompson of Raleigh would probably be glad to get the job," Swain wrote. "He is ordinarily so extravagant in his charges, however, that I do not like to employ him. It recently occurred to me, that Evans (the freeman of color) of your town, might answer our purposes. I know nothing of him personally and will be greatly obliged to you, if you consider him a suitable person to secure him down here." It is not clear whether Henry was invited to submit a bid for the work, but the contract was eventually given to Thomas Day of Milton, a man whose reputation was already well established.[48]

Despite his failure to win the university contract, Henry continued to add staff. In May 1843 he had apprenticed eight-year-old William Mayo (Mayho), son of Melinda Mayo, a free woman of color.[49] It is not entirely clear what ultimately happened to William. He does not appear in the 1850 census as living in Henry's household and was too young to have finished his apprenticeship. He may have died or run away. But it is also possible that Henry found the young man unsuitable for training as a furniture maker and asked the court to find him another place. The court apprenticed a fourteen-year-old William Mayo (identified as the son of Simmons Mayo) to John F. Lyon, a white farmer, in May 1847, and there was a William Mayo living in Lyon's household in 1850.[50]

While the court had the authority to issue apprenticeship bonds, hearsay among free people of color kept track of the opportunities available to their young people to train to be farmers, domestics, or skilled craftsmen. Lyon's next-door neighbor was a free nonwhite laborer named John B. Mitchell. It was probably through him that Adaline Mitchell, a single woman of color living in Chapel Hill, heard of the opening for an apprentice in Henry's shop. Whatever the case, the court bound out Adaline Mitchell's thirteen-year-old son William to Henry in March 1851. His apprenticeship bond provided not only training as a cabinetmaker but also at the end of his apprenticeship "a set of bench tools and a good suit of clothes."[51] Sometime in the interim, Henry also employed James Allison, a sixty-six-year-old white cabinetmaker from Delaware, to help in his shop.[52]

Once he was established, Henry was in a position to use his real estate, inventory, and accounts payable as collateral in order to raise the funds necessary to expand his business. By 1848 he had purchased "a comfortable carriage, a hack, and a buggy" and good horses to provide a transportation service for the citizens of Hillsborough. His ads declared that he had an experienced driver on call to convey passengers to and from town. Two years later he began offering undertaking services, boasting that he could construct a coffin in only three hours. Time was of the essence. Embalming did not become common until the latter part of the Civil War, so in the 1850s it was necessary to dispose of bodies as expeditiously as possible, particularly in the summertime.[53]

At the same time, Henry further integrated himself into Hillsborough's economic life by entering the credit market. Access to readily available credit was crucial in a society that was cash poor. To be considered cred-

Accommodation for Travellers.

THE subscriber is now prepared with a comfortable Carriage, a Hack, and a Buggy, to convey Passengers from Hillsborough to any other place, or to bring them here, by the day, week, or job. He has good horses and an experienced driver, and thinks he can give entire satisfaction. He can be found at his shop, two doors above the Union Hotel.

HENRY EVANS.

February 1.   15—

"Accommodation for Travelers," *Hillsborough Recorder*, January 31, 1849.

Notice.

AS I am obliged to raise money to carry on my business and pay my debts, those who are indebted to me, by note or account, are earnestly requested to call and make immediate payment.

HENRY EVANS.

N. B. I have on hand a large assortment of well made Furniture, which I will sell low for cash.

I am also prepared to furnish Coffins at three hours' notice, of the plainest or finest style, of Walnut or Mahogany.

Persons at a distance may rely on being served here sooner than they can be at home.

H. EVANS,
Cabinet Maker and General Undertaker.

Nov. 13.   07—

"Notice," *Hillsborough Recorder*, March 27, 1850. In 1849 Henry Evans was expanding his business to include providing the citizens of Hillsborough with transportation services. A year later, he began an undertaking business by making coffins.

itworthy was a sign of respect no matter a person's color. And to lend out money or guarantee someone else's financial obligations was a way to support existing business networks and manage community resources.

Throughout the 1840s the judges of the Orange County Court of Pleas and Quarter Sessions sent a clear message to the rest of the community that Henry's guarantee was credible and that they believed him to have access to the cash necessary to fulfill his obligation as a guarantor. In August 1845 whoever was sitting on the bench accepted Henry's bond to secure the pledge of Evans Chaves (Eavins Chasom, Eavins Chavous, Evin Chavous), a mixed-race carpenter from Granville County, to support his out-of-wedlock child, who was living with his mother in Orange County.

A few months later, a judge allowed Henry to guarantee a bond of five hundred dollars for James M. Palmer, a white, slave-owning farmer in the Hillsborough area, who wanted to apprentice Samuel Benton (Barton), an eight-year-old free child of color.[54] And sometime before May 1847, the court allowed him to guarantee a bond for John R. Minnis, a white millwright, and James Jackson, a white farmer. That particular arrangement turned out to be a mistake on Henry's part. He misjudged the creditworthiness of Minnis and Jackson, who defaulted on their bond, and he had to sue them for the money. The outcome of the case is unclear.[55]

Henry's guarantees expose the ways that class and race influenced the use of credit. Henry served as guarantor for both white men and those of color in the middle and lower ranks of Hillsborough society and beyond. For a free nonwhite man to have been asked by a white man to secure his financial obligations was a complicated transaction. Certainly, it was a sign of respect. At the same time, however, the prevailing racial power dynamic meant that such a request both placed the white man (or men) in the humiliating position of having to ask a person they considered a social inferior for financial assistance and made it difficult for Henry to refuse to comply with such an entreaty. The caste difference between the two also meant that, in case of default, Henry might face an uphill battle in his attempt to induce his white debtor to pay up.

Despite the fact that Henry's business was flourishing in the early 1850s, he and his brother became increasingly dissatisfied with their lives in Hillsborough. Some dramatic but unrecorded incident may have prompted their discontent. Certainly the town commission made it clear throughout the 1840s that the town's white inhabitants considered free people of color second-class citizens. In October 1843, for example, it passed an ordinance requiring free people of color to post a bond of one hundred dollars for good behavior. Other ordinances passed between 1843 and 1854 included forbidding them from being buried in the town cemetery and establishing special fees for free nonwhite vendors at the Market House.[56] Such official hostility combined with the persistent and daily indignities that Hillsborough's white citizens were predisposed to inflict on local people of color no doubt made their lives increasingly difficult. Being called "boy," having a handshake refused, or having to bite one's tongue in response to verbal abuse had to have been wearing on the spirit. As it became increasingly apparent to both of them that no matter what they did, their presence in town would never be more than grudgingly accepted, they began to consider joining Delilah and her family in Ohio.

The decision was not an easy one. Leaving Hillsborough meant breaking long-standing community ties, abandoning a successful business, and risking the dangers of traveling through multiple slave states in order to reach their destination. Nevertheless, Henry began liquidating his assets, which in 1850 amounted to about $1,400, or the equivalent in 2023 of about $52,100.[57] In January 1853 he advertised his desire to sell 185 acres of land 2.5 miles southeast of town. A few months after Henry's brother, Wilson Bruce, married Henrietta's sister, Sarah Jane Leary, and brought her to live in Hillsborough, Henry announced in the *Hillsborough Recorder* that he was planning to move out of state and began efforts to sell his home and cabinet shop. Thomas and James Webb bought the property for $479.25 ($17,829 in 2023) during courthouse week in October. Henry ended the year by selling his tools, inventory, and household goods at auction. At the same time, he called in all debts owed to him.[58] By New Year's Day in 1854, he was ready to pack up his family's remaining possessions and move to Oberlin.

Leaving the state was a problem, however. Depending on the route they decided to take, Henry and his party had to travel through the slave states of North Carolina then Virginia or Tennessee and Kentucky in order to get to Ohio. In these states, anyone traveling from one place to another who could be taken for an enslaved person was assumed to be one. Unless they could produce a pass or free papers, they had reason to fear harassment and capture by patrollers or slave catchers whose job it was to hunt down and capture runaways. As Hillsborough men who married into the Leary family of Fayetteville, both Henry and his brother had done some traveling and would have known from experience the hazards inherent in being a stranger caught on the open road without the protection of some kind of testimony regarding their free status and the legitimacy of their journey.

Sensitive to the dangers that might await them on their long trip to Ohio, they asked John H. Cook and Alfred A. McKethan of Fayetteville as well as John Kirkland of Hillsborough, all of whom could testify to their reputation for respectability, to ask Governor David Settle Reid to do what he could to guarantee their safe passage. Cook was a wealthy merchant, and McKethan manufactured coaches with the help of thirty-three enslaved workers, ten apprentices, a wheelwright, a painter, and two blacksmiths.

Kirkland was one of Hillsborough's largest landowners and knew the governor personally. Dated April 22, 1854, the letter from Fayetteville said:

> The bearer, Henry Evans, a free man of color, his wife and children, are about to emigrate to Ohio and desire to make arrangements to pass by public conveyance from the Southern States without interruption. He is accompanied by his brother and brother-in law. Himself and brother married in our place into a family of as much respectability as any Colored family in the State and we are pleased to say that the party are entitled to as much respect and regard as any Colored family in our State. Any manner in which you can facilitate their easy passage will be [appreciated?] and will be acknowledged and reciprocated by Your obedient servant John H. Cook and A. A. McKethan.

The second letter, written the next day from Hillsborough by Kirkland, identified the people in Henry's party as "Serena Jeffrys, light mulatto, dark yellow eyes, about 30, from the family of Caswell, William Mitchell, yellow complexion, Edith Mitchell, Henry Evans and wife and children, Wilson B. Evans, his wife and one child; Patsy Freeman; Nancy Jackson; Lee Chavers (Chavois), small boy in company of Henry Evans, yellow complexion, about thirteen years of age." Kirkland said that he believed their papers had been "properly prepared" and was writing "at their request that they may be forwarded before their journey by such a paper writing from your Excellency as will enable them to accomplish it without delay or hindrance."[59]

Having done as much as they could to ensure their safety on their long trip, the Evans party set off for Ohio with William Mitchell, Henry's apprentice, in tow. It is unclear whether Henry had permission from the court or William's mother to take William with him. The general understanding in apprenticeship cases was that a master could not take an apprentice out of the county, let alone the state. But given the fact that Hillsborough's white inhabitants considered the presence of free people of color undesirable, the authorities may have been willing to ignore his removal.

Settling in Oberlin, buying real estate, establishing a cabinet shop, and absorbing the message of abolitionists that slavery was an abomination affirmed their freedom in a way that remaining in Hillsborough could not. By the time the Evanses arrived in Oberlin, many of its citizens were actively engaged in a campaign to thwart the enforcement of the Fugitive Slave Act passed as a part of the Compromise of 1850.[60] In 1789 the U.S. constitution had provided that slave owners had the right to reclaim runaway slaves. But federal laws enforcing that constitutional provision were weak and therefore hard to enforce. In 1850 Congress had agreed to the southern demand that the fugitive slave law be strengthened in return for southern support for a plan preventing the spread of slavery into western territories recently acquired from Mexico. The compromise was intended to put to rest the debate over the future of slavery and slavery expansion. Unfortunately, with the inclusion of a fugitive slave provision, it did just the opposite.

Given the weakness of previous legislation, slave catchers often short-circuited legal processes and simply kidnapped men and women of color who lived in free states and then illegally transferred them across state lines so they could be enslaved. The new law laid out procedures for reclaiming runaway enslaved workers that clearly favored slave owners. It provided that they or their representatives could identify alleged runaways, demand their detention, and bring them before a federal commissioner to determine their fate. Slave owners or their representatives could swear in person or by affidavit that the individual in question was a fugitive. Those accused had no right to testify on their own behalf or bring witnesses in order to prove that they were free. And the magistrates were paid more to order the return of alleged runaways than to confirm their free status. Not surprisingly, those who opposed the law concluded that it was rigged.[61]

In response to this federal legislation, some state legislatures, including that of Ohio, passed personal liberty laws intended to protect the rights of alleged runaways by allowing them to demand a writ of habeas corpus, which protected them from extradition.[62] In 1858, however, pro-southern Democrats gained control of the Ohio legislature and repealed that law, thus increasing the vulnerability of runaways to capture and transportation south.[63] Living in Ohio had a radicalizing impact on the Evans family, who found themselves in the position of being able to publicly acknowledge their opposition to slavery.

The plight of John Price, a runaway from Kentucky, gave them a chance to do something about it. Price appeared in Oberlin in the spring of 1858 seeking refuge. In September two slave catchers spotted him, notified his enslaver, and awaited the arrival of his enslaver's agent so they could facilitate his return to his owner. Working together, the three men abducted Price and took him to the nearby town of Wellington, where they waited in a hotel room for the next southbound train. When word spread about the abduction, Henry, Wilson Bruce, their nephew, John Copeland Jr., and their brother-in-law, Lewis Sheridan Leary, joined some students and other Oberlin residents to rescue Price. Once they had freed him from the clutches of the slave catchers, they sent him via the Underground Railroad to Canada. They were among the thirty-seven men indicted by a federal grand jury in December 1858 for their participation in what became known as the Oberlin-Wellington Rescue. Considering themselves martyrs, they remained in jail for months before their lawyers managed to get the charges against them dropped.[64]

Henry and Wilson Bruce returned to their life in Oberlin. The same cannot be said of John Copeland Jr. and Lewis Sheridan Leary, who engaged in the increasingly violent abolitionist campaign to eliminate slavery. On October 16, 1859, they participated in John Brown's ill-fated raid on the federal arsenal at Harpers Ferry. Neither survived. Leary died of gunshot wounds, and Copeland was hanged for treason on December 16, 1859.[65]

Henry was forty-four years old when the Civil War started in 1861. At that age, he was not a prime candidate for military service. He remained in Oberlin, the proprietor of a furniture-making/undertaking business. In August 1862 he served as chair of a meeting to celebrate the emancipation of the enslaved in the nation's capital. In 1864 he helped plan and inaugurate a new racially integrated cemetery in Oberlin.[66] By 1870 he had accumulated $2,200 ($53,878 in 2023) worth of real estate.[67] He was buried in Oberlin's Westwood cemetery sixteen years later.[68]

Seven years his brother's junior, Wilson Bruce could not enlist during the early stages of the war because northern men of color were not allowed to serve as soldiers in the Union army until Lincoln signed the Emancipation Proclamation on New Years' Day in 1863.[69] He finally enlisted on August 30, 1864, and served as a private in the 178th Ohio Voluntary Infantry. Mustered out on June 29, 1865, in Charlotte, North Carolina, he made his way back to Oberlin, resumed his work as a woodturner, and died in 1898.[70]

Not all free nonwhites were as concerned about their reputations as those in the Evans family. Anderson Mayo (Mayhoe, Mayho), a free laborer of color who murdered his wife in June 1841, is not only a perfect example, but his case also illustrates how a bad reputation could impact a person's claim on freedom.[71]

The crime took place on the Rev. John Witherspoon's plantation just across the Eno River but within walking distance from town. Witherspoon had begun his life in Hillsborough in 1816 when he accepted a pastorate at the Hillsborough Presbyterian Church. He tended his flock until 1833, when, for reasons that are not clear, he left North Carolina to accept a new pulpit in Camden, South Carolina. By the time he returned in 1839, his farm called Tusculum was mortgaged to the hilt, and he was in ill health. Desperate for a scheme that would help him pay off his debts, he bought silkworm eggs, planted five acres of mulberry trees, and built a hundred-foot-long, 1.5-story cocoonery in an ill-fated effort to produce silk.[72] In doing so he became one of hundreds of agricultural entrepreneurs caught up in a craze for producing domestic silk that started in the early 1830s and continued until about 1844.[73]

Witherspoon may have been enterprising, but he had no expertise in the production of silk. Forced to rely on agricultural journals such as the

Having once served as pastor of the Hillsborough Presbyterian Church, John Knox Witherspoon eventually turned to silk production to support his family. Courtesy of the Mary Claire Engstrom Photographic Collection, Wilson Special Collections Library, UNC–Chapel Hill.

American Farmer and an occasional article appearing in the *Hillsborough Recorder* for information relating to the care and nurture of silkworms, he hired local free workers of color to augment his enslaved labor force and shifted some of his workers from farming to tending his trees and silkworms.[74] It was labor-intensive and highly specialized work. Once the silkworm eggs hatched, his workers had to feed them freshly picked mulberry leaves several times a day for about a month until they began spinning their cocoons. Then those who worked in the cocoonery had to monitor the progress of the cocoon-spinning process until the caterpillars were completely encased in silk. Harvesting the silk required experience, perfect timing, and skill in order to bake or boil the cocoons to soften their long, thin fibers and then unwind several cocoons at once while twisting the filaments into one even thread and reeling it onto a wheel.[75] Such constant attention required that enslaved and free workers live side by side on his plantation so that they would have easy access to the cocoonery.

It was in the Witherspoon compound that on the night of Thursday, June 3, 1841, the body of Jesse Tatum Mayo, a free woman of color, was found near the home of her sister, Sally Tatum.[76] Jesse was the estranged wife of Anderson Mayo. Both of them worked for Witherspoon. They had four children: three sons, including an eight-year-old named Jim, and a daughter named Catherine.[77] Jesse's troubled relationship with her husband had no doubt been the talk of the neighborhood for some time. Sensitive about maintaining what he considered to be his male prerogatives, Anderson was an abusive man with a vile temper. His daughter, Catherine, would eventually testify that sometime before her mother's murder, her father had become incensed because his supper wasn't ready on time and ordered her brother Jim to fetch a switch to beat Jesse. Jim left the cabin to carry out his father's instructions, but before he returned, Anderson "seized an iron poker and said that it would answer the same purpose and he would make the blood fly out of her [Jesse's] head." He later "swore he would kill Jesse if she ever put her foot into his house."

Murders were not common in Hillsborough. By the time the authorities held the coroner's inquest the next day, the town must have been abuzz with the news. Dr. Pride Jones testified at the inquest that Jesse had been violently struck on the left temple with a rock, causing several mortal wounds that fractured her skull and caused her death. A coroner's jury comprised of some of Hillsborough's most prominent white citizens, including Dr.

Edmund Strudwick, Dr. James Webb Jr., James Turrentine, sometime sheriff of Orange County, and Dr. Frank Smith, the son of Dr. James Strudwick Smith, heard testimony from at least ten witnesses before charging Anderson with the murder. He was arrested and held in the county jail until he could be tried in the Superior Court of Orange County during their September quarter session. During the summer, the sheriff delivered summonses for witnesses that included white, free nonwhite, and enslaved inhabitants of Hillsborough.

When the court began its business in September, the sheriff delivered Anderson to the court, where he was arraigned. After he pleaded not guilty, the judge ordered that a jury be selected from a pool of fifty men to hear the case *State v. Anderson Mayo, a free negro*.

The testimony that the jury of twelve heard against Anderson was as straightforward as it was incriminating. Slowly the prosecution put together a damning portrait of the man and a plausible narrative describing the circumstances that led to Jesse's murder. According to two witnesses, Anderson's anger and abuse toward Jesse were fueled by an all-consuming jealousy prompted by gossip that suggested that Jesse was committing adultery with a free man of color who lived nearby. Those who spread such stories triggered a response that was as predictable as it was tragic. Nothing was likely to threaten a husband's sense of honor more than the belief that his wife was unfaithful. Whatever the case, Anderson apparently had second thoughts about throwing his wife out of his house, because three or four weeks before her murder, he began a campaign to try to lure her back. He began by eliciting the help of a go-between, Pompey, an enslaved worker owned by Fred Reeves but hired out to Witherspoon, to arrange a meeting with Jesse. As an inducement, Pompey was to tell her that if she met Anderson "at the big oak tree near the spring at dark, he would give her some money, sugar, coffee, and a pair of shoes." Jesse wasn't interested. Her husband, she told Pompey, had threatened to whip both her and her alleged lover, and she was convinced that he might even kill her. Thwarted in his efforts, Anderson then prevailed on Harry, another of Witherspoon's enslaved workers, to offer Jesse three dollars in cash if she would agree to return home. She again refused. Frustrated by Jesse's unwillingness to meet with him, Anderson confronted her on the day before the murder as she and their daughter Catherine were leaving the Witherspoon house and demanded that she return to live with him. His persistence must have been terrifying. Fearing for her life, Jesse informed him that she had no intention of doing what he asked. On the evening of the murder, Anderson again confronted Jesse in public. Harry testified that he had seen the two of them engaged in an angry discussion as they walked together after dinner.

After his confrontation with his estranged wife, Anderson crossed the river and went into town. Pompey, who had just finished his work in the cocoonery, saw him as he returned carrying two jugs of what he described as stolen whiskey. It was near or shortly after sundown, and Witherspoon apparently enforced a curfew for those who lived on his land. Concerned that he had left Witherspoon's property without permission, Anderson begged Pompey to assure anyone who asked that he, Anderson, had fallen asleep in the cocoonery. In order to strengthen his alibi, he then approached Witherspoon, who was finishing up some garden work, so that Witherspoon could swear he had seen Anderson on the plantation that evening. Shortly thereafter, he apparently confronted Jesse outside Manuel Strudwick's house. Within moments, Witherspoon and Susan Strudwick heard a scream coming from that direction. They found Jesse lying on her back with the right side of her head on the ground.[78]

The trial was held in the local courthouse. As Anderson sat with his lawyer, light filtered through the mullioned windows of the courtroom. He and those who filled the room watched as the judge took his seat on the bench. The witnesses appeared one by one. They told a persuasive, consistent, and coherent story. Three of them swore that they had heard Anderson threaten Jesse's life, and the prosecution was able to show that Anderson had a reputation for being violent, manipulative, and dishonest. Gossip used as evidence of his bad temper and jealousy served as the basis for providing a motive for killing his wife.

There is no record that Anderson's lawyer mounted any sort of defense. After hearing the evidence, the jury found Anderson Mayo guilty of murder, and the judge remanded him to jail to await his sentence. According to the court decree, he was hanged sometime between 9:00 a.m. and 4:00 p.m. on Friday, October 9, 1841.

Their father's execution made orphans of the four Mayo children. It is unclear what became of three of them, but in May 1849 the county court apprenticed sixteen-year-old James (Jim) Mayo to Henry Crabtree, an Orange County farmer.[79] We know nothing about James's life as an apprentice. But in 1853 William H. Whitson (Whitsman) and Abner Peace (Pearce), claiming to be descendants of Absolum Tatum, a Hillsborough bachelor, philanthropist, and reformer who had once owned James's grandmother, Sally, tried to enslave James on the grounds that his claim to freedom was not properly documented.[80]

Thus began the legal struggle to preserve James's freedom and by extension that of his brothers and sister. Wills written by propertied white men that freed enslaved women and their mixed-race children were often challenged in southern courts by white relatives of the deceased. As Bernie Jones has pointed out, the issue for judges was whether to honor the testator's desire to atone for his transgressions and provide for his support of his children, thus breaching racial boundaries by giving enslaved women and children wealth and status, or preserve the interests of the white community by keeping wealth in their hands.[81]

This case hinged on the court's handling of Tatum's 1802 will. In that document, he directed that his executors free his enslaved workers, including Sally, her child, and any future children she might bear, in recognition of their "meritorious service" to him. He asked his legal representatives to arrange for their emancipation and use the proceeds from the rest of his estate for their "use and benefit." In May 1803 the Orange County Court of Pleas and Quarter Session freed Sally and the other individuals named in his will and invested them "with all the rights and privileges of free born Negroes." Apparently, however, the county clerk never recorded the emancipation decree, an oversight that eventually led to Whitson and Peace's claim.[82]

It must have come as something of a shock to James and his immediate family that their status as free people was being questioned and that there was a real possibility that he was about to be enslaved. There is no evidence to indicate that anyone in Hillsborough had ever questioned their position as free people. Sally's descendants believed themselves to be free, behaved as if they were, and had apparently been treated as such. But in the absence of legally filed emancipation papers, they had to depend on the fragile thread of their neighbor's memories of their genealogy and community discussion and acceptance of those memories as their only guarantee against enslavement.[83]

James's case, argued by a white lawyer, came to trial in May 1854. The Orange County Court of Pleas and Quarter Session found that the provisions of Tatum's will were valid, that his executors had properly carried out his requests, and that as one of Sally's descendants James was and always had been a free man. It ordered that the court record be amended retroactively to register the emancipation of Sally and her children and by extension her grandchildren, thus confirming James's claim to freedom. Whitson and Peace appealed that decision to the North Carolina Supreme Court, which heard their appeal, rejected their petition, and affirmed the lower court's decision in June 1855.[84]

The case *James Mayho vs. James H. Whitson and Abner Peace* confirmed James's claim to self-sovereignty. At the same time, however, it stands as testimony to the tenuousness of legal barriers that protected Hillsborough's free nonwhite inhabitants from enslavement, a reality that was no doubt clear to the Evans brothers and their families. They had already decided to leave Hillsborough and were going through the process of ensuring their safe passage to Ohio when James and his lawyer first appeared in court to defend his claim to freedom. The knowledge that there was every possibility that the court might rule in favor of two white men against a free man of color and that the claim to freedom that had protected James and the members of his family for the fifty years since the death of Absolum Tatum could thereby be invalidated may only have confirmed their decision to live elsewhere. In the end, while the Mayo family was able to secure its freedom by court order, the Evans family had to secure theirs by fleeing the state.

Unlike the Evans and Mayo families, most of Hillsborough's free people of color lived and died in obscurity, their shadowy appearance in the public record usually confined to the census unless they did something to disrupt the peace and tranquility of their community. Their labor was critical for the economic well-being of their neighbors, and most of them worked hard to support their families and provide for their children's futures. Henry was among the few to own real estate. Those, like the Mayos, the mixed-race Strudwicks, and the Tatums, presumably lived in housing provided by their employers or rented their living quarters. As strategies for survival, many of them nurtured reputations as hardworking and respectable, attached themselves to white people hoping for their protection, and formed networks of support within their own community. When they died, their families and friends mourned their passing and buried them on whatever land was available.

Anecdotal evidence holds that the two-acre plot that is now Margaret

Lane Cemetery in Hillsborough, first mentioned in town records in 1885, was the site of nonwhite burials even before 1854 when Peter Brown Ruffin purchased it as a burying ground for his enslaved workers and those of the Cadwalader Jones family.[85] Put to other uses, the fieldstones that once marked burial sites have long since disappeared, leaving behind a green lawn lying beneath towering oak trees as a silent reminder of a people whose contributions in terms of labor and service helped turn Hillsborough into a small but thriving community in the years before the Civil War.

Restored in 1987, Margaret Lane Cemetery, once known as "The Old Slave Cemetery," is one of the most tranquil spots in Hillsborough. Yet it stands as silent testimony to racial tensions that still beset those who live in the town. Historical gossip perpetuates the belief that the reason there are no longer markers in the cemetery is because neglect of the site in the mid-twentieth century encouraged some of the town's white citizens to repurpose the headstones to pave the approaches to their houses. Whether the story is true or not, its persistence as part of the town's oral tradition subverts the comforting illusion of racial harmony and illustrates a failure to erase memories of the sort of indignities imposed on Hillsborough's people of color by their white neighbors in the postbellum period. A way of undermining white cultural and moral authority, it serves as a reminder of the town's tumultuous past.

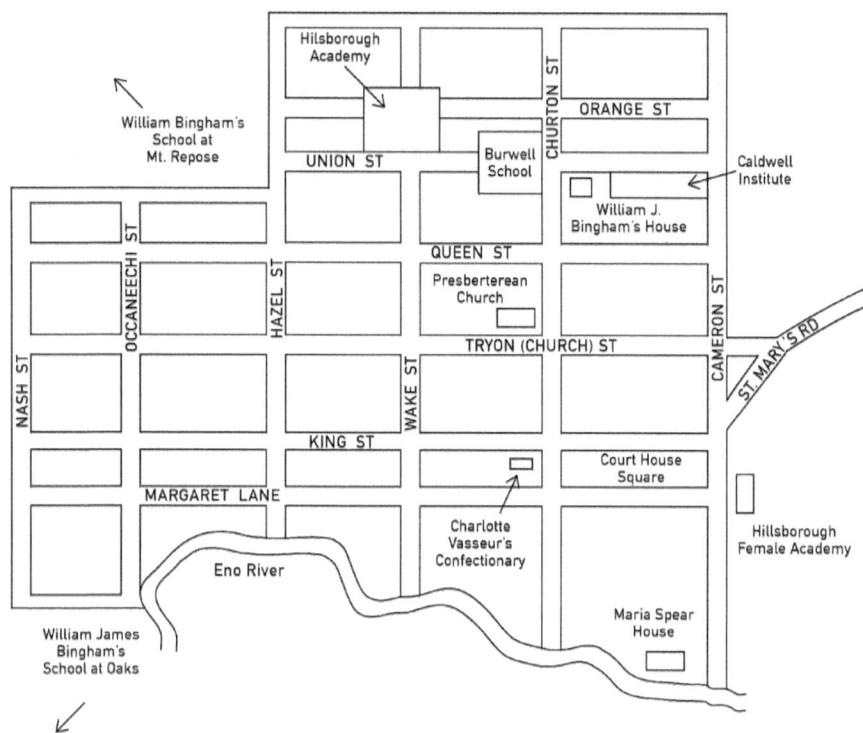

3

SCHOOL DAYS, RULE DAYS

It was a balmy May evening in 1850 when Anna Burwell marched her little army of ten students down Churton Street toward Webb and Long's dry goods store. The girls had spent all day in the classroom reciting their lessons. When their light supper of bread and butter was over, they put on their bonnets to go shopping with Anna as their chaperone.[1] Young William Norwood was working as a clerk at the store that night. While work kept him busy, he longed for a more active social life. "There are very few ladies left in or around Hillsboro," he despondently reported to a cousin in Fayetteville. "We would have quite a solitary village [sic] if it were not for Mr. Burwell's school." The fact that it had twenty-eight boarders was promising, he continued. Some of them were "as ugly as can be imagined," he complained, while the others were "*perfectly lovely*." Presumably, it was the pretty ones who suddenly walked through the door at the end of his working day. Flustered by their presence, he confessed, "I become so *absent* sometimes while waiting on them that I almost forget the difference between the yardstick and my scissors and only come to myself when unsuccessful in getting the yd stick in my pocket."[2]

Female students in Hillsborough were inevitably the subject of idle talk on the part of Hillsborough's single young men looking for female companionship. The kind of parents who were the Burwells' patrons expected that sending their daughters off to school would provide them the opportunity to meet prospective suitors whose education, family background, and economic prospects would make them acceptable candidates for marriage. At the same time, they also assumed that those who ran academies would restrict and monitor their female students' access to young men as a way of protecting their chastity.[3] Everyone understood that attracting attention to oneself and then being talked about was an integral part of the precourtship process. At issue was the trajectory of that talk where respectable young women were concerned. Parents and teachers alike were determined that the young ladies who attended the Burwell School and others like it would emerge from the time they spent there with spotless reputations.

As small as Hillsborough was during the early nineteenth century, the size of its student population was impressive. Dr. James Webb counted 150 students in the town in 1841.[4] And Bell Norwood wrote to her cousin in January 1847, "You have no idea how very literary Hillsborough has become, & if the coming generation are not all able to speak, read and write it will not be because there are no schools in the place." According to her count there were as many as ten trying to recruit students.[5]

Educational opportunities were not evenly distributed, however. Neither enslaved nor free children of color had access to schools before the Civil War. Some learned to read and write as a result of their association with literate white people. A few learned from their literate parents or friends. And some free nonwhite children in the first two decades of the century benefited from the practice of apprenticeship, which often required a master to guarantee that apprentices were literate when they ended their court-ordered term of servitude.[6] But when the Confederacy collapsed, most of the state's free people of color and formerly enslaved could neither read nor write.

Most white children found themselves in much the same situation before 1839 when the state legislature authorized the establishment of tax-supported schools. Before that, white parents with limited resources and a desire to see their children educated taught them at home, sent them to cooperative old field schools, or enrolled them in Sunday schools supported by the Orange County Sunday School Union organized in 1825.[7]

The white elite and those who aspired to that status sent their children to private academies. Some were short-lived proprietary schools, which admitted a small number of children each year. Some of the most prominent families in Hillsborough were involved in such enterprises. Rev. John Knox Witherspoon, who would later try his hand at producing silk, ran a boarding school between 1826 and 1828 on his property Tusculum near town. William and Walker Anderson ran a boarding school at their home Lochiel from 1830 to 1836.[8] Such enterprises were not always successful. When Witherspoon attempted to open another school in 1841, he failed to attract any students.⁹ The same was true of the efforts of Mary Waddell and Anna Kirkland, who each tried unsuccessfully to open a school in her parlor.¹⁰

Other private schools prospered and lasted longer. Girls could get an education at the Hillsborough Female Academy sponsored by the Episcopal church beginning in 1825 and then at the Burwell School for Young Ladies starting in 1837. Boys studied classics at the Hillsborough Academy beginning in the first decade of the century. After that the Bingham School and then the Caldwell Institute prepared them for admission to the University of North Carolina and other seats of higher learning.¹¹ Whether they were locals or boarding students, they found themselves for the first time in their lives under the tutelage of adults who were not their parents, subjected to rules that may have not been typical in their households, and exposed to gender-specific curricula intended to produce well-educated, self-disciplined, Christian adults whose leadership would benefit their communities, advance the economy, promote the political interests of the white elite, and uphold the social and racial status quo.

Despite the South's conservatism regarding gender roles, there was little resistance to the idea of women's education in the region as long as it did not threaten the social, economic, or racial structures that served as the basis for white patriarchal authority. While going away to school could delay marriage and the assumption of adult responsibilities, the parents of school girls did not expect their daughters to use their education as a way to evade the authority of their family, avoid marriage altogether, or support themselves.¹² At the same time, however, in the unlikely event that a woman might find it necessary to provide for herself and her children, an education could give her the opportunity to do so through teaching, particularly if she was skilled in music or art.¹³

Anna Burwell opened her school for girls at the Presbyterian manse on Churton Street in 1837 as a favor to a neighbor, Dr. James Webb, because she needed the money, or so the widely accepted story has it. Twenty years before, Webb had built a little log cabin on his property so that another neighbor and fellow Presbyterian, Mary [Polly] Burke, could conduct a day school for his children and their friends. When Burke moved to Alabama in 1834, Webb sent his daughter Mary across town to the Episcopal school run by Maria Spear. For whatever reason, he appears to have been unhappy with the arrangement and was searching for an alternative.¹⁴

Anna Burwell opened a school for young ladies in her parlor in 1837. Courtesy of the Burwell School Historic Site, Hillsborough.

Anna and her husband, Rev. Robert Burwell, pastor of the local Presbyterian church, had been in town since 1835. Already the mother of three children, she found Robert's yearly salary of four hundred dollars totally inadequate to meet her growing family's needs.[15] Expected to entertain graciously, feed, clothe, and educate her children, and display the trappings of gentility without the means to do so, Anna, like other ministers' wives, struggled to make ends meet and were well aware that their efforts often were likely to fall short in the opinion of their neighbors and the members of their church.[16] Gossip was the bane of a minister's wife's existence. Warned by her aunt shortly after she arrived in Hillsborough that "a pastor's wife will be much observed," Anna could not avoid being the target of it.[17]

A number of ministers' wives wrote about how their self-presentation and activities fed their local gossip mills.[18] In her novel *From Dawn to Daylight: The Simple Story of a Western Home by a Minister's Wife*, Eunice White Bullard Beecher, the wife of Rev. Henry Ward Beecher, wrote of how

The Presbyterian Church and its session house were located just off Churton Street and served as one of the centers of religious life in nineteenth-century Hillsborough. Courtesy of the Mary Claire Engstrom Photographic Collection, Wilson Special Collections Library, UNC–Chapel Hill.

exasperated the newly wed Mary Lighton Herbert was when she realized that among her first callers were those who came "to spy out the land" and "make reports" on their first impressions of the new minister's wife.[19] In her *Jottings from Life*, Helen R. Cutler's main character, the wife of a Methodist minister, complained, "Every body [watches] the minister's wife, and [speaks] to others of what she says and does." She deeply resented being scrutinized by her neighbor, the widow Baker: "Whenever I went out I could feel her black eyes watching me from her window, to see if she could detect, in my dress or deportment, anything upon which to hang censure. I felt that she was taking note of my apparel, to see if I had proper regard for economy, or had failed on the score of neatness."[20]

When word spread that Anna was about to open a school in her parlor in order to supplement her husband's income, four students enrolled. They included Webb's daughter Mary, by then age fourteen, and Mary Susan Burwell, Anna's daughter, age six. Local lore places Sarah Kollock, age eleven, and Annabella Norwood, age six, in that first class as well. Shortly thereafter, Anna welcomed Caroline Cowen, an orphan from New Bern, into her home as her first boarder.[21] Through advertising and word of mouth, the Burwells eventually recruited the daughters of slave-owning farmers, businessmen, and professionals into their home, promising parents that they would provide the girls with a formal education in the liberal arts and informal instruction on how to be a southern lady.[22]

It took the cooperation of her neighbors, a willing workforce, and a community of widely varied businesses to accomplish this. In order to run a household and school that at one time or another housed as many as forty people including Anna and Robert, their growing family, their free and enslaved servants, and their boarding students, the Burwells needed access to a wide variety of local resources.[23] In order to recruit students, the Burwells depended on Dennis Heartt to publicize their notices in his newspaper and distribute their advertisements to newspapers throughout the state. When they needed extra help with their classes, they hired neighbors such as Anne (Nancy) Cameron, who taught Burwell students piano in her home.[24] They purchased meat and produce from local farmers and supplies from local merchants. They employed free people of color such as Umstead Mayo to tend the garden and Eliza Chavis (Chavious) to do the laundry.[25] And they negotiated with their slave-owning neighbors to rent or lend them enslaved workers to cook, clean the house and schoolrooms, and perform other domestic chores.[26] Charlotte Vasseur's confectionary on King Street, mercantile establishments, fancy goods shops, milliners, and dressmakers all provided valuable services to the Burwells and their students.[27] The Burwells counted on neighbors such as Julia Minor and her mother, who had extra rooms, to board their teachers and some of their students during the school term.[28] And when the boardinghouses were full, they depended on hotel owners such as Thomas Howerton, the father of two of their students, to take care of the overflow.[29] Local ministers such as William Mercer Green and Moses Ashley Curtis helped the Burwells tend to the young peoples' spiritual lives. Together, all of these people created an educational community intended to prepare young women for adulthood.

Technically speaking, Anna and Robert ran their school as a partnership. As a full-time, if underpaid, pastor, Robert knew that his congregation had first claim on his time and energy. That combined with his retiring, bookish personality meant that during the school's early years, Robert was not much of a presence at the school.[30] That Anna was the one in charge was cause for comment. As Ann Strudwick Nash later put it, "Mr. Burwell was

Robert Burwell divided his time between his duties as the Presbyterian minister and those connected with the Burwell School. Courtesy of the Burwell School Historic Site, Hillsborough.

supposed to be principal and his wife assistant principal, but in reality it was the other way around; for in this as in their other joint undertakings it was Mrs. Burwell who took the lead, with her husband as adviser and on occasions, co-worker."[31]

This point was illustrated by the Burwells' eldest son, John Bott, who wrote in his memoir that one day his father and a number of other gentlemen were on their way to a meeting of the Orange Presbytery in Caswell County when they stopped for lunch. Seated around the table, they began teasing each other about who among them was a henpecked husband. Each denied being dominated by his wife. "During a lull in the conversation," John Bott continued, "a countryman standing by and hearing my Father's name called, stepped up to him and asked if he was any kin to the Widow Burwell who lived in Hillsboro. He had been in the habit of carrying eggs, butter and other country produce to our house and, never having any dealings with anyone but Mother, naturally concluded she was the 'man' of the family and that there was no Mr. Burwell. This was voted by the party as proof positive that at least one member was ruled by his wife."³² Thus was Robert's reputation as a henpecked husband established.

It is not surprising that the supplier mistook the situation. Standing almost six feet tall, the robust Anna was as imposing a figure as any man.³³ And she presented herself as a thoroughly competent businesswoman able to negotiate the best prices for the supplies she needed and was clearly in charge of the material resources of her business and its labor force. In short, she possessed the self-assurance and administrative expertise that her husband was not yet willing or able to display.

Anna may have been very much in charge, but there were some matters relating to the school that she could not take care of. When she and Robert married she lost the right to control property or sign contracts.³⁴ Although Anna wrote the recruitment advertisements for the school, it was Robert who signed the contract placing them in the area newspapers such as the *Hillsborough Recorder*, the *Wilmington Advertiser*, the *Raleigh Register*, the *North Carolina Standard,* and the *Newbern Spectator*.³⁵ He was ultimately responsible for settling the school's accounts, but Anna paid many of the bills since he did not do it as efficiently as she did. In a letter to one of their daughters, Anna wrote, "Your Father somehow don't dispatch the business in school & tho I get done my share at two o'clock he is every day till three & after."³⁶ And since contracts were involved, Robert also hired the teachers.³⁷

While her husband negotiated school contracts and taught an occasional class, Anna assumed responsibility for all other matters relating to school administration. Her schedule left little time for leisure: "I get up at six, we breakfast about eight, it takes me till eleven to keep my house & set all strait, then I dress & teach till two. Then from three when we finish dinner to four, I have to do one little thing & another—from four to five all the girls sew in my room. They walk from five to six, then comes supper & by that time I am done over."³⁸ "Done over" or not, she might still have to run errands and shop for the girls as well as plan meals and lessons for the next day.³⁹

Her duties were numerous. She evaluated the academic preparation and accomplishments of her students, allocated classroom space, scheduled classes, ensured that Burwell students were properly housed, fed, clothed, medicated, and evangelized, ordered school and domestic supplies, kept detailed records of her students' progress, expenses, and spending money, accounted for school income and expenditures, dealt with dissatisfied parents, and tried to manage the household help. She performed all these duties while she bore a child every other year or so, supported her husband's ministry, attended church and prayer meetings, visited the sick and needy, and worried about the state of her soul and that of her children and students.

A wide variety of challenges faced Anna as she negotiated her way through the school year. There were no admissions standards for young women hoping to enroll, for example. Sometimes parents wrote to announce that they intended to send their daughters to study in Hillsborough. Other times, they just arrived with their daughters in tow. Whatever the case, it was Anna's job to assess their preparedness and appearance and determine the best way to educate them while she turned them into ladies. Take the case of the young woman who arrived unexpectedly at the beginning of the spring term in January 1856. "Yesterday afternoon as I was sitting in my recess at work one of the little boys said 'Mother a man wants to see you,'" she wrote to her daughter Fanny. By his side was a girl who turned out to be totally unpresentable. You could smell her hair, she wrote, "& the girls say she sleeps in every thing she wears except her dress & shoes & stockings. . . . She plays on the Piano—that is puts her foot on the Pedal and makes a rumbling—I'll report her improvement which I flatter myself will be perceptible in a short time—at any rate her hair is to be cleansed & oiled instead of wet—& her clothes made to fit her."[40] A few weeks later she reported that the girl "still looks like a stray one, so dirty that it will take a month to get her skin & hair to look like other people's."[41]

Another challenge was trying to change her students' speech patterns and teach them to write using the proper punctuation, capitalization, and spelling. Some of her students came from wealthy, refined, and well-educated families. But others were farm girls, brought up in the country among people who did not speak standard English and used colloquialisms to make themselves understood. Such habits were hard to break. Her reputation and the success of her school depended on her ability to instill in her students an appreciation of the proper use of the English language, so that "I reckon" became "I think," "a heap" became "a lot," "I would er went" became "I could have gone," and "no how" became "anyhow," as well as to teach them to say "ask" instead of "ax" and "yesterday" instead of "yistiddy."[42]

Without admissions requirements, maintaining both rigorous academic standards and high enrollment was a challenge. Some girls flourished, but others had difficulty. When parents were dissatisfied, it was up to Anna to smooth their ruffled feathers for fear that their complaints could undermine her school's reputation. "We have had, I suspect, a final difficulty with the Jones children," she wrote to her daughter in 1856. "I wrote you that Mary Jones had come back to school. Mrs. Jones requested that she should join the class she left a session ago. I told her I was afraid the studies would be too hard for Mary, as the class had progressed steadily. . . . Well! She joined the class, & sure enough could not recite a single lesson just sat looking about & fooling while Mr. B. and I would be trying to explain the lessons." Mary complained to her father that her lessons in astronomy were too difficult, so he sent a message to the Burwells asking that she be excused from the class. When Robert refused his request, Jones sent another note announcing that he was removing his daughter from school. Concerned about the financial and social repercussions of the incident, Anna wrote a note to Mary's mother: "I told her . . . that I did not write . . . to induce her to send Mary back, for Dr. Jones had once before seemed dissatisfied with our assignments, but merely to show her that Mr. B. said what he did without intending any offence."[43]

Since word-of-mouth support was as important as advertising in attracting students, managing information about themselves and their enterprise was critical for ensuring their school's success. It was in Anna's interest to do what she could to placate the Joneses in the hope that they would not say anything to discourage others from sending their daughters to the school. Good press was always welcome, of course. The Burwells could not have asked for a better testimonial than that delivered by their colleague Alexander Wilson, headmaster of the Caldwell Institute for boys, when he wrote an unsolicited support letter that was eventually published in the *North Carolina Standard*. "I have very little confidence in newspaper puffs about schools," Wilson began, "but it seems sometimes to be expedient to attempt to notice a school so worthy of patronage as that of Mr. and Mrs. Burwell." On the spur of the moment, he said, he had taken the opportunity to observe Anna Burwell teaching one of her classes. As he watched her students read and interpret Milton's *Paradise Lost*, he was impressed by their command of the English language.[44] And it was always gratifying when the Burwells heard that people thought well of their educational efforts. "Mrs. S[trudwick] told me she had a letter from Mrs. Ashe [Sarah

Ann Ashe of Wilmington] the other day in which she said that our school was under discussion & a lady remarked she was 'sure Mrs. Mary [Burwell] Strudwick [Anna's daughter] being educated there was a sufficient recommendation.'"[45]

Gossip based on misinformation could be a problem, however. In December 1855 Anna wrote to her daughter that one of their Virginia friends had been asked "if it was a fact that I did not allow our boarders to wear collars, that I made them wear brown ribbon round their necks to save washing!! & to day Lou Smith wanted to know if it was a fact that we would take no more boarders, as such was the report in Fayetteville.... It seems to me strange what credence people give to every rumor. Common sense is a scarcer article than is generally supposed."[46] Since their source was obscure, such gossip was hard to counter. "It just shows how people can get the wrong end of a story," she wrote a few months later. "Nothing tho' seems unaccountable to me since the 'Brown ribbon' story."[47]

It is through the letters written by Burwell students, complete with misspellings and lack of punctuation, that we gain some impression of what their lives at school were like. When Burwell girls wrote to their loved ones and friends, they talked principally about adjusting to student life, coping with the academic demands made on them, seeking diversions outside the classroom, their lack of access to boys, and arranging their wardrobes.

Boarders found themselves separated from family for the first time in their lives. The more adaptable among them adjusted to school life quickly, accepted Anna as a surrogate for their mothers, and made deep and satisfying friendships with the other girls. "We are just like a family," Mary Murphy from Sampson County wrote to her mother shortly after she enrolled in 1848. She found Anna easy to talk to and was delighted in the affection she showed toward her boarders. "We talk to [Anna] just like we would our mother evry night she goes in our room and kiss us all we girls kiss [one] another evry night before we go to sleep." Mary liked Hillsborough "tolerabley [sic] well," but her homesick twin sister Susan did not. She had only been in school for a few weeks when she wrote to her mother, "I donot like to stay here atall I think to much about home but I cannot help it Sometimes I ball like my heart would break It appears like I have been here 5 months allready I never wanted to see home so bad in my life I cannot stay here any longer than next winter nohow but Pa says I shall stay untill I am done here tell him if he dont send for me I will go in the stage for I cannot

The Burwell School was home to the Burwell family, their students, and their enslaved workers from 1837 to 1857. Courtesy of the Mary Claire Engstrom Photographic Collection, Wilson Special Collections Library, UNC–Chapel Hill.

stand it I must go home if I have to walk."[48] When her parents reenrolled her for another term, she continued to protest but to no avail.[49] The same was true of Annie Kerr from Alamance County. She had been enrolled in the Burwell School for about six weeks when she wrote to her half sister that she was studying hard but was tired of being in town and missed her niece Lizzie.[50] When her parents sent Lizzie to join her, the poor child was afflicted with homesickness as well.[51]

Their studies kept Burwell students busy. The reputation of the school depended on the rigor of the curriculum, which focused on math, geography, history, science, and the history of Christianity and related theological issues as well an appreciation of literature and the proper use of English.[52] Mastering these subjects was intended to instill in students intellectual discipline, civic pride, an appreciation of the natural world, and a moral compass that would encourage temperance, philanthropy, and community service. Burwell students also studied French, art, music, and needlework. These so-called "ornamental" subjects were designed to meet the needs of the elite in preparing their daughters to enter society, attract suitable husbands, travel, and run large households.[53]

Some students found their daily routine tedious. "It is 'powerful' dull times in Hillsborough at present, for my part I see nothing but books from morning till night," Bell Norwood wrote to her cousin in 1846. "I rise early in the morning and get my lessons, go to school at nine." She and the other students attended morning classes until twelve and then sat down to dinner. They returned to the classroom at two and continued their studies until four. On Tuesdays and Thursdays after school, Bell took drawing lessons, and on Mondays and Wednesdays she spent the late afternoon writing her compositions. Friday evenings were reserved for vocal music or voluntary society meetings.[54]

The girls who wrote about their classes seemed to have enjoyed them even if they found them difficult. Bell wrote to her cousin, "You will remember that I was studying Latin when you were here. I can't brag I don't think about my progress, for I have only read the life of Joseph & fifty-two fables. I think it a very interesting study and great deal easier than English." She was also studying algebra but found it "right hard" as opposed to Mag Walker, who considered mathematics problems a challenge and whose success in solving them earned her the highest marks in her class.[55]

Burwell students enjoyed tea parties, skating parties, and impromptu dancing in the parlor when they needed to let off steam. "The girls are 'kicking up a dust' literally in the other room," Anna wrote to her daughter in February 1856. "They have been so confined that I told them to night to dance for exercise. Bettie Carrington is playing, and I went to the door just now & could hardly see across it for the dust."[56] Sometimes there were surprise excursions. "We had a picnic on the mountain, some time ago," Mary Pearce told her cousin. "We were assembled in the school-room as usual, not even suspecting we were to have holydays, when Mr. B. entered and told us we could go to the mountain, if we wished. I can tell you we quickly concluded, (as one of the girls remarked) that 'unexpected pleasures were better than unknown quantities,' and joyfully assented. We spent a delightful day—took our dinner, sitting on the grass around the Mountain Spring—quite romantic."[57]

Others sought out entertainment in town. An occasional community-sponsored fair provided one source of amusement.[58] Parties held near or at the end of school sessions provided yet another. "The young people

Bettie Carrington from Halifax, Virginia, attended the Burwell School in 1855–56. Courtesy of the Burwell School Historic Site, Hillsborough.

here have been quite gay for the last month; we had four parties," Bell Norwood reported. "You know Dr. Wilson [of the Caldwell Institute] and Mrs. Burwell do not like their scholars to attend parties during the session, but at the last part of it we always manage to get round them."[59]

Given their ages, interest in boys was predictable and talk about them inevitable. The Burwells responded by discouraging their students' romantic fantasies and making sure they were always chaperoned when they went out. According to Mary Murphy, the girls could not go anywhere "with out Mrs. Burwell go with us." The Burwells also restricted the visitors the girls were allowed to entertain on school property. "Ther is a male school a bout a quarter of a mile from Mr. Burwell," Mary reported to her mother. "They [the boys] are passing about the house all the time Mr. Burwell don't allow them to go to his house. They went last session but they will not come this session."[60] It is not clear what the Caldwell Institute boys did to deserve banishment, but they remained unwelcome for some time. In 1850 another student reported, "We are not allowed to go out without Mrs. B. for fear we will meet an [Caldwell] Institute boy and we are not to stay in the piazza when the Chapel Hill students are up here."[61]

Young male relatives also found themselves unwelcome when they came to visit. "Mr. & Mrs. Burwell do not like for the brothers from Chapel Hill to visit their sisters and as for letting cousins see each other here she never thinks of such a thing. I have two cousins there and both of them have been up here but I could not go to see them," one student complained.[62] Male friends from home met the same fate, although Robert Burwell appears to have been more concerned about their visits than his wife. In 1849 Susan Murphy told her father that a boy from New Bern had come to see one of her New Bern classmates. "Mrs. Burwell told her she might go and see him, but Mr. B. called her out and asked her what business she had in the parlor." When it turned out they were unrelated, he asked the young man to leave.[63]

Burwell girls may have found such restrictions annoying, but they did have ways of subverting the rules, which included opening the parlor door and sneaking a young man in when the Burwells were not paying attention.[64]

The presence of single male teachers combined with the romantic naiveté of their students posed a potential threat to the Burwells' ability to protect their students' reputations and by extension the reputation of their school. It was with great consternation that Anna wrote in her diary in October 1855 that she had just learned that the music teacher, Mr. Rudolph Vampill, had engaged in "improper conduct to some of the girls." It is unclear exactly where she heard about it, who told her, or what kind of behavior she was referring to. But she clearly understood that if such damaging information made its way into the community, it could do serious harm. Their immediate response was to dismiss Vampill.[65]

Evangelical parents were concerned about the state of their daughters' souls and hoped they would embrace the possibility of spiritual rebirth and a religious conversion while they were at school.[66] Parents who had qualms about the dangers of transferring their spiritual stewardship to someone else had little reason to be concerned that their daughters' religious education would be neglected at the Burwell School, which was, after all, run by a Presbyterian minister and his wife. Anna's efforts to enrich her students' spiritual lives were ceaseless and heartfelt but went largely unappreciated. Her students sat through her Bible study classes because they had no choice. Few seemed inclined to spiritual self-examination. Their lack of receptiveness to her spiritual ministry was a constant disappointment to her. "I spent the evening in the Parlor with the girls," she wrote in her diary one cold January night just before she went to bed. "Oh that I could realize more my responsibility about these young immortals, that I care more for their souls." She continued to be discouraged about the impact of her efforts, noting that her scholars seemed relatively unconcerned about "eternal things."[67]

Burwell students spent more time gossiping with each other and their families about fashion than they did on matters relating to religion. Those from wealthy, well-traveled families or small towns like Fayetteville probably came to school with a sense of fashion. But girls from families of modest means, who lived in the country, and whose mothers had never been to school, may have found themselves at a disadvantage in determining what clothes they would need as a student and assessing the appropriateness of those they brought with them. They and their parents depended on Anna to help them select clothes that were modest, practical, and in good taste.[68] In April 1852, for example, Elizabeth Coit wrote to her sister that Anna had ordered white linen bonnets from a milliner in Petersburg for the girls at the school. "Mine is going to be trimed with pink," she said. "I told Mrs. Burwell that I had thought some of having it trimed with white, but Mrs. Burwell said that she thought that white looked too old for a school girl, and it is also going to do for a summer and a winter bonnet."[69]

By the 1850s, Hillsborough's young women had a number of ways to acquire new clothes and accessories. In 1854 Lizzie Glass wrote to her mother asking if she could buy a new dress from a local merchant who was selling them in a range of prices.[70] Another option was to take fabric to a dressmaker and have a garment custom made. Such was the case with Sarah Kollock, who wrote to her grandfather in 1841 that she wanted a calico dress. She could find no suitable fabric in Hillsborough, she said, so she asked him to purchase some and send it to her.[71]

Some of the Burwell girls hired "country" women to make their dresses.[72] But in the 1850s, those with more sophisticated tastes and money to spend could commission one of Hillsborough's dressmakers, who had the creativity and technical expertise to design a garment without the use of a pattern and fit it to her customer's body. Mary Easley, Susan Murphy, and Lizzie Glass consulted Mary Waddell when they wanted custom-made clothing and accessories.[73] "I will take my dress to Mrs. Wodell this evening," Lizzie wrote to her mother in 1856. "Miss Bettie says it must be made with [more?] flounces. She has had a spencer [short jacket] made with edging all around the skirt. I [told] her you said you would have sent some but you did not know whether it was the fashion. She told me to send for two yards and a half, I think her spencer is the prettiest one I ever saw."[74]

It was Mary Waddell's reputation as an accomplished seamstress that attracted the patronage of Burwell students. But her neighbors gossiped about her unfortunate domestic circumstances. Bell Norwood wrote in a letter to her cousin that Mary's husband Haynes "does nothing on earth, but frequently takes a dram."[75] A woman without capital, she had to appeal to the goodwill of local merchants to let her buy on credit even though they knew that collecting the money she owed them might be a challenge. "I have had several difficulties with the Waddells," William Norwood wrote in

From Sampson County, North Carolina, Susan Murphy and her twin sister Mary attended the Burwell School in the late 1840s. Courtesy of the Burwell School Historic Site, Hillsborough.

1850 about collecting accounts receivable for Webb and Long's dry goods store. He confessed that his most successful strategy toward that end was to "make them mad" so that they paid him "out of spite" in order to be able to say they were no longer under an "obligation" to the store. He sympathized with Mary, whom he described as "an honest hearted woman" forced to support "Old Haynes (a complete buzzard) and a house full of worthless children which had been better off if drowned like puppies when younge."[76] That William had a low opinion of Haynes might have been expected given what appears to have been his well-deserved reputation as a poor provider and a drunk, but what the Waddell children (three girls and two boys ranging in age from five to eighteen) could possibly have done to deserve such a mean-spirited, venomous characterization remains a mystery. It may have been that, as members of a desperately poor family, they had even less social capital than Mary Ruffin Smith to protect them against derogatory remarks made by those who considered themselves their social betters. Or it may have been that there was bad blood between the Norwoods and the

Haynes Waddells. Whatever the explanation, what seems clear is that the Waddells were fair game for gossip and that the gossip that swirled around them did nothing to make it easier for Mary to support her family.

Despite the fact that the Burwell School was flourishing by 1856, Anna was becoming increasingly unhappy living in the town, and teaching was beginning to wear her out. "Teaching worries me a great deal. I am not as strong as I used to be & I am so tired when I come out of school that I am really lazy," she wrote in February 1856.[77] Those factors combined with the prospect of living debt-free may have been one of the primary incentives that induced the Burwells to accept the directorship of the new Charlotte Female Academy in 1857. Anna gave up teaching to become the matron. Robert served as principal.[78] Their school survived the Civil War and eventually became Queen's University of Charlotte. When Anna died in 1871 at the age of sixty-one, Robert left Charlotte for Raleigh where he and his son, John Bott, became coprincipals of Peace Institute, now William Peace University. Robert retired in 1875 and died in Raleigh on March 4, 1895, at the age of ninety-three.[79]

Only a few rules regulated the school lives of young women who came to study with the Burwells. Those whose letters have been preserved had little to say about them except to mention that they were expected to make their beds and put back their chairs when they got up from the dinner table and were required to deport themselves with quiet dignity. One student wrote that she and her classmates had been out walking when "a dog barked at me and liked to bit me and I screamed and got a scolding."[80] There was always the possibility of being dismissed because of bad behavior, of course, but the threat of a scolding seems to have been enough to keep most students from breaking the rules or challenging the Burwells' authority.[81]

Anna considered herself to be a better disciplinarian than her husband. "I am more strict in keeping good order & more keen sighted & keen eared than your Father," she wrote her daughter.[82] But neither of them expected their students to misbehave, and when they did, it was notable. "Mary Garrett misbehaved & I was too harsh & hasty," Anna wrote in her diary on September 29, 1855. A month and a half later, she wrote that she was "mortified by some conduct of B[ettie] Carrington & [Lizzie] Watkins—but both apologized & all is well."[83] While the Burwells wrote nothing about their disciplinary regimen in their advertising, there is every reason to believe that they would have agreed with their contemporary, William Mercer Green, principal of the Hillsborough Female Academy, when he wrote in his Prospectus that he expected his teachers to inspire so much respect from their female students that corporal disciplinary measures would be unnecessary.[84]

The same attitude did not prevail among the headmasters of classical academies for boys throughout the United States, particularly in rural areas. In the South, teachers had every reason to be concerned about issues of discipline, partly because many among the elite were often unwilling to impose discipline on their sons at home and expected schoolmasters to inculcate the principles of obedience and self-discipline in the children seated before them. The result was that classrooms in college preparatory schools could easily become battlegrounds where teachers pitted their wills against boys who refused to respect their authority.[85]

Boys, some as young as nine or ten, arrived at school to find themselves unexpectedly bound by strictly imposed rules of conduct, subjected to a dull and inflexible curriculum, and forced to endure a tedious schedule of classes and recitations. Used to doing what they pleased, some of them did not like taking orders or submitting to any sort of disciplinary regimen. The older they got, the more sensitive they became to the ideals of the southern code of honor that encouraged them to take exception to any gesture or comment, real or imagined, that might have the potential for besmirching their reputations or threatening their autonomy. The defense of either sometimes prompted acts of violence.[86]

Southern schoolmasters at respected classical academies typically took their responsibilities as stand-in parents seriously and acknowledged the importance of inculcating respect for authority in their male students both as a matter of principle and as a practical matter, knowing that an orderly environment helped ensure that learning could take place. The reputation of schoolmasters and their ability to recruit students was likely to hinge on their ability to control their classrooms. So when they could not persuade or charm their students into following the rules set down for them, some resorted to the use of force to establish order. The use of corporal punishment as a disciplinary tool meant that the relationship between a schoolmaster and his most troublesome students was fraught with frustration and resentment.

We know virtually nothing about the disciplinary regimen of Alexander Wilson, a Presbyterian minister and headmaster of the Caldwell Institute.

He and his board set high academic standards for those admitted and demanded that character witnesses testify to the good morals and behavior of their prospective students. He forbade his students from frequenting Hillsborough's taverns or tippling houses, theatrical exhibitions, and horse races. And he required them to read the scriptures, pray morning and night, and attend chapel on Sundays where he quizzed them on their knowledge of the Bible and the Presbyterian Assembly's Shorter Catechism.[87] It is not clear that these strategies were entirely effective in ensuring their good behavior. The Burwells' eldest son, John Bott, prepared for his admission to Hampden Sydney College in Virginia at the Caldwell Institute. "There was a large number of boys from a distance in attendance and a pretty wild set," he recalled in his memoir. "I cannot say much for the morals of that school."[88]

John Bott does not mention how Wilson handled the "wild set" when they disrupted his classroom, but the students of William Bingham and his son William James Bingham of the Hillsborough Academy and the Bingham School had vivid memories of experiencing corporal punishment when they misbehaved or did not prepare thoroughly for class.

William Bingham began teaching in the 1790s. An Irish-born, Scottish-educated Presbyterian minister, he established college preparatory classical academies for young men in both Wilmington and Pittsboro, North Carolina, after his arrival in the United States. In 1801 he accepted a position as professor of ancient languages at the newly established University of North Carolina in Chapel Hill.[89]

Shortly after William began teaching at the university, the faculty tried to introduce a new disciplinary system that shifted responsibility for monitoring student behavior from the faculty to the students. Convinced that snitching on their classmates was dishonorable, forty-five students refused to cooperate and signed a remonstrance explaining their objections to the proposed plan. Violence against the faculty ensued. It was a case, wrote one indignant observer, of ignorant boys of sixteen or seventeen taking it on themselves to judge the actions of their superiors in regard to morality, government, and education. By the time the so-called Great Rebellion of 1805 was over, most of the university's students had withdrawn.[90]

Having experienced the unpleasant consequences of student unruliness, William resigned his teaching position and eventually moved his family to Hillsborough, where he became head of the Hillsborough Academy. We know virtually nothing about his tenure there, but his subsequent behavior suggests that the use of corporal punishment as a disciplinary tool was part of his pedagogical repertoire.

In 1818 he left the academy and established a boarding school at Mount Repose, a three-hundred-acre property northwest of Hillsborough.[91] There, his thirty or forty students, some from as far away as Louisiana and Georgia, lived and studied in log cabins built on the property. The closely supervised environment and rigid routine of prayer, recitation, study, dining, recreation, and sleep left students little time for mischief.[92]

William Bingham believed that instituting a strictly enforced, uniform system of discipline was the key to learning. There is no evidence to suggest that he looked for alternatives to corporal punishment. If fatherly concern, gentleness, and forbearance did not prompt his students to study hard and comport themselves appropriately, he was perfectly willing to punish them physically, a practice condoned by the Bible and based in part on traditional religious notions about the need to break a child's will.[93] One of his students, Giles Mebane, reported that the headmaster "whipped with well-trimmed hickories, of which he kept a supply equal to the demand." He did not necessarily do so out of pique or anger, he said. Nor did he do so merely to punish the boys under his care. According to Mebane, his headmaster whipped his students out of a sense of "duty to his patrons."[94]

That duty was multifaceted. When parents sent their children to William to be educated, they did so at considerable expense and with high expectations. Preparatory schooling under the careful stewardship of a learned and conscientious scholar, they hoped, would not only prepare their sons for entrance into the university but also begin the process of turning their offspring into Christian gentlemen. They expected him to provide his students with the social skills, moral sensibilities, and intellectual training that would allow them to avoid the temptations for dissipation that awaited them in places such as Chapel Hill and to make the most of their opportunities as members of the state's social, political, and economic elite.[95] William tried to fulfill his duty to his students and by extension their parents by preparing his scholars to govern and discipline themselves, lessons he believed were best learned by being subjected to routine, predictable, and dispassionately applied corporal punishment.

William's son William James followed his example. Born in Chapel Hill on April 6, 1802, he attended his father's school in Hillsborough and endured his approach to discipline like the other students. After he graduated from the University of North Carolina, he began pursuing a career in law but had to leave his studies when his father died unexpectedly in February 1826. William James returned to Mount Repose to finish the term and apparently found the role of schoolmaster so fulfilling that he abandoned his goal of becoming a lawyer and traveled to New England and Virginia in order to study the pedagogical methods used at some of their more prominent private college preparatory schools. It is unclear what he learned during his trip, but when it ended, he accepted a position as head of the Hillsborough Academy and began teaching there in January 1827.[96]

William James Bingham became headmaster of the Hillsborough Academy in 1827. He developed a reputation for being a strict disciplinarian. Courtesy of the State Archives of North Carolina, Raleigh.

When parents sent their sons to the Hillsborough Academy, they abdicated their disciplinary responsibilities to him.[97] Ebenezer Pettigrew, a planter from Washington County, North Carolina, who sent three sons to William James Bingham to be educated, was among them. "Minors are to be governed by those persons of mature age. . . . You will govern, and that is the reason why I have valued it [your school] so highly," he wrote in 1842.[98] A few days later, he continued, "Where there is flogging (with your temperance) there is order & government, without which a school is worth nothing."[99]

A series of letters written by Pettigrew to his son James Johnston provides some insight into tensions that could plague the relationship between a teacher and an unruly student, a student and his parents, and a parent and a teacher as a result of the use of corporal punishment. James Johnston Pettigrew did not hesitate to break the rules and then complain to his father about being punished. The elder Pettigrew responded to his complaints by assuring his son that his headmaster cared for his students and that he had their best interests at heart. "Your brother William, once thought that Mr. Bingham hated him," Ebenezer wrote. "If you will conduct yourself in a proper manner (as you are well able to do) then he & Mrs. Bingham will treat you with all the kindness you could ask."[100] Despite his father's advice, James Johnston continued to do as he pleased and suffer the consequences.

The consequences did not always include the use of corporal punishment. In July 1839 William James felt it necessary to write to the elder Pettigrew to explain his efforts to control James Johnston's rebellious behavior. He had caught James Johnston "beating on a bench in the Acad'y with sticks, in imitation of a drummer," he said, and explained that such behavior was "strictly forbidden." He excused this breach of the rules, he continued, on the grounds that James Johnston had been drumming quietly and did not expect to be heard. The young man's sense of entitlement and propensity to put on mannish airs when it went unrecognized was a more serious matter, however. When James Johnston went into supper one night, his place had been taken by a guest, William James reported. Instead of waiting for another place to be set, he left the house in a huff announcing that he could be found in the school building. William James ordered him back to the dining room and made plans to "switch him" after he had eaten, but, seeing that he was "deeply mortified" by his behavior, he "let him off with a lecture" and made him promise "never to assume another air while in my charge."[101]

The threat of pain rather than the infliction of it does not seem to have been effective in inducing James Johnston to behave himself. When in August 1839 James Johnston wrote to his father that William James intended to whip him, Ebenezer responded: "You think that Mr. Bingham is geting [sic] more strict, but my son you are mistaken you are geting more self willed, and do not know it, and will not believe it when you are told so by others. I know Mr. Bingham loves you Johnston, and that he is anxious to overlook little errors as far as he consistently can, but to let a boy have his own way, is to ruin him forever and that I never could allow in my children."[102]

James Johnston was not the only student to take umbrage at the punishments he was subjected to. The associations and loyalties that developed among students at preparatory schools were no less intense than those at the nation's colleges, where they often served as the basis for challenging the authority of those in charge.[103] Such was the case when in September 1839 some of the older boys at the academy began fomenting a rebellion. A rumor spread among the faculty that some of the students were willing to use force to resist William James's authority. Armed with a pistol, the schoolmaster carried on his teaching duties, but, having been forewarned, he was sensitive to any sign of "insubordination and dissatisfaction" among his students.

On Thursday, September 12, one of his students, Alexander Croom, disturbed early morning prayers by "scraping and stamping the floor with his feet." William James confronted Croom outside after the service and dismissed him from the school. As the furious Croom left the scene, he threatened the headmaster. Later that morning, as William James and his assistants were returning to class, someone informed him that Croom was still at the academy, he was armed with pistols, and he and other similarly armed students intended to attack him as he reentered the east wing of the school. William James's assistants responded by arming themselves with whatever was at hand. Meanwhile, someone told the rebellious students that their headmaster was aware of their conspiracy and was prepared to defend himself. Before he entered the school and confronted Croom, William James ordered any student who was willing to abide by his authority to gather in a grove nearby and then sent a message to the rebels demanding that they come out of the building. One by one they complied, emerging slowly from the school and joining the boys in the grove, leaving Croom alone inside. William James entered the building and ordered Croom to leave the premises. When the rebel leader drew his pistol, the headmaster responded by drawing his as well. Croom fled, hurling insults and epithets as he went. William James immediately called a meeting of the trustees, who ordered the dismissal of all of the students who had taken part in the conspiracy.[104] Following their instructions, he expelled twenty students, leaving ninety-six still at the school.[105]

The rebellion had little perceivable impact on William James's disciplinary methods or James Johnston Pettigrew's recalcitrance. It took until the end of the term in 1841, but William James was finally able to report to the elder Pettigrew that his son was at last willing to submit to his authority. "A more submissive & docile pupil no teacher could desire; yet it is necessary he should feel the justice as well as the weight of authority exercised over him," William James wrote to a father apparently willing to join him in the conviction that in loco parentis authority exercised judiciously had achieved its goal.[106]

William James stayed in Hillsborough until the mid-1840s but found it increasingly difficult to adequately monitor the behavior of his students, who boarded with local families or in hotels. Interested in farming, determined to reduce his enrollment so he could devote more time to the intellectual and moral development of his students, and hoping to rear his children in the country as his father had done, he established a boarding school in Oaks, a small farming community twelve miles southwest of Hillsborough, thus removing his students from the temptations of small-town life.[107] His reputation had preceded him and the school was immediately successful, netting him two thousand dollars in 1845. From more than two hundred applicants, he accepted only thirty.[108] Most of his students boarded with neighbors and attended classes in the three-room brick academy building he erected just to the east of his house.[109]

Despite the change of venue, William James continued to whip his students. Sawney (William Robert) Webb, the son of one of his neighbors, entered the Bingham School at Oaks in 1856 at the age of fourteen. Webb apparently adjusted quickly to the regimen of the school and to what he described as William James's parental firmness. The headmaster made his expectations clear and punished those who failed to fulfill those expectations with a smack of a hickory stick, Webb wrote years later. "His theory

William James Bingham left Hillsborough in the mid-1840s and moved his school out into the country. Courtesy of the Mary Claire Engstrom Photographic Collection, Wilson Special Collections Library, UNC–Chapel Hill.

was that the boy knew," Webb remembered. "When a boy missed declining a word, he thrashed him. . . . He wasn't mad. He thrashed a boy, all the time looking nice and sweet like he was doing the nicest job he ever did in his life. I would watch the old man sitting back and smiling like he was eating peaches or Georgia watermelons. I never heard him stand and lecture boys. . . . That's the only school I ever saw where thirty or forty boys knew their lessons every day, never missed."[110]

William James Bingham's career as a schoolmaster continued through the Civil War, although by that time he had abdicated primary responsibility for running the school to his two sons, William and Robert. As early as 1862, the Binghams began to include infantry tactics into the curriculum. At about the same time, they moved their facilities to a large piece of land south and west of Hillsborough near Mebane, where they built a barracks to house the students and laid out a drilling field. In December 1864 they applied to the state legislature to formerly incorporate the school as a military as well as a classical academy.[111]

Shortly after the war ended in 1865, William James Bingham, a man who had spent his entire adult life trying to establish and sustain order in his classroom, succumbed to disorder of the mind, and his family committed him to the North Carolina Asylum for the Insane in Raleigh.[112] After his release, he died on February 9, 1866.[113] His eldest son William took over as superintendent of the school. Robert taught on the faculty.[114]

William James Bingham's use of physical violence as a disciplinary tool outlived him. As the head of the school, his son William employed a disciplinary regimen and educational philosophy that mirrored that of his father. Both Walter Hines Page, who began attending the school in 1868, and Paul Barringer, who enrolled in 1871, remembered disciplinary punishments imposed on their classmates. William Bingham's rules were unwritten but perfectly understood, Barringer recalled in his memoir, and the schoolmaster whipped his students whenever he thought it necessary. "He flogged me something like a dozen times," Barringer wrote, "but never without reason nor when in a rage. This punishment consisted of ten or twelve strokes on the right hand with a well-trimmed hickory switch about the size of a lead pencil."[115]

After William died on February 8, 1873, at the age of thirty-seven, Robert became superintendent. He moved the school to Asheville in 1891. Described as "a beautiful little city of barracks on a hill," the Bingham School managed to survive the 1890s depression. By then an honor code served as the basis for what was described as a system of discipline based on fairness and uniformity, moderated by an appeals process under the supervision of the superintendent.[116] The school closed after Robert's death in 1927.[117]

The Burwell School, the Hillsborough Academy, the Bingham School, the Hillsborough Female Academy, and the Caldwell Institute had reputations for maintaining high academic standards and the sort of gendered discipline deemed important for producing the next generation of the state's social, economic, and political leaders. They succeeded because they fulfilled their patrons' expectations that they serve as a culturally stabilizing force by perpetuating traditional gender roles, reinforcing prevailing ethical and religious values, perpetuating a society based on white domination, and, in the case of young men, encouraging a commitment to public service.

The Burwells did their best to position their ladies-in-training to become housewives and teachers as well as a positive moral force in their families and communities.[118] Some such as Mary Susan Burwell Strudwick and Anna Robertson (Nannie) Burwell Crow found jobs teaching before they married. Others established their own schools or served as school administrators.[119] Former student Susan A. Webb founded Almeda Schoolhouse in nearby Oaks in 1849.[120] When the Burwells closed their school and left Hillsborough, Sarah Kollock helped establish the Nash-Kollock School to take its place.[121] In the 1860s Bell Norwood Huske opened her own school.[122] And in 1902 the board of Greensboro Female College elected Burwell School graduate Lucy Henderson Owen Robertson their president, making her the first female president of a southern college.[123]

The Binghams and Alexander Wilson of the Caldwell Institute focused their efforts on turning self-absorbed, disobedient boys into self-disciplined young men prepared to assume adult responsibilities. John Bott Burwell, who studied with Wilson, went on to become a schoolmaster himself. Edmund Strudwick, who studied with William Bingham in the second decade of the century, became one of North Carolina's most respected and influential doctors, a man who supported advanced training for physicians, organized and became president of the North Carolina Medical Association, and helped supervise the building of the North Carolina Hospital for the Insane, which opened in 1856.[124] Nathaniel Hill Burgwin and John Tillinghast, both of whom studied with William James Bingham, became respectively a prominent corporate lawyer and an Episcopal priest.[125] Walter Hines Page became an internationally recognized journalist and served as ambassador to Great Britain.[126] And Sawney Webb went on to establish the Webb School in Bell Buckle, Tennessee. By 1896 it was one of the most respected boarding schools in the South.[127]

Schoolmasters and mistresses used advertising to recruit students. But they depended on word-of-mouth support to establish and sustain their standing as educators and the reputation of their schools. The Burwells benefited from the goodwill of their mostly compliant students and the general satisfaction of their parents with the education their daughters received under their tutelage. And they did what they could to mitigate the impact of talk that might reflect badly on them or the way they ran their school.

In a society where people believed that young, privileged men were likely to be unruly and contemptuous of authority, the reputations and prospects of Wilson and the Binghams would have been damaged had word spread that they could not maintain discipline in their classroom. Parents like Ebenezer Pettigrew sent their sons to classical academies in the hope that as their sons learned to master Greek and Latin verbs, they would also learn to master themselves. If agreeing to subject their sons to corporal punishment was the price they had to pay to accomplish that goal, they were willing to pay it.

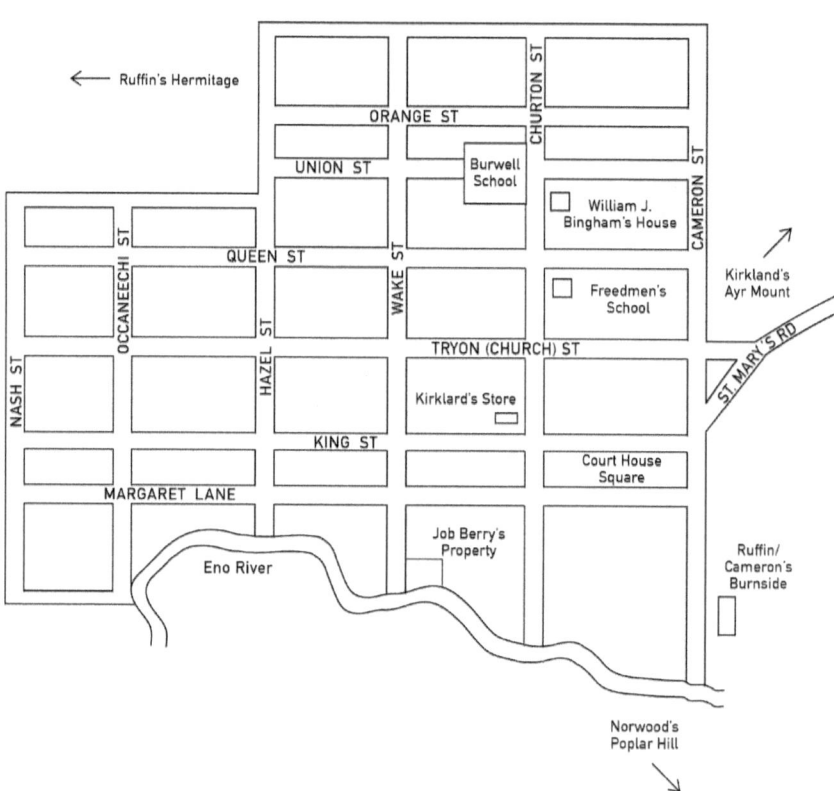

4
TO WORK THE LIVELONG DAY

Gossip and rumors were no less important in the lives of those held in bondage than they were in those of their free counterparts. The enslaved may not have been able to protect each other from the violence and indignities that accompanied their enslavement, but they witnessed them, talked about them, and were not likely to forget the suffering each of them endured. Since most of them were illiterate, word-of-mouth communication was critical to their efforts to form a community based on shared values. It offered the opportunity to come to some understanding of their situation and offered them the possibility of anticipating, even if they could not control, what the future held for them. Gossip in the household, barnyard, or fields about supervisors and work expectations helped acclimate new workers to unfamiliar living arrangements and adjust to the demands of their duties. The use of it could help them try to resist and subvert the power of those who held them in bondage.[1] And as we saw in chapter 1, gossip among their white neighbors about ill treatment of the enslaved could be used to put pressure on their abusers to modify their behavior. That was certainly the case as far as Harriet Jacobs was concerned. Enslaved more than 150 miles from Hillsborough in Edenton, North Carolina, Jacobs credited her ability to resist the advances of her enslaver to the fact that she lived in a small town where everyone knew each other's business. As a married, professional man, she said, her enslaver Norcom knew he had to preserve appearances and forego using the "lash" in order to avoid the gossip that would have ruined his reputation.[2]

Rumors about the indebtedness or imminent death of their owners spread quickly through enslaved communities, heightening concerns about potential sale and imminent separation from friends and loved ones. The same was true in the case of weddings or the birth of a child in white households where the enslaved might be given away as gifts as a part of the celebration. Word that a master, mistress, or overseer went to bed early and slept soundly provided information useful in allocating what little time the enslaved had to themselves. Gossip about the sexual predilections of the white men in their midst put them on guard. And common talk about their reputations as workers had the potential for expanding the freedom to move about for those believed to be loyal, dependable, and industrious or subjecting to increased white surveillance and hostility those considered insolent or insubordinate. Information derived from overheard conversations and passed on provided the enslaved with a tool that could be used to develop strategies as individuals or as part of the enslaved community for surviving a brutal labor system that exploited their labor and denied their humanity.

A look at the Burwell household provides the opportunity to explore the role of gossip and its impact on the relationships between enslavers and those they held in bondage. In 1840 Robert Burwell reported to the census taker that he had six enslaved workers in his household. By 1850 that number had risen to eleven, although it is unlikely that any of these people actually belonged to him. While they lived in Hillsborough, the Burwells never had much money and were always economizing. There is no deed transfer of property in the form of enslaved laborers to Robert in the Orange County records, although he may have purchased some in Richmond or Petersburg. We know that he borrowed some from his family. The others he hired or borrowed from his neighbors.[3]

What we know of the lives of the enslaved in the Burwell household begins with an enslaved teenaged domestic servant named Elizabeth Hobbs, whom the Burwells brought on loan with them from Virginia in 1835. In her gossipy memoir, *Behind the Scenes, or Thirty Years a Slave, and Four Years in the White House*, published in 1868 three years before Anna Burwell died, Lizzie, as she was called, devoted a whole chapter to the abuse she suffered at the hands of the Burwells. She chronicled in vivid and lurid detail the physical violence she endured in Hillsborough. "I did the work of three servants," she wrote, "and yet I was scolded and regarded with mistrust."[4] Precisely what prompted Anna Burwell's low opinion of Lizzie is unclear. Enslaved domestics like Lizzie had any number of passive-aggressive strategies designed to resist the demands made on them. A smirk, a job poorly done, and dithering were enough to drive a mistress wild. When verbal abuse proved ineffective in changing Lizzie's behavior, an exasperated Anna demanded that she be whipped.⁵ Unwilling to perform the task himself, Robert sent Lizzie across the street to William James Bingham, the village schoolmaster known for his disciplinary expertise. "Recollect," Lizzie wrote, "I was eighteen years of age, was a woman fully developed, and yet this man cooly bade me take down my dress." When she refused, he tore it from her back, picked up his rawhide, and plied it freely across her shoulders. With blood dripping down her back, she returned home bruised and battered only to have Robert throw a chair at her when she asked why she had been beaten. The beatings stopped, she said, only when word of them became "the talk of the town and neighborhood." Lizzie wrote to her mother, Agnes, known as Aggy, in April 1838 that she "could fill ten pages" with her "griefs and misfortunes" and wished more than anything to be gone from Hillsborough.⁶

The threat of physical punishment or verbal abuse became the least of Lizzie's worries when Alexander Kirkland of Ayr Mount plantation began pursuing her. A member of Hillsborough's elite, Alexander was not a man

Elizabeth Hobbs Keckly, enslaved by the Burwell family, suffered every indignity imaginable during the years she spent in Hillsborough. Courtesy of the Burwell School Historic Site, Hillsborough.

It was to this house and its owner, William James Bingham, that the Burwells sent Elizabeth Hobbs Keckly to be disciplined. Courtesy of the Mary Claire Engstrom Photographic Collection, Wilson Special Collections Library, UNC–Chapel Hill.

to be trifled with. At six feet, eight inches tall with a physique to match, he was used to getting his way. He was twenty-eight years old and a married man when Lizzie arrived in town with the Burwells in 1835. His lack of ambition, bad temper, excessive drinking, sense of entitlement, and sensitivity to slights made him difficult to live with and impeded his success in business. By 1839 he was the father of two sons but did little to support his family. Instead, he spent his time seeking pleasure wherever he could find it.[7]

Unfortunately for Lizzie, he initiated a game of cat and mouse in which the cat held all the cards. There was little she could do to avoid him. When Anna Burwell ordered her to go to the Kirkland store she could not refuse. The same would have been true when she was asked to run an errand or deliver a message that took her to Ayr Mount. Alexander had power and freedom of movement. She did not.

It is unclear what role the Burwells played in this particular drama. Robert held Lizzie in trust for his father and was responsible for her well-being. Given the size of the town and Alexander's reputation, it is unlikely that Robert remained ignorant of what was going on. Certainly as a clergyman, he was obliged to object to Alexander's adultery on moral grounds. Without the power to stop such behavior, Anna may have found it easier to deny the idea that a man she knew was capable of sexual assault, to view Lizzie as a seductress, to attribute the presence of mixed-race children in town to the moral laxity of the enslaved, or all of the above than to take any action.[8] In any case, neither of the Burwells seems to have done anything to shield Lizzie from Alexander's unwanted attentions.

When Lizzie discovered she was pregnant, there were few people to whom she could turn for help or advice. There were three enslaved females above the age of ten working in the Burwell household in 1840, but there is no way to determine what her relationship with them was.[9] And even if they were sympathetic, there was not much they could do except perhaps relieve her of some of her duties. Others in the free Black and enslaved community could have offered moral support, but we have no way of knowing whether they did so. She had been separated from her mother and the rest of her family at the age of fourteen when the Burwells brought her from Virginia to Hillsborough. And given her animosity toward Lizzie, it is unlikely that Anna gave her much comfort or sympathy.

As Lizzie's pregnancy advanced, she almost certainly became the subject of tittle-tattle as the town's busybodies speculated about who had fathered the child she was carrying. Such talk would have been humiliating for Robert since he was as likely a candidate as anyone else. It was perhaps to put an end to such speculation that Robert sent Lizzie and her light-skinned son George back to Virginia in about 1841, granting her wish to be gone from Hillsborough and reunited with her mother. Lizzie, George, and Aggy eventually moved with Robert's sister and her family to St. Louis. There, Lizzie supported them all by designing and constructing dresses for the city's elite. She married James Keckley, earned her freedom, and moved to Washington, D.C., where talk among politicians' wives about her exceptional dressmaking skills brought her to the attention of Mary Todd Lincoln. This ensured her financial success and allowed her to make a place for herself as a member of the capital's Black and mixed-race elite.[10]

The market for slave narratives provided the context for the publication of Lizzie's memoir *Behind the Scenes*.[11] By publishing the book, she did as much public damage as possible to the reputations of the perpetrators of the violence directed against her but also to those who must have known about it and talked about it but did nothing to stop it. What she had to say about them was damning. There is no way to know if the Burwells, the Binghams, the Kirklands, or anyone else they knew ever saw a copy of her book. But if word of it circulated either in Hillsborough or in Charlotte, where the Burwells were living in 1868, it would surely have focused on the way she weaponized her story in an effort to discredit them.

Lizzie's replacements at the Burwell School continued to bear the brunt of Anna's temper tantrums. On the first Monday in January 1846, Anna wrote in her diary, "I was very impatient with Mary Ann, scolded her for a fault." The next day, she scolded Mary Ann again. A week later she failed to curb her temper once more. On January 24 she complained that Mary Ann was "negligent and fretful." And on the last day of the month, Mary Ann got another tongue-lashing because Anna thought her "very lazy and careless." Anna knew she was being unreasonable and acknowledged that her "intemperate temper" was her "besetting sin." She claimed to be sorry for her outbursts and pledged to be more forbearing in the future.[12] But her good intentions did nothing to ensure domestic tranquility in her household.

It is unclear to whom Mary Ann belonged or when she began to work as a housemaid at the Burwell School. But like Harriet, Mary Ruffin Smith's enslaved housemaid discussed in chapter 1, she lived in an abroad marriage. In February 1846 Mary Ann's husband Mitchell ran away from his owner, came to see his wife, and begged Robert to arrange for them to be together. It is not clear what Robert's response was, but a few days later Mitchell was still on the premises helping draw off the water from the Burwells' muddy well. Whether Robert could not afford the arrangements Mitchell and Mary Ann wanted him to make or whether he was unsympathetic to their situation is not clear. But Robert informed Mitchell that he had to return to his master. Mary Ann and Mitchell said their goodbyes the next morning.[13]

Desperate to be reunited with his wife, Mitchell may have unintentionally condemned himself to a life without her. Enslavers often sold those who left their property without permission because they feared that running away was a chronic behavior, and they were unwilling to spend the time and money needed to recover runaways. We don't know if this was the case with Mitchell, but Anna Burwell never mentions him again in her letters or diary. Nine years later she identifies a man named Alfred as Mary Ann's husband, suggesting that in Mitchell's absence, Mary Ann had found another partner.[14]

Mitchell and Mary Ann knew when they pledged their love to one another that their vows were conditional. They may or may not have said "Till death or distance do us part," but they knew, as did every enslaved couple, that they could be involuntarily separated at any time. The result was that serial monogamy was common among the enslaved, many of whom did what they could to regularize their relationships as circumstances allowed.

Despite her dissatisfaction with Mary Ann's work, Anna does not appear to have been willing to replace her. Her labor was critical to the success of the Burwell School, and she was valuable as a piece of property. In 1850 Robert used Mary Ann, her children, and any children she might conceive in the future as part of the collateral he needed to borrow the money to renovate and expand his property so that he and his wife could accommodate more students.[15] Mortgaging enslaved workers was common in the antebellum South since it allowed slave owners access to local credit while retaining the labor, appreciation, and reproductive potential of those held in bondage.[16] The enslaved could be sold if their master failed to pay off the loan, but Robert was able to come up with the cash he needed when his note came due, and Mary Ann remained in his household.

Anna was still describing Mary Ann as "insolent" in the spring of 1855, but she was becoming increasingly dependent on her. "Mary Ann [is] my mainstay," she wrote in her diary, acknowledging that it would have been impossible for her to have run the Burwell School without her help. Mary Ann's position of housekeeper was a time-consuming job, one of great trust, responsibility, and authority. Under Anna's supervision, she was responsible for managing all of the household's resources, distributing food supplies, and supervising the household staff. She spent her days ensuring that the household ran smoothly. It is not surprising, then, that when Mary Ann was temporarily away, Anna lamented her absence.[17]

Mary Ann was pregnant in the fall of 1855 and was approaching her confinement when Anna wrote, "Mary Ann is poorly hardly able to get about but does the best she can, sews, and helps me in the morning."[18] In early December Anna was anticipating the need to attend the birth of Mary

Ann's baby.[19] She was so worried about her housekeeper that she contracted with Patsy Freeland, a free woman of color, to sit with Mary Ann and help with the housework that she could no longer do.[20] Mary Ann went into labor on the evening of December 28. Anna reported to her daughter that Mary Ann had been "very sick" and that she had sent for Dr. Edmund Strudwick. When he could not come, she settled for Dr. Osmund F. Long, who lived farther away.[21]

Calling in a doctor to attend an enslaved woman giving birth was somewhat unusual. Anna, the mother of twelve children and clearly familiar with the normal course of labor, must have been willing to bear the extra expense because she believed Mary Ann had developed complications that she or a midwife could not handle.[22] It is unlikely that she consulted Mary Ann about the matter. Historian Marie Jenkins Schwartz has suggested that enslaved women resisted the intervention of doctors, whom they viewed as agents of their enslavers.[23] Nevertheless, with the doctor and Anna by her side, Mary Ann delivered a son at seven o'clock in the morning of the 30th. Given all her other duties as the headmistress of a flourishing boarding school, it would have been difficult for Anna to personally provide postpartum care for Mary Ann, so she hired a nurse named Mary Palmer to stay for a month and take care of the new mother and her baby, thereby incurring yet another expense.

The birth of Mary Ann's baby was a valuable addition to the Burwell household, but her confinement was accompanied by the inconvenience and disruption involved in temporarily replacing her with someone who could perform her duties. As Anna juggled her staff to ensure that the house ran smoothly, the brunt of that inconvenience was borne by the other domestic servants, both free and enslaved. William found himself waiting tables in the dining room while Ann added doing the housework to her dining room duties. And Anna had to hire someone temporarily to look after the needs of the students. Fortunately, Mary Ann's recovery went well, if slowly. By the middle of January, she was sitting up but had not yet gone out.[24]

Despite Mary Ann's reputation for insolence, the Burwells were dependent on her housekeeping skills. So they took her with them when they gave up their school and left Hillsborough to run the Charlotte Female Academy in 1857. After emancipation, she remained in their household and died in October 1868. "This past week was a sad one," Anna wrote in her diary. "Mary Ann died on Wednesday, was buried on Thursday. She was more of a friend to me than a servant."[25] After all the unpaid service she rendered to the Burwell family and the verbal abuse she suffered in the process, it is unlikely that Mary Ann felt the same way.

One of Mary Ann's coworkers in Hillsborough was a woman named Hannah, the Burwells' enslaved cook. Mistress of the kitchen, it was her responsibility to prepare three meals a day for the Burwell family, their boarders, and the rest of the household; supervise the serving and cleaning up; and produce pastries and other delicacies for holidays, weddings, and parties held at the school. Like Mary Ann, Hannah's origins are unclear, but she may have come on loan from the Virginia Burwell household along with her sister Lucy.[26] In any case, she was part of the Burwell household in early 1846 when Anna referred to her in her diary as being "impertinent."[27]

If Anna thought Mary Ann was difficult, she found Hannah utterly impossible. With her insolence, Mary Ann disrupted the lines of authority Anna tried to establish. Hannah did the same and added persistent claims of ill health and drunkenness to her list of transgressions. It is difficult to tell from the documents available when Hannah was really sick and when she was feigning illness. Pretending to be sick was an everyday form of resistance that temporarily relieved the enslaved of their duties and irritated their enslavers beyond measure.[28] "Hannah is sick," Anna wrote in her diary on February 26, 1855. Her illness lasted most of the week. Ann, Hannah's substitute, could not manage to serve meals on time and sent the food into the dining room raw. Not a woman noted for her self-control, Anna predictably lost her temper. When Ann got sick at the end of March, the illness spread rapidly through the household. Hannah again took to her sickbed along with the Burwell children, at least one of the Burwell students, and three of her coworkers. Ann slowly recovered but was not well enough to cook, so Anna had to turn to Jane to work in the kitchen. Unfamiliar with her new duties, Jane accidentally set herself on fire. Had it not been for the fast action of another Burwell bondswoman, Aunt Feriby, she might have died. It took until April 5 for most of the staff to recover and the household's routine to return to normal.[29] At the end of April, Anna reported that Hannah was sick yet again.[30] She returned to her sickbed two months later and remained there for more than a week.[31]

It is not clear when Anna became aware of Hannah's alcohol problem, but at the end of August 1855, she wrote in her diary: "Hannah absolutely drunk, so much so that she could not cook supper—greatly harassed to know what we ought to do."[32] We have no way of knowing how and where Hannah got access to liquor. There is nothing in the Burwell papers to suggest that they kept it in the house, although alcohol was often used for medicinal purposes at the time. Whatever her source, Hannah apparently had the means to acquire liquor and imbibed whenever she had the chance.

Hannah's tumultuous relationship with a man called Phillip may have encouraged her to seek solace in the bottle. It is unclear who Phillip was. He had some freedom of movement, so he may have been a hired laborer. Within days of her awareness of Hannah's alcohol problem, Anna wrote, "This afternoon Hannah & Phillip got to fighting & greatly disturbed us." Whatever the cause of the quarrel, Hannah was still in distress the next day. Shortly thereafter, Phillip created a "great disturbance" when he returned "for his things."[33] The crisis in Hannah's love life apparently did little to discourage her from drinking. Two weeks after Phillip's departure, Anna went to the kitchen to check on supper. She must have suspected something when she did not hear the usual clatter. Much to her dismay, she found Hannah "too drunk to know what she was doing."[34] Hannah did not stop drinking in the weeks that followed, but she learned not to get caught by her mistress. "She has had no more drunken frolics," Anna wrote in a gossipy letter to her daughter in late November, "does very well but smells so strong of spirit that some days I am afraid to look at her. Mary Ann tells me she [Hannah] and Phillip want to live together again & I wish your father would let them—it will do no good to hinder them & may be Hannah might do better."[35]

While the Burwells were considering whether to allow Hannah and Phillip to cohabit, Hannah continued to imbibe. In early December Anna wrote to her daughter that she had gone into "the wash-house to see about the Lard" and found Hannah "so tipsy that she was too foolish for me to put up with so I ordered her to her own Kitchen or out of my sight." Realizing that Hannah was in no shape to prepare dinner, she recruited Eliza Chavis, her free mixed-race laundress, to help cook the food.[36]

Matters did not improve as the school term came to an end. "Hannah drunk & worried me greatly," Anna wrote on December 11. Convinced that the most sensible way to handle the situation was to get rid of her cook, Anna wrote to James Bridges in Virginia to arrange the sale.[37] Word of her alarming intentions spread quickly through the household, and when she went down to dinner, Hannah convinced her that if Anna allowed Phillip to return, she would try to stop drinking.[38] Phillip's presence appears to have helped the situation but did not dissuade Anna from the course of action she had decided was the best. "Hannah was drunk enough Christmas day but has been sober ever since," she wrote in late December. "She I think will certainly be sold this spring—we can stand it no longer."[39]

The loss of Hannah's labor at the same time that Mary Ann was convalescing from the birth of her baby meant that the house was in turmoil. This situation prompted Robert to become increasingly critical of Anna's ability to manage both the school and the household. In late January he gave her an ultimatum and demanded that she hire someone to help her or he would forbid her to teach. The next time Hannah claimed to be sick, he said, he would insist that Anna take Ann's place while she took Hannah's. Anna responded by hiring Julia. For forty-eight dollars and clothes for a year, the new domestic was obliged to clean the parlor, wait tables at breakfast, help wash up afterward, and sew until she was required to help with dinner at midday and supper in the evening. When Mary Ann had fully recovered, Anna expected Julia to do the sewing full time "for Mary Ann must be my housekeeper," Anna wrote in January 1856.[40]

Just as Robert had predicted, Hannah soon claimed to be sick and took to her bed. Anna was even more determined to sell her. "She is killing herself drinking & we can't afford to loose [sic] all her work. To Richmond she goes as soon as we can make arrangements. It will be a trial & I dread the day, but I have fully made up my mind that we ought to do it, & I'll go thro' [with] it," she wrote to her daughter.[41]

Why Anna planned to send Hannah all the way to the Richmond slave market when she could have arranged a sale locally is unclear. One possibility is that since Anna complained openly and frequently about Hannah to her daughter, she probably did so to her neighbors as well. Any of them who might have been looking for a cook would have known through the grapevine how difficult it was to manage her. Potential buyers in Richmond were unlikely to have had access to such information.

By the middle of March, plans to sell Hannah were in place. Anna wrote to her daughter,

Dr. Ashe expects to get a pair of Vermont horses, & Mr. Tommy Anderson is to go to Petersburg to bring them here, & when he goes, we expect him to take Hannah to Richmond to James Bridges who will attend to selling her for us. I do wish it was over, I can't feel easy 'till it is. I am satisfied we ought to sell her but still I dread the time for her to know it & go. I don't believe she cares a fig for us or any one, but still I feel sorry that any one should be as she is.[42]

Whether Anna changed her mind or Hannah gave up the bottle, the situation remained at an impasse. The sale never took place. Hannah moved with Mary Ann and the rest of the Burwell household to Charlotte and continued to work for them throughout the Civil War. By that time both of them had learned how to use Anna's dependence on them to mediate the conditions of their servitude. In February 1865 Anna wrote to her son that her school in Charlotte was "dirty beyond endurance." Mary Ann and Hannah had "taken their usual spell," she explained. "Hannah has not cooked for three weeks & Mary Ann has not been in the house more than two days since you left."[43]

Lizzie Keckly, Mary Ann, and Hannah lived and worked in close contact with their owners, which meant that they were always on call and could not escape white supervision. Enslaved workers whose labor took them away from the household experienced bondage and community somewhat differently. Take, for example, Jesse Ruffin, a mixed-race enslaved man born in 1806 to a woman owned by Thomas Hunt, an Orange County farmer. The Orange County deed books show that Hunt transferred ownership of Jesse, one of his five enslaved workers, to Thomas Ruffin in 1823.[44]

Born in 1787, Ruffin studied law with Archibald Murphey and set up his law practice in Hillsborough in 1808. He cemented his claim to social prominence when he married Anne Kirkland, the daughter of William Kirkland of Ayr Mount, in 1809.[45] By 1810 there were four enslaved laborers in his household. By the time he brought Jesse to Hillsborough, he had at least seven.[46] The teenaged Jesse went to live in one of the cabins located near the barn and kitchen garden on Judge Ruffin's Hill on the east side of Hillsborough where his enslaver had his home and law office.[47]

Ruffin was rarely home in those days. As a lawyer and eventually a superior court judge, he had to ride the legal circuit, arguing cases and holding court in various locations, sleeping and eating in taverns and inns, and socializing with other lawyers. Because his absence made it impossible for him to effectively manage his enslaved workers, he hired an overseer.[48]

Doing so was risky. It was the overseer's job to manage and discipline enslaved workers in order to get as much work as possible out of them at the least possible expense, a situation that put his priorities in direct conflict with the owner's interest in preventing damage to his very valuable human property.[49]

Because of Ruffin's frequent absences, Jesse's contact with his master would have been limited and sporadic. It was the overseer who determined his working conditions, monitored his private life, and meted out whatever punishment for real or perceived transgressions he thought necessary. Less than a year after Jesse arrived in Hillsborough, Ruffin's mentor Archibald Murphey, a man predisposed to mind his own business, felt compelled to inform Ruffin about gossip regarding his overseer's "cruel and barbarous treatment" of his enslaved laborers. Admitting that he had no personal knowledge of the matter and was relying on the word of others, he told Ruffin: "Your negroes are in the first place worked to death; in the sec'd place they are whipped both cruelly and barbarously." Moreover, he continued, they were given almost no time to prepare and eat their meals. The most damaging of the stories held that Ruffin's overseer "has been literally barbequing, peppering, and salting [his victims]," Murphey reported.[50] While a slave owner could treat his enslaved workers any way he liked, an overseer could be found criminally liable for excessive punishment of those held in bondage under his supervision.[51] It was with that in mind that Murphey warned Ruffin that "without your interference," a charge of murder might be brought before the court.[52] It is unclear what action, if any, Ruffin took to remedy the situation. But whatever it was, Jesse would have found himself in the middle of it and could not have emerged from the experience without an appreciation of the potential danger he faced.

In 1828 Jesse married Rebecca, a domestic worker enslaved by William Norwood, whose plantation Poplar Hill was located across the Eno River from Ruffin's place.[53] How Jesse and Rebecca negotiated with their respective masters for permission to marry is unclear. In general, masters were ambivalent about slave marriages. They appreciated the fact that the birth of children that resulted from such unions enhanced their wealth and that the relationships established through marriage helped tie the enslaved to those they lived and worked with. But many did not take slave weddings seriously because they knew that the marriage vows of the enslaved had no legal standing and could be easily broken.[54] For enslaved couples, however, wedding rituals, whether they involved jumping a broom or saying vows in the presence of a minister, offered them a claim to social respectability within their own community.[55]

Once married, the couple was haunted by the threat of separation. It was well known that Ruffin had little concern about separating families. Earlier in the decade, he made an agreement with Benjamin Chambers to provide the capital for Chambers to purchase enslaved people in places such as Virginia and North Carolina and sell them for profit in Georgia, Mississippi, and Alabama. The business flourished at first but ended with Chambers's death in 1827 just before Jesse and Rebecca's marriage.[56] Ruffin's callous attitude toward separating families did not change. In 1838 William Hooper wrote to ask him to hire or purchase an enslaved worker named November so that he could live with his wife, who did sewing for the Ruffin household. Testifying that November was "sound and strong," "honest and sober," and a "good house servant," Hooper wrote, "He seems to think his fate a hard one that he can go only once a month to see his wife, and then have to walk such a distance or hire a horse" to make the trip.

Enslaved by the Norwoods, Rebecca [Ruffin] managed the household at Poplar Hill across the Eno River from Hillsborough until emancipation. Courtesy of the Mary Claire Engstrom Photographic Collection, Wilson Special Collections Library, UNC–Chapel Hill.

Ruffin was predisposed to reject Hooper's request on the grounds that he did not believe that reuniting a married couple was sufficient grounds for taking a chance on finding November's work ethic unsatisfactory, which, he explained to his wife, would require him to sell both November and his wife. There is no record in the deed books of the county clerk that Ruffin ever purchased November.[57]

Jesse and Rebecca's fear of separation was realized when Ruffin moved his household out of Hillsborough in the winter of 1829–30. At about the same time that Ruffin was elected to the North Carolina Supreme Court, he purchased an estate ten miles west of town on Great Alamance Creek called the Hermitage. The purchase was prompted by an effort on his part to help his friend Archibald Murphey cope with pending financial disaster. The property included two thousand acres, a gristmill and sawmill, and a distillery, as well as a large home and a law office.[58] The vast estate needed a large labor force to be productive, so Ruffin sent Jesse there to work as a wagoner, coachman, and sometime gardener and occasionally rented him out as a stagecoach driver.[59]

Being allowed to leave the estate unaccompanied was a privilege given to only the most trusted of enslaved laborers. As a teamster, Jesse's job included transporting products between the Hermitage and town, retrieving and delivering packages and purchases for the Ruffin family, and moving goods and supplies traded with or purchased from the Ruffins' neighbors. As he traveled around the county, he could also carry notes, letters, and documents from one place to another. In order to go about his work, he needed a pass or a permission ticket from Ruffin or his overseer stating his date of departure and return as well as his destination and the route he was supposed to take. Without it, he would have been subjected to the whims of the slave patrollers who could whip him or worse for being abroad without permission.[60]

Jesse's mobility gave him access to news and gossip useful for those isolated on individual farms and plantations about friends and loved ones who were living elsewhere. It also gave him the chance to visit his wife and children, who remained on the Norwood plantation. And if he chose to take advantage of it, he could facilitate an underground and invisible market economy where the enslaved exchanged produce and other property with those who lived beyond plantation boundaries. Slave owners did their best to prohibit such trade, but it was an uphill battle to stop it.[61]

The struggle between master and enslaved workers that characterized life in the Burwell household could also be found at the Hermitage. Along with the purchase of Murphey's plantation, Ruffin bought Bridget, which turned out to be a mistake on his part.[62] According to Ruffin, she had a reputation as a troublemaker who did what she could to spread discontent among those in the quarters. What she did, how she did it, and how Ruffin knew about it is unclear. But by disrupting established routines and lines of authority, she challenged his position as master and undermined his peace of mind at a time when North Carolina slave owners were particularly sensitive to the threat of slave insurrections. Shortly after the Nat Turner Rebellion in 1831, Ruffin was so angry at Bridget that he wrote to Murphey describing her as a "detestable character" and a "vile fiend." Convinced that her disruptive influence was undermining plantation discipline and worried that local gossip about the disorder he believed her to be fomenting might result in the decline in the value of his labor force, he had decided "to sell her at a great distance," he said, and if that was not possible, he was willing to give her away on the condition that whoever got her promised that she "would not be sold or live short of a thousand miles from the Hermitage."[63]

Murphey apparently agreed to take her off Ruffin's hands but either did not appreciate his friend's antipathy toward Bridget or simply neglected to honor his friend's desire to be rid of her forever. Having left his wife, who was ill, in the care of the Ruffins, Murphey returned to visit her, bringing the banished Bridget with him. Someone saw her on the property and reported it to Ruffin. Incensed that she was "prowling about" and unsettling those he held in servitude, Ruffin ordered his overseer to find her and whip her. When that did not happen, Ruffin went looking for her himself and found her near his mill. He reported that when he confronted her, she gave him "a look of insolent audacity which Patience itself could not swallow." He responded by giving her "a good caning."[64]

Insolence in the form of a facial expression or a disrespectful comment served as a reminder to masters and mistresses alike that power did not necessarily beget respect. As communications scholar William Wiethoff has pointed out, insolence on the part of enslaved workers such as Elizabeth Hobbs Keckly, Mary Ann, Hannah, and Bridget had economic, social, and moral repercussions for slave owners like Anna Burwell and Thomas Ruffin. It limited the productivity of their workforce, represented a small-scale rebellion that could sow the seeds of more organized resistance, and belied the idea that slavery was a paternalistic labor system based on the deference inherent in familial attachment. In short, insolence was part of a limited repertoire of strategies that enslaved workers could use to shame those who held them in bondage.[65]

Jesse may or may not have witnessed Bridget's insolence, but word about it would have spread quickly in the quarters. He could not have remained ignorant of her presence, his master's sensitivity toward preserving his authority, and his exasperation with the woman. All Jesse could do was keep his head down and go about his business, which frequently took him away from Ruffin property.

In 1832 Jesse's fortunes improved when Ruffin's daughter Anne married Paul Cameron.[66] The couple spent part of their time at Stagville, the Cameron plantation located north and east of Hillsborough, and part of their time living in the Ruffin homestead in Hillsborough, which they named Burnside. Since the house was inhabited at least part of the time, it had to be staffed with a maintenance crew, so Jesse may have been able to work there. By that time, he and his wife had at least three daughters, Margaret, Nancy, and Julia, who lived across the river with their mother on the Norwood property.[67]

Rebecca's life with the Norwoods revolved around her expanding duties as the head housekeeper. As in the case of Mary Ann, she managed the Norwood household. The symbol of her position were the keys to the pantry and the smokehouse that she carried around in her pocket.[68]

When William Norwood died in 1842, Rebecca became the property of his son John Wall Norwood and his wife Annabella.[69] Added to her responsibilities was the care of her new mistress, a woman of delicate health and unstable mind who was terrified about being left alone at night. When John was away tending to his law practice, she demanded that Rebecca spend the night with her and sleep in her bed.[70]

Rebecca's domestic duties limited the time she could spend with her children. It is unclear what arrangements she was able to make for their care or, for that matter, whether she had anything to say about it. When they were infants, she had to negotiate the time to feed them, a duty that by its very definition ensured they were close by.[71] In the absence of Jesse, it was Rebecca's responsibility to ensure that her children survived the condition of servitude into which they were born. She had to teach them to

When Anne and Paul Cameron resided at Burnside on the edge of Hillsborough, Jesse [Ruffin] had the opportunity to visit his wife and children at the Norwood plantation. Courtesy of the Mary Claire Engstrom Photographic Collection, Wilson Special Collections Library, UNC–Chapel Hill.

respect their elders, obey white people, keep secrets that might put themselves, their family, or their enslaved neighbors in danger, and develop a strong work ethic. By doing so, she helped transmit attitudes, values, and traditions that integrated them into the enslaved community and attempted to protect them from the hazards that enslavement imposed on them.[72]

The possibility of being permanently separated from their children must have been a constant concern for both Jesse and Rebecca. The Norwoods never sold those they held in slavery, but they had a reputation for giving them away.[73] When the Norwoods' daughter Robina married Thomas Webb in November 1854, she received three of Jesse and Rebecca's grandchildren, Jesse, Caroline, and Sallie, on her wedding day and took them to her new home in Georgia. In 1859 she received another enslaved individual from her father.[74] And in 1862 John Norwood gave five enslaved workers to another of his married daughters.[75]

It must have been some comfort to Jesse when Paul Cameron decided to move his family permanently to Hillsborough in 1859. With Rebecca and his children living just across the river, Jesse was able to see them whenever he could. Paul was an unenthusiastic supporter of secession and did not join the army or seek a position in the Confederate government. So Jesse

JOHN WALL NORWOOD
(1803-1885)

Owner of Poplar Hill, John Wall Norwood was a lawyer and a politician as well as a trustee of the Burwell School, the Bingham School, and the Caldwell Institute. Courtesy of the Mary Claire Engstrom Photographic Collection, Wilson Special Collections Library, UNC–Chapel Hill.

spent the war years working in Hillsborough where much of his time was spent laying out new gardens at Burnside.[76]

The destruction that accompanies war and the realities of dealing with invading armies did not affect Hillsborough until the very end of the war. When Union soldiers approached Raleigh from the south, Confederate troops retreated north through Orange County. As the Yankees approached, a remnant of Confederates camped in the woods outside of town and took what they wanted to eat from the Norwood plantation, as Jesse's grandson Lindsay Faucette recalled. But what he remembered most was the lice that that they brought with them. "It took fifteen years for us to get shed of de' lice," he said, noting that the only way to get rid of them was to burn your clothes.[77] Confederate General Joseph E. Johnston surrendered his troops to Major General William T. Sherman at Bennett's farmhouse between Hillsborough and Durham Station on April 26, 1865. When the Union troops occupied Hillsborough, Jesse sold their quartermaster some of his vegetables.[78]

The Emancipation Proclamation issued in 1863 was intended to free the Confederacy's enslaved labor force. Whatever rumors may have made their way through the enslaved community living in and around Hillsborough about the possibility of freedom, it wasn't until the Thirteenth Amendment was ratified in December 1865 that Jesse and his family were technically free. Adjusting to freedom was a complicated process that required assuming responsibility for supporting themselves and working out new personal and economic relationships with former enslavers. Jesse was eager to explore the possibilities that freedom offered.

Some of the formerly enslaved in Hillsborough turned to Freedmen's Bureau commissioner Isaac Porter for advice and assistance.[79] Established by the federal government in March 1865, the Freedmen's Bureau was set up to assist the formerly enslaved and impoverished white people adjust to the new social, political, and economic realities they faced. Porter's job was to supervise the distribution of food and clothing to those in need, legalize employment contracts for those in search of work, promote education, investigate racial confrontations, and register the marriages of the formerly enslaved. In March 1866 the North Carolina General Assembly passed an act instructing local justices of the peace to collect and produce a record of the cohabitation of former enslaved couples to ratify their state of marriage.[80] Jesse and Rebecca were among the first to comply with the law, registering their commitment to each other with the Freedmen's Bureau on May 1, 1866. Eventually four other Ruffin, one Norwood, and thirty-one Cameron couples added their names to the list.[81]

Jesse may or may not have consulted Porter about possibilities for employment, but he did believe the rumors that the federal government might distribute land to the formerly enslaved in North Carolina, thus emancipating them economically from their former masters. His hopes were not entirely misplaced. On January 16, 1865, Gen. William T. Sherman had issued Special Field Order no. 15 setting aside thousands of acres in the coastal area from Charleston, South Carolina, to Jacksonville, Florida, for settlement by freedmen and their families.[82] The promise of forty acres and a mule may have been an illusion, but it had a powerful influence on the behavior of formerly enslaved workers who hoped to become landowners in their own right and were not predisposed to sign labor contracts tying them to someone else's land.[83]

Shortly after he registered his marriage, Jesse visited the Cameron plantation to spread the word about the possibility of landownership. Paul Cameron was not pleased. Like many large landowners, he was not about to allow the aspirations of his former enslaved workers to interfere with the normalization of what had been an agricultural empire. "Very few of the negroes have gone off [but are] idle and indisposed to work or return to their former duties," he wrote to Thomas Ruffin. "Perhaps it is my duty to tell you that it is reported that Jessie in a recent visit to this place is said to have excited the negroes to demands and expectations and hopes that had not been thought of—such as a freehold interest in the soil on which they reside. I saw him but for a moment . . . on his way to the Station. I beg that you will not connect my name with this man."[84] Ruffin, who by 1860 held one hundred people in bondage, was facing his own labor crisis.[85] It is not clear how he responded.

Jesse also sought the advice of Rebecca's former owner, John Wall Norwood. In August 1865 Norwood wrote to Ruffin, "Jesse has applied to me to assist him with advice and otherwise, in settling himself, and I have told him I could have nothing to say to him until he first sees you upon the subject. If he decides to leave you, I will endeavor to fix him here, if I can. Beccy, his wife, is the only one of my negroes who even talks of remaining with us. She is so absolutely necessary to my wife that I do not see how she can possibly do without her."[86]

It is unclear what arrangements, if any, the Norwoods made with Rebecca. Land rich and cash poor, their circumstances were greatly reduced, and they had little to offer her as an inducement for staying. Her name does not appear in their household in the 1870 census, but she may have continued to run their household.[87]

Local gossip provided news of work opportunities for Jesse. Sometimes he hired himself out to his former enslaver, Thomas Ruffin. In a letter dated December 1865 and written from Norwood's Poplar Hill, Jesse, who somehow had learned to read and write during his enslavement, wrote deferentially, "My Dear Master, I have written to ask you if you will please have everything ready for killing hogs Monday morning. I will be up Saturday night, and will be obliged to return on Wednesday evening. I hope that you will have everything ready so that I can get along as fast as possible."[88] Helping with the hogs not only provided him with some income but also helped put food on his table, since those who participated in the process took home lard and whatever leftovers the hog's owner did not want.[89] Some years later, Jesse advertised his expertise in gardening and sold turnip seeds, cabbage plants, and asparagus roots to anyone willing to buy them.[90]

Meanwhile, his daughter Margaret's husband, William Faucette, negotiated a contract with John Wall Norwood to farm eighteen acres of his land. It was a year of great sacrifice for Margaret's family of twelve. Her son Lindsay worked on the land with his father and recalled that there was not a scrap of bread, let alone meat, in his mother's pantry. The family may have gone hungry, but they persevered. William "made a good crop" of wheat and corn, sold it, and began to save his money to buy his own farm. He eventually bought land in the Hillsborough area and continued to grow cash crops to sell and food to feed his family. Like his grandfather Jesse, Lindsay became a hack driver and teamster and finally went into business for himself by purchasing his own dray to cart people and supplies from one end of Durham to another. By the 1930s he had turned the hauling business into a trucking firm with a payroll of six thousand dollars a year.[91]

Through it all, Jesse and Rebecca continued to live in the Hillsborough area.[92] By 1900 Rebecca had died, and Jesse was living on Pettigrew Street in Durham.[93] He died at his grandson Lindsay's home on March 6, 1901, at the age of ninety-six. His body was returned to Hillsborough on the morning train. It is unclear where he was buried.[94]

Jesse, Rebecca, and their children were not the only victims of slavery to establish themselves as respectable members of the Black community in the Hillsborough area after the Civil War. Among Jesse's contemporaries was a man who became known as Job Berry.[95] Born around 1810, Job's original owner was probably George W. B. Burgwin (Burgwyn), a wealthy planter from Hanover County who apparently brought his family to live in Hillsborough in the summers in order to escape the heat, humidity, and ague that characterized living along the eastern coast of North Carolina. An Episcopalian, Burgwin sponsored the baptism of his son, Nathaniel Hill Burgwin, and the enslaved Job at St. Matthew's on October 6, 1833.[96] After enrolling Nathaniel in William James Bingham's Hillsborough Academy, the rest of the Burgwin family returned to their Hanover County home. Considering Job honest and trustworthy, they left him behind in Hillsborough.[97]

While the boy spent his time learning Greek and Latin in preparation for entry into the university in Chapel Hill, the twenty-three-year-old Job prepared for his confirmation under the direction of William Mercer Green, the Episcopalian rector. With Green as his tutor, he mastered the tenets of faith to be found in the church's catechism, the Creed, the Lord's Prayer, and the Ten Commandments, and he familiarized himself with the Bible and Episcopalian prayer book. Green also may have taught Job to read and write, a practice that was illegal but unofficially tolerated in some circles. As Job became more and more involved in matters relating to St. Matthew's Church, it would have become painfully obvious that while he might be admitted to membership in the congregation, it was unlikely that he would ever be given the opportunity to assume any position of authority or leadership in the church hierarchy.[98] Nevertheless, he persisted, and after six months of study, Bishop Levi Silliman Ives confirmed him on April 13, 1834.[99]

What Job did for the next few years is unclear. Since the Burgwins were related by marriage to the Nashes, the Waddells, and the Moores, all prominent Hillsborough families, and since slaveholding families were in the habit of selling, renting, or loaning their enslaved workers to each other, he could have lived in any number of households.[100] Whatever the case, Francis Waddell, a Hillsborough lawyer, or Sarah S. Moore, a member of Waddell's household, held him in bondage in 1839. Before that date, Waddell and Moore had used him as collateral to borrow $9,600 from the Bank of Cape Fear and $5,000 from a bank in Raleigh. Their notes had been guaranteed by some of the most notable citizens of Hillsborough: William Cain, Edmund Strudwick, John U. Kirkland, Hugh Waddell, Andrew Mickle, and Joseph Norwood. When Francis Waddell and Sarah Moore found it impossible to pay off their debts, the court stepped in and appointed Stephen Moore as trustee in charge of selling some of their property to cover their obligations. By February 1841 Moore had disposed of thousands of acres of their land in Tennessee and twenty-six of their enslaved workers, including one named Job. Hugh Waddell purchased Job at auction for $775.[101]

Waddell gave Job permission to marry in the mid-1840s. His new wife, Rebecca Nash, was at least ten years his junior. She bore Richard, the first of their eight children, in August 1847.[102] In 1853 Waddell and his family left Hillsborough for Chapel Hill.[103] If Job went with them, he did not remain long. In 1855 he apparently used his reputation for dependability and loyalty to negotiate an agreement with his owner whereby he was able to return on his own to Hillsborough to be near his family. In March he was working as a day laborer for the Burwells helping plant potatoes.[104]

At some point before the Civil War, Job felt called to preach the Gospel. Thwarted by the limitations placed on him by the Episcopal Church, Job appears to have served as a lay preacher among the enslaved and thereby began to establish his credentials as a trusted voice within Hillsborough's enslaved community. His opportunity to do so rested on a number of factors. As early as the 1830s, white evangelical Christians were deeply engaged in efforts to convert the enslaved population of the United States. Their efforts were largely successful because those held in bondage were willing to incorporate Christian theology and rituals into religious traditions that had their roots in African culture. In the South, the enslaved officially worshipped under the supervision of white people. Some enslavers such as Burgwin took their enslaved workers to church with them. Others like the Norwoods required that their workers come up to the "big house" every day to listen to someone read to them from the Bible.[105] Still others tolerated or hired preachers who had reputations for trustworthiness to tend to the spiritual needs of those they held in bondage. When such arrangements proved unsatisfactory, the enslaved held their own worship services with their own preachers either in their quarters or in the seclusion of so-called brush harbors away from the prying eyes of their enslavers. Black preachers like Job helped them practice a form of Christianity that incorporated two religious traditions designed to bring spiritual comfort to a people ensnared in a society that held them in subjugation.[106]

After the Civil War, Job took the surname Berry. Naming oneself was an important event for the formerly enslaved as they transitioned from a state of bondage to one of freedom. Slave owners reserved the right to name their enslaved workers and their children, although they might defer to the mother of a newborn. Before emancipation, the U.S. census listed the enslaved under the name of their owners. During that same period, public records such as deeds and wills referred to the enslaved by their first names only, often appending the name of their master in order to identify them. For example, since at the time of her emancipation Elizabeth Keckly was living in St. Louis in the household of her enslaver's daughter, Anne Garland, her emancipation documents referred to her as "Lizzie Garland" or "Garland's Lizzie" and to her son as "Garland's George."[107] Freedom offered people like Job and Rebecca the opportunity to establish their own identity and lay claim to themselves. Choosing a surname was one of the first gifts they could bestow on their children and grandchildren.

Some freed persons chose a surname seemingly at random for reasons known only to themselves. Others such as Jesse Ruffin chose their former enslaver's surname. Still others, like Job and Rebecca, chose the surname of a man in the community for whom they clearly had a great deal of respect. Job identified himself as a painter after the Civil War, suggesting that he had acquired a trade at some point, probably under the supervision of John Berry, a highly regarded builder in Hillsborough.[108] Their decision to identify themselves with John Berry had practical repercussions. Association with a prominent family who could serve as your protector, testify as to your character, loan you money, or help you arrange for employment and housing had its advantages, particularly in the sort of social and economic environment that existed during Reconstruction when the rules of social engagement and the structures of power were being redefined.

Only a few months after the Civil War ended, Job Berry assumed a position of leadership in Hillsborough's Black community by placing an advertisement in the *Hillsborough Recorder* to announce that a fair was to be held to raise money to found a freedmen's school.[109] As historian James Anderson has pointed out, the formerly enslaved showed exceptional initiative in establishing schools to educate themselves and their children.[110] Soon after the end of the war, Hillsborough's Black leaders began negotiating with newly established northern freedmen's aid societies to arrange for the employment of teachers. They opened their school in the old Orange County courthouse building, a structure that had been moved to the corner of Queen and Churton Streets sometime after January 1845. For some years, this property had served as the place of worship for Hillsborough's white Baptists. But in 1862 the Baptists sold it to George Bishop of Newbern, who in turn sold it to the Society of Friends in Philadelphia for twelve hundred dollars in 1866. The Quakers held the property in trust for the "relief of colored freed men," established a freedmen's school on the site, and hired two teachers appointed by the Friends Freedmen's Association.[111]

One of the first of them was Robert Fitzgerald. Originally from Delaware, educated in Pennsylvania, and a veteran of the Union navy, the twenty-seven-year-old received an offer from the Philadelphia Friends in early January 1868 to serve as assistant teacher in Hillsborough for twenty dollars a month plus any expenses he incurred for board, laundry, and travel. He arrived a few weeks later and worked with the school's head teacher, Miss B. V. Harris of Oberlin College. The challenge he and Harris faced was both pedagogical and social. The school enrolled over three hundred students, both adults and children, who could attend both day and night sessions.[112]

Hillsborough's freedmen's school was a thorn in the side of some of the town's most prominent white citizens. They resented the aspirations for self-improvement that it represented and believed that for many members of the Black community, schooling was taking precedence over working. "It is very difficult to hire them at any price since the 'cussed' Nigger School commenced," one of them wrote in early 1867.[113]

Southern white people resented freedmen's teachers and did what they could to make them feel unwelcome. And those in Hillsborough were no exception. Whether they were white, Black, or mixed race like Robert, whether they were male or female, freedmen's schoolteachers were essentially shunned by the white community when they were not being harassed and threatened with violence. Finding a room in one of Hillsborough's white-run boardinghouses was out of the question, so Robert stayed with the family of Heywood Beverly, a twenty-six-year-old, free-born, mixed-race tanner who owned property in town. Robert worked in Hillsborough with Job for only a short time before he moved to Goldsboro, North Carolina, to superintend a freedmen's school there.[114]

While Job worked to provide a place to educate Black children, he also looked for ways to stabilize his family's domestic life. On October 9, 1865, he purchased part of lots 17 and 20 for a total of one acre from Henry N. Brown for three hundred dollars.[115] It is not clear where he got the money or why Brown sold him the property, but the purchase meant that he and his family now had a home of their own.

About one and a half years later, on April 2, 1867, he was admitted as a "local preacher" in the African Methodist Episcopalian (AME) Church at the denomination's annual conference in Wilmington, North Carolina, thus enhancing his position as a community leader.[116] The AME Church had been organized in 1816 in Philadelphia by Black Methodists as a protest against the limits that white Methodists placed on their ability to function as equals within the structure of the church. Emancipation provided the opportunity for the AME Church to expand their missionary activity in the South. One of their first efforts was to organize the South Carolina conference in 1865 to facilitate their evangelical work among people of color, including those in North Carolina. Church leaders approved the appointment of exhorters and licensed preachers and authorized them to organize new congregations among people anxious to free themselves from the control that white Christians had previously exerted over them. AME preachers not only provided religious leadership for those in their congregations but involved themselves in both Reconstruction politics and efforts to provide educational opportunities to those in their communities. They helped recruit support for the Republican Party and did what they could to ensure that people of color had the right to vote. Like teachers, their efforts did not go unnoticed by local white racists, who did what they could to intimidate AME congregations by burning down their churches and brutalizing their ministers.[117]

It is hard to overstate the importance of having their own church for the free Black population of Hillsborough. It provided a safe public space for those used to being monitored and gossiped about by their white neighbors. It served as a center for the distribution and redistribution of community resources and offered its members strategies for improving themselves. A community center for worship, education, political activities, and cultural events, it served as an important marker of respectability in a white-dominated society.

According to oral tradition, Job served as the first pastor of Hillsborough's AME church.[118] By November 1868 the church had grown to two hundred members, and Rev. Henry Polke had replaced him, although Job apparently continued to preach in the area and through his ministry probably remained active in the affairs of the freedmen's school.[119] S. B. Williams was both pastor of the church and a teacher at the freedmen's school in

September 1869 when he complained to North Carolina Governor William W. Holden about Ku Klux Klan activities in the area and expressed concern for his safety.[120] Whether the Klan ran him out of town or the AME Church reassigned him to a different congregation is unclear, but Williams had left the area by the summer of 1870.[121]

By 1872 Job Berry was deeply involved in state politics. The new state constitution, ratified in 1868, opened the doors for Black ministers like Job with reputations as community leaders to serve as spokesmen for the newly emancipated. Toward that end, he joined the Republican Party, attended its Orange County meeting on March 30, and was elected to a committee to draft resolutions expressing support for President Ulysses S. Grant and North Carolina Governor Tod R. Caldwell in their bids for reelection. At the same meeting, Job was selected to serve as a delegate to the party's convention in Raleigh.[122] Together with white Republicans, men like Job worked to elect representatives who would implement policies to protect the interests of the poor and uneducated of both races by guaranteeing their political and legal rights, promoting their economic interests, and laying the basis for their social equality. White resistance to their political activism was swift in coming and brutal in its execution.

It is not clear where Job preached after 1868 when Polke took over his pulpit. But his self-possession and courage are suggested by a reminiscence published by De Bernier Waddell, who became an Episcopal minister in Mississippi.[123] Reverend Waddell, the nephew of Hugh Waddell, remembered that shortly after the Civil War, he and "twenty or thirty" of his white friends heard through the grapevine that Berry was preaching and decided to attend one of his services. Waddell does not say who his friends were, why so many of them decided to join him, or whether the group contained both men and women. Sparked by curiosity or boredom with the more ritualistic and reserved forms of worship they grew up with, they may have simply considered such an outing a lark. Or given the size of the group and the timing of their visit, they might have had some sort of intimidation in mind.

It is hard to imagine what Job and his congregation thought of the entrance of a large group of unexpected white visitors at a time of such racial tension. According to Waddell, as he and his friends sat on the benches surrounded by Job's Black congregants, they listened to his sermon, "Dividing the Sheep from the Goats," based on Matthew 25:31–46. The thrust of the text was that the charitable (sheep) would receive the keys to heaven while the uncharitable (goats) would be condemned to Hell. As Job was finishing, Waddell reported, "Berry paused, looking at his white brethren and then at his colored brethren, and then rather reluctantly said: 'My brethren I was going to say it anyway, and I might as well say it, notwithstanding our white brethren, and that is that when they go to dividing out the sheep from the goats, we sure belongs to the wooly crowd.'"[124] His decision not to change his message to accommodate the presence of the white people in his audience stands as testimony to his determination to help define for the members of his church what freedom really meant. It was not often, after all, that a Black preacher had the opportunity to put white folks in their place.

There appear to have been no repercussions for Job's outspokenness. He remained in the community, conducted at least forty wedding ceremonies in the Hillsborough area between September 1867 and May 1878, and presumably continued to preach as long as he was able.[125] Job and his wife were not listed in the 1880 census and are listed as deceased on their daughter's marriage license in 1887, so they probably died sometime in late 1878 or 1879.[126]

Gossip and rumors complicated the already complex interpersonal relationships that existed between those held in bondage and their enslavers. Overheard by chance, gossip could generate considerable anxiety if not outright desperation among the enslaved when talk of sale or separation made its way through the household or quarters. It also exacerbated the fears of the white community about racial unrest both before and after the Civil War. It could provide the enslaved with news of changes in workplace conditions. As in the case of Archibald Murphey and his friend Thomas Ruffin, it could be used to try to shame abusive enslavers into modifying their treatment of those they held in bondage. It could influence the reputations of the enslaved, determining the way they were treated, the amount of freedom of movement they were allowed, and their value as property. As a communication tool, it provided the enslaved with the information they needed to get a sense of the parameters within which they could maneuver their way through the minefields that characterized their lives in bondage.

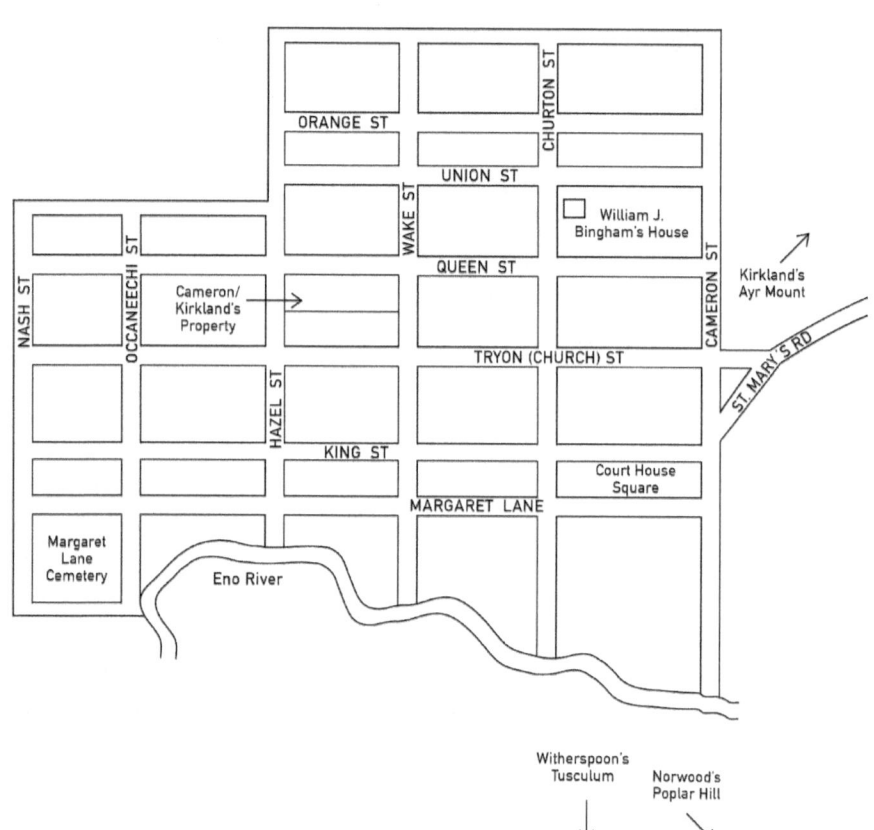

5
THE PLAGUE OF MADNESS IN OUR MIDST

There is nothing that feeds a town's gossip mill like people whose self-presentation diverges from the norm. Like most small towns, Hillsborough had its share of eccentrics, people whose odd, sometimes quite bizarre behavior provoked their neighbors' interest, comment, and occasionally their censure. It was gossip within the community about a neighbor or family member's mental instability often accompanied by physical incapacity and drug addiction that led to the diagnosis of madness. As awareness of unusual behavior gave way to growing concern, family and friends tried to evaluate the seriousness and persistence of the symptoms they were observing and began speculating about their cause and the possibilities for treatment.

Such was the case with schoolmaster William James Bingham, whose career as an educator was discussed in chapter 3. Bingham's questionable judgment, excessive excitability, and neurotic fears became a source of gossip in the days that followed rumors about the possibility of a slave insurrection in Hillsborough during the Christmas season in 1830. Despite the fact that no rebellion occurred, Bingham apparently convinced himself that the threat persisted and that, as an enslaver, his safety remained at risk. One of his neighbors, Alexander Kirkland of Ayr Mount, concluded that he had gone quite mad: "It is questionable whether the former gentleman will be able to resume his station as teacher in our Academy this season, as he is presently mentally deranged; facts speak for themselves. He has lately placed himself under the immediate tuition of an imposter who pretends to learn and teach the English language by steam. This circumstance alone is enough to condemn him. The boys say he walks backwards to & from school for fear a negro might creep up behind him and knock him in the head."[1] Kirkland had no expertise in diagnosing cases of mental illness, but, given his observation of the man's behavior, he was more than willing to share his opinion that Bingham was out of his mind.

Anxiety about the state of Bingham's mind was not misplaced since he was the sole support of his family, and the success of his school depended on public confidence in his abilities as an educator. He was not violent and did not disrupt the lines of authority within the community, however, so he was not confined to the jail in the courthouse square at county expense.[2] Instead, the town's residents speculated about his state of mind, tolerated his behavior, and left it to his family to monitor and supervise him.

It is not clear how long William James remained terrified of his shadow and infatuated with the pedagogical applications of steam, how long gossip about his paranoia dominated the popular imagination, how well he was able to run his school, or how his family responded to his behavior. If they agreed that he was mentally deranged, there was little they could have done about it at the time. Consulting domestic health manuals such as William Buchan's *Domestic Medicine* or turning to a local doctor to provide treatment would have proved futile since neither could offer effective remedies. And despite the national movement to build mental health hospitals to care for the insane, North Carolina did not yet have one. All the Binghams could realistically do was try to minimize whatever disruption William James's paranoia inflicted on their household, his classroom, and the community, deal with the strain it placed on their emotional resources, and hope that he would eventually recover his wits.[3] He apparently did, at least temporarily, and continued to support his family as a schoolmaster.

For those in Hillsborough with long memories and an interest in such matters, however, it may have come as no surprise when they heard that the Bingham family committed him to the North Carolina Hospital for the Insane in August 1865 after he was diagnosed with mania.[4] It is unclear what specific set of symptoms prompted them to send him to the hospital in Raleigh to seek confirmation of his mental breakdown. A study of Alabama hospital records, however, suggests that doctors who diagnosed cases of insanity in men typically looked to the public aspects of their lives as the source of their mental illness. Among the factors they identified as precipitating causes in men were excessive political excitement, overwork, and business troubles.[5] Bingham's mental health could have been negatively impacted by all of them. There was political excitement in abundance during the months following the Civil War. He had always been excessively conscientious about his work, and anxiety about the survival of his school must have been enormous given the fact that he and his sons now had to recruit students from once prosperous but now impoverished southern families.[6]

Illnesses affecting both mind and body were pervasive in the nineteenth century, particularly in the South where malarial fevers and agues were common. Those without an identifiable cause and clear diagnosis were especially problematic. Complicating the issue of assessing a patient's condition was the fact that once consulted, doctors' treatment of choice for almost every known ailment, including mental instability, was the administration of opium or one of its derivatives such as morphine or laudanum. Doctors chose such therapy because opiates were widely available with or without a prescription and because their patients found that taking them was easier and less debilitating, unpleasant, and painful than so-called heroic treatments such as bleeding and purging. Unfortunately, while patients may have appreciated the degree to which such drugs masked their symptoms, extended use of the substances could easily result in addiction, which made treatment and cure more difficult.[7]

Another complication was the impact of prevailing anxieties concerning women's bodies that led doctors to assume that well-bred white women were predisposed to invalidism and insanity because of their childbearing capacity.[8] As one of them put it, a woman's reproductive organs exercised "a controlling influence upon her entire system, and entail[ed] upon her many painful and dangerous diseases."[9] Once doctors armed with forceps and anesthesia slowly began to replace midwives in the birthing room, they began to define the natural process of childbirth as a problem requiring medical diagnoses and interventions. Convinced that childbearing posed a threat to a woman's mental health, they diagnosed a woman's "unnatural" emotional response to childbirth in the form of postpartum depression or overexcited, aggressive, or disruptive behavior (mania) as puerperal insanity.[10] They also thought that menopause was a time when women were increasingly likely to suffer from depression and insanity as well as diseases such as dyspepsia (indigestion), diarrhea, and rheumatism. Of no less danger was puberty when the onset of menstruation and unfamiliar sexual urges forced young women to deal with their bodies in new ways and to confront their future as wives and mothers.[11]

Young white women in the middle and upper classes had to learn about sex on the fly despite the fact that the evidence of reproduction was everywhere around them. There was little privacy at school or in their homes. It was hard to miss the pink-tinted rags hanging up to dry on the clothesline. And both domestic and farm animals copulated on a regular basis in plain sight. But as the products of a Christian tradition that considered lust to be a sin and members of a society that considered the frank discussion of sexuality off limits, young ladies were expected to enter the marriage market as virgins without having the benefit of knowing much about human sexuality and the realities of marital intimacy. Under those circumstances, they had every reason to approach womanhood and all it entailed with some degree of anxiety.

Doctors would have considered the case of William Kirkland's eighteen-year-old daughter Phebe classic.[12] Phebe's invalidism and mental instability started in late 1829 when she began suffering from muscular cramps, paralysis, and convulsions that affected her mind. Her incapacity changed the dynamics of the Kirkland household. As a young, unmarried daughter, her job was to help run the household, prepare herself for marriage, and be of service to those in her community. Her illness gave her the power to make demands on her family's time, emotional reserves, and economic resources to which she would have had no claim under normal circumstances.

Her parents consulted Drs. James Webb, Edmund Strudwick, and James Strudwick Smith, who at first attributed her condition to an "internal injury" (gynecological problem) and applied blisters to her skin. Their treatment was ineffective, but consultations with her minister, Rev. William Mercer Green, seemed to sooth her troubled mind and ailing body. It was not until the spring of 1830 that her symptoms began to diminish. By March she seemed to have recovered completely.

Having regained her equilibrium, she traveled to Fayetteville where she again fell ill. When she awoke one night weeping uncontrollably and quoting the lines of a familiar hymn, her hosts sent for a doctor. She seemed to have no idea where she was and did not recognize people who were familiar to her. Her spasms resumed. The fact that her mouth clenched shut leaving her unable to speak or swallow only added to her misery. The doctor diagnosed lockjaw and administered blisters to her head, jaws, ankles, and wrists. Her muscles eventually relaxed, but her tongue remained paralyzed until a bout of vomiting made it possible for her to take liquids. After that she could only communicate by "spelling with her fingers."

After her father brought her back to Hillsborough, convulsions and lockjaw continued to plague her. Dissatisfied with their original diagnosis, her local doctors identified a displaced uterus as the culprit and prescribed astringent douches and a pessary to support her vaginal tissue. Her condition gradually improved, but in 1835 her spasms returned again. Friends and neighbors gossiped about how "silly" she had become and commented on "a great expression of wildness out of her eyes." They all agreed that she was "not herself."

By 1839 she had recovered completely and was well enough to travel to Columbus, Georgia, to visit her sister for what turned out to be an extended stay. Still single, her illness had allowed her to postpone marriage and childbearing for ten years. It was in Columbus that she met and fell deeply in love with Nelson McLester. They married in 1841, and she gave birth to a daughter called Maggie. Whatever anxieties she carried with her about childbirth were only confirmed by that experience. "I had often heard it said that labour was the worst suffering that poor females are subject to, but I know it now from bitter experience, and had I known as much as I do now I would have staid single all my life," she wrote. Phebe got only a taste of the so-called joys of motherhood. She died in 1844 at the age of thirty-three from unknown causes.[13]

Her family had to assume responsibility for Phebe's care in the 1830s because they had no other options. By the 1840s, however, doctors such as Hugh Lenox Hodge, a professor of medicine at the University of Pennsylvania in Philadelphia, had begun to specialize in the care of women whose physical complaints were often accompanied by drug addiction or some sort of perceived mental or emotional disturbance. Word-of-mouth recommendations brought them the patronage of patients from Hillsborough and other areas of the South.[14] In addition, the construction of insane asylums provided an attractive alternative to home care for Hillsborough families forced to deal with invalidism, opiate addiction, and mental illness, thus relieving them of direct responsibility for dealing with their difficult, often disruptive relatives.

The doctors who worked in such institutions expressed great optimism that whatever its cause, mental illness could be cured. The therapy they recommended was called the "moral treatment." It was based on the premise that the causes of mental disturbance originated in the way society was organized. So in order to cure a mentally ill patient, their environment needed to be changed. The asylum, they believed, provided just such an environment. There the insane could be placed under a doctor's absolute authority and provided with a pleasant environment isolated from the social, political, and economic tensions that were believed to have brought on mental instability. In the asylum, order could be returned to their bodies and minds by requiring them to follow a rigidly prescribed regimen of medical treatment combined with a strict schedule of activities and amusements.[15] The families of invalids, drug addicts, and the mentally ill now had alternatives to home care that promised to be both humane and effective.

Among the first of Hillsborough's families to take advantage of such alternatives were the Witherspoons.[16] Born on July 9, 1827, Mary was the youngest of the Witherspoon children. Her home life was unsettled from the beginning. Just before her birth, the Witherspoon house at Tusculum burned to the ground. She was six when her father moved the family to Camden, South Carolina. They returned in 1839, and soon thereafter Mary went to live in town with Dr. Edmund Strudwick and his family. While her father John searched for a way to support his family and pay off the debts he had accumulated, Mary attended the Burwell School and tutored the Burwells' youngest children in order to pay for her tuition.

The Panic of 1837 and the depression that followed had exacerbated the Witherspoons' financial distress. Business was slow, credit was hard to get, and over extended businessmen like James Strudwick Smith found themselves on the verge of bankruptcy. To get access to cash, John mortgaged Tusculum to Edmund Strudwick, but his inability to pay off the debt forced Strudwick to foreclose in 1845. By that time, eighteen-year-old Mary was so ill that he did not have the heart to evict the family, so he allowed them to stay on the property.

As a young woman just emerging from adolescence, Mary's situation mirrored that of Phebe Kirkland. In July 1846 Mary's father wrote to her married sister in Camden that nineteen-year-old Mary was suffering from excruciating headaches. He feared, he said, that she was suffering from "an affliction of the spine" that deprived her of both health and happiness.[17] It is not clear how the Witherspoons heard about Dr. Hodge, but within a month Mary was in Philadelphia with her mother to consult with him to see if he could offer treatment for her pain, "spasms," and the emotional stress that accompanied them. Consulting a physician like Hodge, whose lucrative practice included a great many southern women, served to both legitimize Mary's condition with a diagnosis of illness and find a medical intervention to cure it. Predictably, Hodge looked to the state of her reproductive organs to explain her physical symptoms and told her mother that once her womb was "relieved," her accompanying "nervous symptoms" would eventually disappear.[18] But her convulsions continued, and when she "lost herself," as her mother put it, she lost her ability to reason and did not recognize anyone in the room. By the middle of September, Hodge was so concerned about her condition that he asked Dr. Samuel Jackson, one of his colleagues, to consult on the case. Both doctors agreed that the problem lay in her displaced womb, treated her with warm baths and warm toddies, and again assured the patient and her mother that when her womb was relieved, her mental state would also improve. When that did not happen, her mother wrote that she was under considerable pressure from friends to send Mary to an asylum but that she could not bring herself to do it.[19] Mary's convulsions had become less frequent, her cousin Elizabeth Rice reported in October, "but she has still but a short interval of reason through the day, from an hour and a half to two hours."[20]

Mary had returned home to Hillsborough by November, but her spasms continued, and she developed such a severe case of indigestion (dyspepsia) that she could not keep food down. Her mother reported that she was so desperate to get well that she had begun to take seriously the suggestion that she be admitted to an asylum.[21] By April 1847 she had taken her treatment into her own hands, and in an attempt to stabilize her womb, she was lacing her corset so tightly that her local doctor warned her that she was making herself worse.[22]

Desperate for a cure, Mary's parents found the means to return her to Dr. Hodge's care. Mary and her mother, accompanied by a neighbor, Susan Waddell (wife of Hugh Waddell), who also intended to consult Dr. Hodge regarding her own health, traveled north in May and established themselves in a boardinghouse near Dr. Hodge's practice.[23] Unfortunately, Hodge's attentions did nothing to improve Mary's condition. In June her health deteriorated when she began suffering paralysis of her legs, feet, and left arm. Hodge, who visited her every day despite his busy schedule, assured her mother the condition was merely "a nervous affection" that would "pass off."[24] By mid-July she appeared to have spontaneously regained the use of her arm, was walking again, and was no longer misidentifying the people she knew.[25]

It is not clear how long Mary and her mother stayed in Philadelphia. Money was always tight in the Witherspoon household, and boarding in Philadelphia was an extra expense they could not really afford. In the summer of 1850 they were both living at home in Hillsborough. Mary had taken in students, although she sometimes found it necessary to take her pupils into her room and give them their lessons from her bed, an unusual arrangement to be sure and one that could only have exacerbated talk about her situation.[26] Because her condition had not improved by December 1852, her parents again bore the expense of sending her to Dr. Hodge for the third time.[27]

In August 1853 Mary's father's health began to fail.[28] When her mother returned home to care for him, her sister Susan became her caretaker in Philadelphia.[29] John Witherspoon died on September 25, 1853, in the Tusculum farmhouse. Mary was still in Philadelphia when her mother died just six months later on March 31, 1854. Her tenure there caused judgmental talk among her friends and relatives. M. G. Nash wrote to Mary's sister to say that "a public boarding house" in Philadelphia was "a very improper place for" Mary and offered to take her into her home. It is unclear who cared for Mary after her mother's death or when she regained her health and mental capacity.[30]

But recover she did in a manner reminiscent of Phebe Kirkland some fifteen years before. Throughout most of her twenties, Mary had been an invalid like Phebe whose chronic physical suffering was accompanied by mental disability. At the age of almost thirty, she, like Phebe, married. Her husband was William G. Bowers, an Orange County farmer known as Green Bowers.[31] There is nothing to suggest that she was unable to function as a farm wife. She bore two children and ran the homestead while Green served in the Confederate army. In 1871 she and her husband tried unsuccessfully to persuade the federal government to compensate them for losses suffered during the Union army's occupation of their land during the Civil War. By 1900 she was widowed and living with her daughter in nearby Chatham County.[32]

Just about the time Mary Witherspoon's health began to decline, their neighbor Anna Cameron Kirkland also began to suffer troubling symptoms of mental distress. Born in 1817, Anna was a timid child who grew up believing that she was less articulate, less intelligent, and less physically attractive than her siblings.[33] At the age of ten, she was diagnosed with what was known as brain fever, an illness similar to scarlet fever, meningitis, or encephalitis, which manifested itself in high fever, violent headaches, intolerance of noise or light, quick pulse, convulsions, and mental confusion. Treatment consisted of bleeding and purging. She grew to adulthood in a permanent state of ill health.[34]

In 1835, at the age of seventeen, she married the highly indulged son of William Kirkland of Ayr Mount, Alexander McKenzie Kirkland, a man ten years her senior.[35] Letters full of family gossip provide some insight into Anna's domestic situation and relationship with her husband. In March 1836 Catherine Ruffin, who was traveling with the Kirklands, wrote to a relative that they had had to interrupt their journey when Anna, who was almost six months pregnant, became "indisposed." They stopped and immediately consulted a physician, who warned them that Anna "was threaten'd with an accident [miscarriage]" and treated her pain and fever with niter and laudanum. The threat turned out to be a false alarm, and she was able to travel a few days later. It appears that in the midst of the crisis, however, Alexander decided to leave the two women to fend for themselves. Of all "the cowardly husbands I ever saw in my life uncle Alexander exceeds," the outraged Ruffin declared.[36] Anna was able to carry her first child to term.[37] Her second experience in childbirth in 1838 was no less traumatic. Robert was a very large baby, the birth was difficult, and she never fully recovered, thus adding gynecological problems to her state of ill health.[38] It was during this period that her husband began to pursue Lizzie, the Burwells' enslaved domestic servant.

At about the same time, Alexander began his slow descent into alcoholism. Catherine Ruffin described his condition: "It grieves my heart to find uncle Alexander so altered; he has the appearance to me of a very intemperate man. He is fat and unnaturally flushed and is really stupid." Ruffin alluded to Alexander's abusive behavior toward Anna in the same gossipy letter: "I am glad to hear she bore it so meekly for she is a high-spirited woman and I was afraid would resent such treatment."[39]

By the spring of 1843, Alexander's health was deteriorating. Confined to his bed, he required around-the-clock nursing, but his doctor, Edmund Strudwick, had no reason to think that his death was imminent. If Alexander's sudden death in early May 1843 was a shock to his doctor, it was a catastrophe for Anna. She had assured him that she would be by his side in his last moments. As it turned out, however, he expired while she was tak-

Anna Cameron Kirkland lived at Ayr Mount on the outskirts of Hillsborough after her marriage to Alexander Kirkland. Courtesy of the Mary Claire Engstrom Photographic Collection, Wilson Special Collections Library, UNC–Chapel Hill.

ing a few minutes' reprieve from the sick room. Consumed by the guilt she felt for having let him die without her, she was inconsolable. She mourned his loss by idealizing a man who could not have been easy to live with. "He was a man of modest merit," she wrote. "Few knew his real worth & none save the wife of his bosom appreciated his gentle & endearing virtues." Like many abused wives, she blamed herself for provoking his rage. "He was generous & forgiving almost to a fault & bore with the infirmities of my temper and disposition as no other man on earth would have done. I do not remember that he ever spoke harshly to me during the whole of our wedded life except once when I richly deserved it & then the words had scarcely passed his lips when he begged my pardon with tears in his eyes.... How I worshiped him. He was my *life* my *all*."[40]

Anna later claimed that she lost her mind the night her husband died, when she found herself unable to accept God's decision to take him away from her. "In my heart I almost cursed my God," she wrote. The spiritual underpinnings of her life as well as her emotional equilibrium crumbled when she found it impossible to submit to God's will. She interpreted her feelings as a sign of His abandonment, began to despair of her own salvation, and convinced herself that she was damned.[41] She tried to ignore the emotional distress that plagued her by caring for her two children, attempting to support herself by teaching school, and engaging in acts of charity, but as time passed she became despondent, then melancholic, and began contemplating a violent death.[42]

Her alarming behavior frightened her family, whose letters are full of descriptions of her distress. She could not sleep and would not eat or drink water. And she prayed incessantly and tore at her hands until they were raw and bleeding.[43] When a cousin visited just after Christmas in 1845, she found Anna "to be the most wretched miserable creature I ever beheld. To use her own strong language she thinks she 'is a lost, damned being for all eternity.' . . . She has lost all interest in her children and friends. . . . Her poor mother is overwhelmed with trouble, she looks as if her mind too was unbalanced." Something needed to be done at once, she concluded, or "she [Anna] will soon be a *maniac*."[44]

Anna's family was desperate to find someone who could help alleviate her torment. At first they turned to Robert Burwell, the Presbyterian minister and schoolmaster, to provide her with spiritual counseling. But in a gossipy letter to her daughter, his wife reported that after talking and praying with the disturbed woman, he came away convinced that the best way to deal with her obsession was to carefully avoid talking to her about religion.[45] Anna's brother William Cameron was a doctor, but he had no training in treating mental illness.[46]

It was typically gossip among family and friends that eventually led them to define persistent, disturbing, atypical behavior as insanity. When Anna's condition did not improve, her mother Anne Cameron (called Nancy) consulted her brother-in-law Duncan Cameron, the family's wealthy patriarch. He agreed that Anna was mad and needed to go to an asylum. There was no such institution in North Carolina, so he wrote to the Western State Hospital for the Insane in Staunton, Virginia. Asking its staff for a confirmation of his diagnosis, he offered to pay for her treatment.[47] Anna did not resist their efforts. Writing to Margaret Mordecai, she said, "I do not believe I am insane.... Still I turn my eyes towards Staunton and try to awake even the feeblest shadow of hope."[48]

Authorized by the Virginia state legislature in January 1825, the hospital provided spacious grounds and a tranquil atmosphere where its nonchronic, paying patients could live comfortably, exercise regularly, and find gender-specific, useful employment to occupy their time while they recovered from their afflictions.[49] Francis T. Stribling was the man in charge. Born in 1810, he attended the University of Pennsylvania Medical School and in 1836 became the superintendent of the Western State Hospital, where he introduced moral treatment as the regimen most likely to restore his patients' sanity.[50]

Anna and her mother traveled from Hillsborough through Petersburg, Virginia, to Staunton in early 1846. Given that the association between religiosity and madness dated back to ancient times and the early nineteenth century was an age of revivals and destabilizing religious enthusiasms, it is not surprising that asylum superintendents like Stribling gave considerable weight in their diagnostic process to the religious nature of Anna's symptoms.[51] In the end he agreed with the Kirkland/Cameron family's diagnosis that Anna was insane. Officially diagnosed as being in "ill health," Anna became patient number 504 on February 8. One of Duncan Cameron's sisters spent time with them and reported that "such an object of heart rending pitty [sic] I never beheld."[52]

Stribling visited Anna once a day and wrote regularly to her family about her progress. His treatment included injecting alum water into her vagina as well as administering regular doses of morphine, laudanum, and opium. The drugs calmed the nerves and induced sleep but also caused constipation, so he prescribed calomel in the form of blue pills to loosen her bowels.[53]

The administration of opiates seems to have had the anticipated calming effect on Anna. Ten days after she arrived, Stribling wrote to one of her brothers that she had been understandably distressed at the prospect of living among strangers and that, in the first few days in the hospital, she had continued to manifest the disturbing symptoms that had led to her commitment. She seemed obsessed with her "morbid reflections," he wrote, did not want to eat, and refused to stay in bed at night. Instead, she "placed herself on her hands and knees on the floor, insisting that 'she was unworthy of the comforts furnished her & that her suffering's [sic] hereafter would be aggravated by her indulging therein." She forced her nails into her thumb in the apparent belief that "self-torture was a duty." Nevertheless, he assured the family that she was gradually improving. She was, he reported, eating well and regularly, sleeping through the night, and knitting him a pair of socks. She seemed pleased, he said, to have something productive to do. She was willing to socialize with the other patients, he continued, and expressed contentment with her circumstances. But he warned them that her recovery would take time.[54]

Anna's letters confirmed Stribling's belief that she was adjusting to her new life. "I understand that patients sometimes blame their friends for bringing them here, but I have no feeling of the kind, on the contrary shall forever bless the day that brought me to this 'house of refuge,'" she wrote to her uncle. She had developed great confidence in Stribling, she said, and was willing to remain in the hospital until he thought her fully restored to sanity. Her only regret was that her absence might somehow injure her children and "weaken the bonds of parental authority" she had over them.[55]

In October Stribling wrote to Anne to report that Anna continued to improve. Her anguish and irritability were so diminished, he wrote, that "her whole demeanor has been that of a rational, amiable lady." Her physical health had also improved, he said, and he anticipated that she might be able to leave the hospital by the end of the year.[56]

He released her in November, and she went to live with her mother and children in a rented house in Petersburg.[57] For a while, she was able to maintain her equilibrium. It was with great relief that Anne wrote to her brother-in-law on New Year's Day that Anna showed no signs of her former affliction, "continues perfectly calm, and self-possessed of her faculties, her bodily suffering is much slighter that it was, and I hope with care she may pass the remainder of her days in more comfort that she has known for years."[58]

Unfortunately, Anne's hopes were misplaced. Two months after her release, Anna wrote a long, incoherent letter to Stribling in which she claimed that her mental state was threatened this time by "a painful idea which has haunted me for eleven or twelve years, & while I am under its influence every source of enjoyment is poisoned." Thinking about it was a torment, she said, and doing so was making her feel "wretched." After describing her condition in great detail, she concluded: "I suppose 'tis not necessary that you should know the nature of this idea; I can only say 'tis not of a religious nature."[59] It is not clear how Stribling responded, but he must have sensed that her distress did not portend well for the future.

Anxiety about money during this period also posed a threat to Anna's fragile state of mind. Because Alexander had no property to leave his widow, she became financially dependent on her mother Anne after his death. In 1826 Anne's father had bestowed on her considerable real estate and enslaved workers, but, like many women, she had never been taught how to manage money or property and depended on her male relatives to manage her affairs.[60]

Once she was out of the hospital, Anna became concerned about her ability to support her children. Her mother had promised to give her the title to her house and lot in Hillsborough as well as enslaved workers and cash, but thus far she had made no effort to make good on her pledge. The unsettled nature of her financial situation caused Anna much anxiety, resulting in "loss of appetite, broken & unrefreshing sleep & a high degree of nervous irritability" until her mother finally turned over to her the deed to the house and its lot, three enslaved workers, and one thousand dollars.[61]

The need for a regular income still needed to be addressed, however. Anna tried to open a boarding school, but the effort failed.[62] In the summer of 1848 she wrote to her uncle Duncan Cameron that she couldn't really afford to live in Hillsborough and that she suspected her brother-in-law was trying to defraud her mother. Anna claimed that her continuing struggles over money were threatening her mental stability and that, because of it, she expected to be "subject to occasional fits of insanity all my life."[63]

Her fears were realized. Her mother wrote to Duncan Cameron on Christmas Day 1849 that Anna had been delirious for a month, was convinced that she was dying of cancer, and once again believed that she was damned: "She raves day and night that she is lost, and doomed to eternal suffering."[64]

Anna's brother William wrote to Stribling in Staunton, reporting that Anna had relapsed, her religious melancholy had returned, for the past four months she had been convinced that she was about to "commit certain acts of violence" for which she and her children would be "publicly executed," and she would "bring disgrace on her friends by her wanton deportment and impure acts." He could detect no physical ailment, he said, so he was treating her nervous excitability with opium and blisters and was stimulating her liver with "Blue Mass," a concoction with a mercury base. He asked that she be readmitted to the asylum, and Stribling agreed.[65]

By the time Anna arrived back at the asylum in March 1850, she had become dependent on the opium her brother had prescribed and begged for it when it was withheld.[66] Despite her addiction, Anna was happy to be in Staunton. She wrote to her cousin: "I am *perfectly* satisfied with my quarters & only wish I could . . . feel sure I might spend the remainder of my days here."[67] Stribling continued to prescribe opium, morphine, and blue pills. As time passed, he added blistering and cold "plunging baths" to her regimen.[68]

Within weeks of Anna's second arrival in Staunton, Annabella Norwood (known as Anna), the wife of John Wall Norwood and the mistress of Jesse Ruffin's wife Rebecca, joined her. Born in 1805, Annabella married in January 1826 and bore eight children at Poplar Hill between 1826 and 1843.[69] Complaining of an unidentified malady, she sought treatment from a doctor in Buffalo, New York, in 1841. She returned home unimproved. When her battle with ill health continued, some of her family suggested that she was malingering. William Tillinghast opposed the suggestion that she find respite by spending the winter in Wilmington. "I am doubtful of the efficacy of the plan," he wrote, "as she commonly divests herself of the cares and anxieties of home by leaving it."[70] Without an effective treatment, she remained an invalid. In 1846 Robina Norwood wrote, "Poor Anna has been ill for nearly three weeks with this *vile neuralgia* the worst disease except cancer that I know. . . . She is now suffering greatly & the remedy's [sic] are almost as bad as the disease."[71] By early 1847 she was suffering from dyspepsia and rheumatism as well.[72] In the summer of 1847 her sixteen-year-old daughter Bell interrupted her education at the Burwell School to accompany her mother on a trip to Philadelphia where Annabella joined the small cadre of Hillsborough women who were seeking treatment from Dr. Hodge.[73] "She has taken tea twice at the table," Bell wrote when she got home in August, "& seems cheerful. Dr. Hodge does not doubt but what she will be entirely restored but says it will take time & I truly hope Pa will keep her there until it is thought by the physician that it would be right to return."[74] Her health did not improve rapidly. In October Bell wrote to her cousin: "If you were to witness the scenes of suffering that [we] do, you would not wonder. Uncle William Giles said he had seen & he thought had heard of real pain but had never realized any thing like this—he went into Ma's room but came so near fainting that he was forced to leave it."[75] A year later she appeared to be on the road to recovery: "No one but those that have witnessed them can form any idea of her sufferings. We all feel as if we had come to life again. I actually had forgotten how to laugh aloud," Bell wrote.[76]

Annabella eventually returned home to Hillsborough, but Bell did not believe that she had a firm hold on her sanity. "We all feel very low spirited," Bell wrote. "You can form no idea what her sufferings are both of body and of mind. I do not think for almost eleven months she has had a comfortable home. She has dyspepsia to a *dreadful* degree & with the effects of that & her *gloomy* disposition, she never feels cheerful, never expects anything pleasant but always the worse that would befall her. She thinks she will never recover."[77]

Annabella returned to Philadelphia in summer of 1849 to seek further treatment. By that time she was addicted to opium and in such pain that she had to be carried to her destination on a feather bed. Bell wrote to her cousin from the Quaker City,

> The doctor was horrified to hear of the quantities of opium she was taking for you must know there was one day she took nine teaspoons. He has taken it entirely from her and tis true She does badly enough without it. She begs most imploringly for it but never succeeds in getting it. She was worse one day than she ever was at home & for three nights two of us were up & she never pretended to sleep for three or four days except occasionally would doze for about three minutes & then would wake so terrified that I dreaded to see her sleep.[78]

Unable to cope with Annabella's illness and depressed spirits, her family finally decided to commit her to the Western State Asylum in Virginia. She was admitted on April 17, 1850, and was diagnosed with melancholia. After living together in the same institution for more than a year, Anna Kirkland and Annabella Norwood were both released on the same day, July 8, 1851, and returned together to Hillsborough.[79]

Neither of them flourished. Annabella's ill health and mental instability continued to tax her family's resources and disrupt their domestic tranquility. In 1852 one of her relatives wrote to her cousin that her daughters were "to be pitied to have such a charge on them when they are so young." Despite her disability, she lived for another twenty-four years and died on March 28, 1876.[80]

Anna Kirkland's affliction returned in 1854.[81] Unable to afford to return to Staunton and pressured by her children to seek further treatment, she was determined to enter the North Carolina Hospital for the Insane being constructed in Raleigh even if she had to do so as a pauper.[82] Toward that end, she had herself declared "of unsound mind and incompetent to manage her affairs" and asked that a guardian be appointed to dispose of her property. The county court appointed Dr. Osmund F. Long to sell her assets, a process he began on June 16, 1856, by advertising her real property, an enslaved male, and some of her household furniture in local newspapers, including the *Hillsborough Recorder*, the *Weekly Raleigh Register*, the *Weekly Standard* (Raleigh), and the *Semi-Weekly Standard* (Raleigh). The ads ran through July and early August. "The lot is pleasantly situated, and the House large and commodious, and well suited for a private residence. Families in the Eastern part of the State, desirous of securing a summer residence in a healthy country, are invited to examine the property," they said. C. M. Latimer and Israel Turner eventually bought the property for $1,250.[83]

When it was finished, the Raleigh asylum stood on a hill in a parklike setting of 182 acres one mile outside Raleigh. It was a three-story brick and stucco structure with two wings, separate rooms with grated windows for each patient, a recreation area inside, gas lighting, and a central heating system.[84] The superintendent, Edward C. Fisher, had treated both Anna and Annabella in Staunton.[85]

Anna was admitted in March 1856.[86] She was contented living at the hospital: "I am satisfied that under existing circumstances I am as comfortable & happy here as I could be any where unless I had a home of my own." She found some aspects of her situation disagreeable, but she seems to have been a model patient. Compliant and cooperative, she was occasionally even allowed a furlough to spend the holidays with her family.[87]

As time passed, Anna's doctors' optimism about curing patients of their afflictions declined. They were treating chronically ill patients and held out little hope for their recovery. It was clear by that time that Anna was no longer a danger to herself. She had spent much of her adulthood living among the insane. And while she must have out of necessity grown used to the smells of the wards, the lack of privacy, and the tediousness of hospital regimens, she never quite got used to the noise and disruptive behavior of some of her fellow patients. "There is so much screaming & raving in my ward," she once wrote, "that I scarcely know what I am about—Mercy

Opened in 1856, the North Carolina Asylum for the Insane stood in a parklike setting on 182 acres one mile outside Raleigh. Courtesy of the State Archives of North Carolina, Raleigh.

knows 'tis enough to run a sane person mad to be shut up in such a place much sooner then will it upset one whose nerves are all unstrung."[88]

While she remained confined, she probably lived in what was called a "convalescent ward" intended for patients whom attendants found to be very little trouble and who seemed perfectly sane. She wrote of taking walks on the grounds, planting woodbine around the trees in front of the sitting room windows, and petitioning hospital administrators for permission to establish a flower garden at the end of her building.[89] And when she was in the mood, she had the opportunity to take carriage rides and attend worship services, singing classes, and weekly parties. The hospital staff eventually even organized a small orchestra "composed entirely of crazy people" whose performances, according to one of the attendants, were "better than the professionals."[90]

She continued to suffer from periodic "spells of gloom" during which she lost interest in her usual activities, missed her boys, and felt sorry for herself.[91] And she remained convinced that she was doomed to spend eter-

This image of the interior of the North Carolina Asylum for the Insane reflects the belief that a relatively comfortable environment would help patients recover. Courtesy of the State Archives of North Carolina, Raleigh.

nity in hell. In 1872 she wrote of the morbid "wretchedness" that continued to plague her. "I am considered insane, & and would to God that was the proper name for my malady," she continued. "You know I believe that my Soul is lost and the souls of my children also, & that we are to come to a horrible end in this world, so you See my life is a 'living death.'—Sleeping and waking the awful belief is present with me and no effort that I am capable of can enable me to disbelieve these tenors for a Single instant." She would be "the Happiest of living beings," she concluded, if she could convince herself that she was insane instead of doomed to eternal torment.[92]

Anna may have been confined to the hospital, but she was not cut off from the outside world. She was able to receive visitors, who carried general impressions of her situation back to her family and friends in Hillsborough. As time passed, however, the attentiveness of friends and relatives began to wane. In July 1861 Anna wrote that her formerly attentive cousin Mag often came to the hospital but did not bother to stop by to see her and had ceased bringing her "delicacies." She did not know why and was clearly upset by such neglect. "I shall not make any effort to find out the cause of her alienation from me or to appease her wrath, knowing that intentionally I have done nothing to cause her to treat me as she is doing," she wrote.[93]

Anna had other contacts with the outside world. As in many other asylums, the superintendent of the hospital encouraged the general public to visit the facility, walk the grounds, and observe the patients. The practice was so common throughout the country that historian Benjamin Reiss has characterized such visiting as a "spectator sport." In 1876, for example, 11,794 people toured the New York State Lunatic Asylum in Utica. And a steady stream of local citizens carrying picnic baskets and travel writers carrying pen and paper made their way through the halls, up into the cupola, and into the gardens of the South Carolina Lunatic Asylum in Columbia, disrupting established routines and distracting staff and patients alike.[94]

Visiting asylums was more than "gratuitous spectatorship" and a source of entertainment, however. Asylum tourism connected patients to the outside world, fostered community pride in local institutions, promoted what were considered progressive attitudes toward social problems, and engaged the general public in discussions of social reform and the treatment of mental illness. Superintendents allowed such visits because they wanted to reassure patients that the outside world was concerned about them. At the same time, they used such visits as a way to tie themselves to the larger community and insert themselves and their work into the daily conversations of everyday people regarding the issue of mental illness. By allowing the general public to inspect their facilities and observe their patients, they hoped to ensure that the discourse that emerged regarding their efforts on behalf of the insane would allay suspicion of the institution they were running, reassure the general public of their concern for the welfare of their patients, and encourage private support for their work through philanthropy, admission fees, and sale of consumer goods produced by the patients. Allowing visitors carried with it a number of risks, of course. The appearance of friends and family had the potential to make patients homesick and remind them of associations that had led to their mental deterioration. Doctors also feared that outsiders might interfere with their treatment regimen by prompting demands for a patient's premature release, thus threatening his or her recovery.[95]

Anna had been in the hospital for more than ten years when Mary Alves Long visited the asylum. From 1868 to 1872, she was a student at Peace Institute, the boarding school in Raleigh founded by Robert Burwell and his son. It was the practice during those years to take the students on an outing to visit the insane asylum over the Thanksgiving holiday. Her impressions were vivid and long-lasting. "Once arriving," she wrote in her memoir years later,

> we were greeted by yells from the barred windows above, so terrifying that we started to climb back into the buses. . . . Once inside . . . we were taken to the wards, where the women were sewing, and through the kitchen, where cabbage and fat pork were boiling in huge kettles; into the dining room, where the tables were set with tin plates and cups. . . . Finally we were shown into an immense parlor, where, sitting on the red velvet sofas and chairs, we ate cake and drank wine. Somehow it didn't taste right in that terrifying gloomy building with strange close smells where unhappy people lived in misery and despair.[96]

Mary's mother had grown up in Hillsborough, but she had not, so it is not surprising that she made no mention of Anna Kirkland, who could easily have been one of the women she saw with a needle in her hand.

Whatever her circumstances, Anna's health eventually deteriorated in the hospital. She died there of influenza and heart failure on February 4, 1890. After being intermittently separated from her family first in Staunton and then in Raleigh for thirty-six years, she returned home to be buried on a rainy day at Ayr Mount in the family cemetery next to her husband after a funeral service at St. Matthew's Episcopal Church.[97]

The number of documented cases of mental illness, drug addiction, and ill health among the prominent residents of Hillsborough seems to suggest that the town had more than its fair share of inexplicable and bewildering behavior to gossip about. Family members and those in their inner circle were typically the ones who discussed and diagnosed the mental state of their loved ones and then looked to the medical profession to confirm their diagnosis. They consulted each other about how to interpret what they were observing, kept those they considered interested parties informed about the progress or lack thereof of those afflicted with mental instability and its physical manifestations, shared information about possible sources of relief, and, no doubt, tried to ignore gossip about their difficult situation among the town's busybodies. Before the North Carolina Hospital for the Insane opened in 1856, wealthy white families such as the Cameron-Kirklands and the Norwoods could seek treatment outside the state, but those without the means to do so had to care for their mentally ill relatives at home or depend on the county to provide for their care. That remained the case for Black and mixed-race families until after the Civil War when the mental hospital in Raleigh finally opened its wards to them.[98]

During this period, the field of psychiatry was in its infancy, so physicians had few reliable tools with which to evaluate the mental condition of their patients. Diagnostic labels such as "mania" and "melancholia" were imprecise. The boundaries that separated the sane from the insane were elastic. Physicians were willing to conflate invalidism and drug addiction with mental illness, thus complicating both the diagnostic process and treatment. And the fact that gender played such an important role in the diagnosis and treatment of mental patients meant that it was hard for doctors to look beyond their assumptions about the "nature" of men and women to find alternative explanations for their symptoms. So, despite the initial optimism of asylum superintendents and doctors specializing in the diseases of women, even the most attentive treatment did not necessarily ensure an improvement in the mental and physical state of some of their patients.

There is no evidence to suggest that invalidism, drug addiction, or mental illness, which appear to have been relatively common among the privileged women of Hillsborough, did permanent damage to a family's reputation. The degree to which they disrupted the lives, strained the resources, and tried the patience of family and friends is clear from the letters they left behind. The personal anguish of patients is more difficult to document. Letters concerning the case of Anna Kirkland provide some insight into how she experienced insanity and its consequences and how people talked about it. But a particularly poignant expression of despair can be found in a poem that Sophia Turner, a Hillsborough housewife who was addicted to morphine, wrote shortly after her husband committed her to the hospital in Raleigh in 1878. Entitled "Insanity," it stands as testimony to the sense of helplessness, disorientation, fear, and humiliation she experienced as she tried to adjust to the realities of her new life as well as her awareness of the degree to which she was the focus of gossip among her friends.

Oh say! is there grief any greater
Than to feel that your mind's giving way,
Or can there be Cross any heavier
Than for Reason to yield up her Sway?

To feel that your thoughts are all floating
Away from your grasp one-by-one
Never stopping a Prayer to mutter
Not *even* "Thy will be done."

To feel that your friends are all thinking
T'were better for you to have died
Before this dark cloud came upon you
And *Reason* resigned *Her Pride*.

I hope I humbly will bear
What ever is sent from Above
For I know whatever "*He doeth*"
"*He doeth* it *all* in Love."

But I pray, "Oh Father of Mercy"
"Oh spare me from bearing *That Cross*"
For I fear that if Reason should leave me
My soul will sink under the loss.[99]

CONCLUSION

Have you heard that . . . ? Did you know that . . . ? Can you believe that . . . ? What do you think about . . . ? Do you suppose . . . ? Idle talk by a roaring fire on a snowy winter's day. Tittle-tattle on the steps of St. Matthew's after Sunday services. Hearsay at a quiet corner table in the King Street tavern. Hushed conversations at the back of the Orange County courthouse. Whispers under the quilts in the cold bedrooms of the Burwell School.

Gossip was the mechanism through which the people of Hillsborough and the surrounding area articulated their anxieties, shared their news, perpetuated their grudges against each other, and exposed behavior they deemed to be unacceptable. It was gossip that gave birth to rumors of impending doom and disaster, whether it be a slave uprising or a student revolt. It was gossip that announced pregnancies, betrothals, and deaths and also exposed details about the private lives of friends and neighbors that some may have preferred to keep secret.

No community study can be complete without a consideration of how gossip and rumor affected the everyday life of its inhabitants. In the nineteenth century, small southern towns like Hillsborough were much like small towns in other parts of the country, places where most people lived in large households and worked cheek by jowl. Under such circumstances, informal, judgmental talk between two or more acquaintances about the private affairs of an absent person or persons became an integral part of the social fabric. Whether in casual conversation, their letters to friends and family, their personal diaries, their newspapers, or court testimony, people talked about each other endlessly, exposing their fascination with each other's lives and offering opinions about the behavior and activities of their neighbors. Gossip, whether benign or malicious, reliable or unreliable, knew no boundaries and subverted the power dynamics across race, class, and gender. It bound the community together in an effort to reinforce generally held ideas about how neighbors should relate to each other, uphold standards of what was considered appropriate social conduct, and describe shared experiences. On a day-to-day basis, the shady streets of Hillsborough may have seemed peaceful to the casual observer. But underneath all that tranquility, the social fabric of the town was rent with competition and conflict as the town's white, Black, and mixed-race inhabitants, both free and enslaved, negotiated relationships with their neighbors and places for themselves in the social, economic, and political hierarchy of the community.

However true, distorted, or exaggerated it may have been, idle talk about Mary Ruffin Smith, Thomas Ruffin, William James Bingham, and Robert Burwell's treatment of enslaved workers served as means by which the town's white inhabitants could indirectly express their anxiety about the repercussions of enslaving one-third of Orange County's population. The white inhabitants of Hillsborough may have told themselves and others that those they held in bondage were loyal and posed no threat to their safety. But as a practical matter, they were under no illusion about the resentment simmering under a façade of deference on the part of those they enslaved. Nat Turner's Rebellion of 1831 proved the case on a national level. Rumors of the possibility of a slave insurrection during the holidays in 1830 exposed anxieties about the matter locally. Among Hillsborough's inhabitants, it was no secret that one of Thomas Ruffin's enslaved domestic servants tried to burn down his house twice in one day four years later, first by placing a live coal under the bricks of the hearth and then, when that did not work, by hiding another coal behind a cupboard.[1]

If they needed to be reminded, an article published in not one but two Raleigh newspapers in 1845 exposed the truth of the matter in what was purported to be a joke but was in reality a deadly serious commentary on race relations. The story went that Cudjo's enslaver asked him if he had been to church as he had been told. Cudjo replied that he had but added, "An' what two mighty big stories [lies] dat preacher did tell." Cudjo's enslaver asked what the stories were. "Why, he tell the people no man can serve two massas—now, dis is de fuss story, 'cause you see Old Cudjo serves you, my ole massa, an' also young massa John. Den de preacher says, 'he will lub de one and hate de other'—while, de Lord knows, I *hate you boff.*"[2] This racist caricature written by a white author and read by a largely white audience only added fuel to the fire of rumors and gossip about discontent among the enslaved population that fed the anxiety of a white population desperately trying to convince itself, despite evidence to the contrary, that those they enslaved posed no danger to them and the social and economic power they wielded. Such inflammatory rhetoric exposed the deepest prejudices and worst fears of the white community in general and slaveholders in particular.

Gossip also exposed anxieties about larger changes in social intercourse and standards of social behavior that took place as time passed and the town grew. Early Hillsborough was a backcountry village settled by what has been described by one commentator as "a strong, fearless, independent race, simple in taste, crude in manners, provincial in outlook, democratic in social relations, tenacious of their rights, sensitive to encroachment on their personal liberties, and, when interested in religion at all, earnest, narrow and dogmatic."[3] As well-furnished, two-story houses with wide front porches replaced the rustic cabins of the early settlers, the white people of Hillsborough engaged in a process of discarding the egalitarian social codes that had characterized society in the backcountry and establishing standards of self-presentation and polite behavior that would help elevate society, serve as a basis for social mobility, and provide guidance in incorporating newcomers into the community. The drunkenness, profanity, and disregard for religion that had characterized an earlier age gave way to concern on the part of a certain segment of the community about taste and refinement in dress and behavior, the adoption of new standards for speaking English, and the pursuit of piety.[4]

Generally speaking, it was women like Anna Burwell, herself the subject of her neighbors' gossip, who were responsible for helping promulgate social practices designed to promote these goals. And it was to them that newcomers with social aspirations had to look for acceptance. Whether Delia Smith had social aspirations is unclear. What is clear is that once she moved from the country into town as the new wife of one of its local doctors, Hillsborough's gossips considered it their job to evaluate her qualifications for acceptance in the upper echelons of their society and found her wanting, thus denying her the social capital that might have helped protect her loved ones from the censorious commentary of her neighbors.

In Hillsborough, gossip, rumor, and concern for reputation had profound consequences with significant racial implications. No matter their race, all of the inhabitants of the town were potential targets for local gossip. For whites who cared about such things, being gossiped about was a source of personal embarrassment and the potential source of strained social relations. Such was the case with Mary Ruffin Smith. Gossip about her father had more serious consequences. Talk about his creditworthiness or lack thereof led to fractured relationships with his business partners and creditors, resulted in his bankruptcy, and forced him and his family to move out of town. Both the Burwells and the Binghams were well aware that talk about their effectiveness as educators could enhance or diminish the reputation of their schools and thus influence their ability to recruit students and support their families. Thomas Ruffin was very much concerned that talk about unrest on his plantation would not only undermine his reputation as a competent manager but had the potential for threatening the market value of those he enslaved. Gossip about William James Bingham, Anna Kirkland, Phebe Kirkland, Mary Witherspoon, and Annabella Norwood's odd behavior confirmed prevailing attitudes about gender and class concerning a person's vulnerability to physical and mental illness and served as the basis for their diagnoses and medical treatment.

Concern about gossip's potential impact on one's reputation had an important impact on the interpersonal relationships of Hillsborough's white inhabitants. It worked to inhibit the development of close relationships between school boys and girls as they made their way through their teens and approached the age when they could marry. It shaped the relationships between white men and women by allowing men considerably more freedom of movement and behavior than it allowed their female counterparts, whose claim to honor was based on deference to male authority, avoiding any talk of sexual impropriety before and after marriage, and fulfilling their roles as wives, mothers, and housekeepers. And it had the potential for shifting the interpersonal dynamics and power structure within the family. Public concern about and discussion of mental health issues served to recognize the extraordinary emotional and financial burdens they placed on caregiving relatives while at the same time excusing those afflicted from the censorship that would ordinarily have accompanied their abdication of their family responsibilities.

Gossip, rumor, and concern for reputation had somewhat different implications for Hillsborough's free Black and mixed-race inhabitants. As in the case of their white counterparts, gossip could have a profound impact on their economic well-being. For free Blacks, gossip concerning potential employment, vocational training, or entrepreneurial opportunities could influence their ability to support themselves and their families. A reputation for respectability and dependability could help ensure their access to those opportunities, as in the case of those who were employed by the Burwells and those like Adaline Mitchell who actively sought apprenticeship opportunities for their children. Henry Evans's prosperity, entrance into the credit market, and safe passage to Ohio all depended on public discussion and acknowledgment of his law-abiding respectability.

In this community, gossip and rumor had the potential for both undermining and protecting fragile claims to freedom. On one hand, Anderson Mayo lost not only his freedom but also his life in part because of gossip about his ill treatment of his wife. On the other, James Mayo's reputation as a long-standing member of Hillsborough's free Black and mixed-race community helped him thwart efforts to enslave him. And particularly when it involved rumors about insurrection, Hillsborough's free Blacks could find their personal safety at risk as whites worked through their own insecurities and anxieties about the imbalance in the power structure between them and their Black and mixed-race neighbors.

Because the enslaved had so little control over their lives, information derived from gossip gave them insight into the disruptions and dangers that could seriously threaten their physical and mental well-being. Household gossip would have alerted Hannah about her pending sale. The same could be said of talk in the Burwell household about the potential sale of the Burwell School and the imminent move to Charlotte. It could help ameliorate their situations as in the case of Elizabeth Keckly, who attributed the end of her abuse in part to the impact of town gossip. Gossip about the paternity of her son George could easily have influenced the Burwells' decision to return her to her family in Virginia.

At the same time, gossip could exacerbate the already fraught relationships that existed between enslavers and the enslaved. Anna Burwell's public complaints about Mary Ann and Hannah allowed her an outlet for her frustrations in the wake of their perceived shortcomings as domestic servants but also served as a painful reminder of her own moral and administrative inadequacies. Gossip could also have profound life-altering consequences for those held in bondage. Talk about Bridget and the perceived threat she posed to plantation discipline on Thomas Ruffin's property resulted not only in her sale, which forcibly separated her from her friends and family, but also a brutal beating at the hands of her former owner. Talk that helped establish the reputation of Jesse Ruffin and Job Berry for exhibiting appropriately subservient behavior and apparent loyalty resulted in their ability to avoid constant white surveillance, to convince their owners to let them marry whom they pleased, and some freedom of movement and the opportunity to pursue their own interests. And Job's reputation as a stalwart defender of the rights of freedmen guaranteed him a place of leadership in the Black community after the Civil War. In these ways, gossip and concern for reputation worked in concert with economic interdependence, kinship, and assumptions about race, gender, and class to structure the relationships of Hillsborough's inhabitants.

It should be noted, however, that the power of gossip had its limits. Wagging tongues were not able to ensure conformity to community values unless those who were the focus of gossip cared about their reputations. Such talk had no perceptible influence on Sid Smith's shocking behavior toward Harriet, his brother Frank's insistence on cohabiting with her, or his sister Mary's acceptance of her brothers' mixed-race children as members of her family. And while neighbors complained about Thomas Ruffin's indifference to the suffering of his enslaved workers, their gossip provided no mechanism, legal or otherwise, that could be used to force him to treat them more humanely. Unwilling to adjust their behavior to community expectations, Ruffin and the Smiths embraced reputations distinctly at odds with community values.

The Civil War brought an end to familiar patterns of personal relationships and mutually held but often contested understandings of racial etiquette in Hillsborough. In 1861 the town's white women began sending their husbands and sons off to war. The absence of white men upended the power structure, disrupted kinship relationships, and shifted the South's gender and racial dynamic. Their wives, sisters, and daughters found themselves increasingly unable to depend on their male relatives to support them or to exert authority over their enslaved workers. Wartime conditions undermined the disciplinary system on which slavery depended. And white women found it necessary to expand their range of activities in order to ensure the well-being of their families.[5]

The people of Hillsborough did not face the realities of invasion and occupation until the spring of 1865. Although retreating Confederate troops and the Yankees who pursued them confiscated anything they thought useful and stole anything they thought valuable, there is no record of any houses being burned in Hillsborough. When the soldiers withdrew, Hillsborough looked pretty much the same as it had before their arrival—the buildings a little shabbier and the landscaping a little weedier, perhaps, but not substantially different. Churton Street was still the center of the commercial district. There were still vegetables in the gardens and crops in the fields. Hens still laid their eggs in the henhouses. Herds of livestock, diminished to be sure, still grazed in the pastures. Hillsborough's streets were still choked with red dust in the summer, and clay oozed through wheel spokes when it rained.[6] The Eno still flowed to the sea. And people who had been neighbors before the war were neighbors still. But their relationships had changed irrevocably, and the lives they lived together would never be quite the same.

The tensions that had characterized community life continued unabated as prominent families joined their less affluent neighbors, both Black and white, in facing an uncertain future. The once mighty were brought low or at least lower. As John Norwood told his friend Thomas Ruffin in August 1865, "I am ruined; nothing left to me but my land if I can save even all of that."[7] Federally appointed Freedmen's Bureau officials displaced the town's white elite, who had previously been responsible for organizing the labor force and enforcing the laws. Free Black folks and the formerly enslaved scrambled to learn to read and write, stabilize their families, acquire land to farm, or make new work arrangements with former enslavers or employers. Together with their white Republican allies, they temporarily dominated the state legislature, which wrote a constitution setting up a new government intended to serve the needs of all the state's citizens instead of privileging a few.

As the town's white, Black, and mixed-race inhabitants began to negotiate new rules governing interracial social and economic interaction, the town they lived in lost some of its vibrancy and entrepreneurial spirit. Local businessmen had access to the railroad but were not in a position to attract the investment capital needed to take advantage of it. Tobacco warehouses and processing plants that had been established in nearby Durham before the war expanded, providing employment opportunities for Hillsborough's citizens both Black and white, many of whom would otherwise have worked locally on the land or sought vocational training with local artisans or businessmen.[8]

Though he did not call it by name, Walter Hines Page, the journalist and diplomat who spent his school days sitting in William James Bingham's classroom, may have had Hillsborough in mind when he published "Study of an Old Southern Borough" in the May 1881 edition of the *Atlantic Monthly*. "The whole town," he said, "has a languid and self-satisfied appearance. There is little animation in man or beast. . . . The streets are neglected and in places almost impassable. The paint is worn from most of the houses; the people are slow in their movements."[9] Hillsborough moved through the rest of the nineteenth century with its streets still in disrepair waiting for better times.

Better times did come. In 1896 the Eno cotton mill opened on the outskirts of town in what became known as West Hillsborough, a company town that provided jobs and housing for its workers and a school for their children. While vestiges of the old Hillsborough remained, a new and thriving mill culture emerged as the area's economy slowly shifted to one based in industrial capitalism.[10]

With a population of about seven thousand, today's Hillsborough has recovered some of the vibrancy of its past. When you cross the Eno River on your way into town in the summer, the tree canopy blocks your view of the reconstructed Occaneechi stockade built at the river's edge. Following Churton Street north takes you to the square, which in many years past held a jail, a whipping post and stocks, a jailer's house, and a market house and now serves as the setting for the old courthouse. The business district is still only three or so blocks long and about a block wide but features an upscale grocery store, restaurants, a coffee shop, an old-time hardware store, specialty shops including a chocolatier, galleries exhibiting the work of local artists, and a bookstore proud to display the latest book written by one of Hillsborough's literary celebrities. Along Churton and its side streets are structures that have been there for more than a century—the newly renovated Colonial Inn with its gracious front porch, the Burwell School with its red tin roof and long sloping front lawn, and well-preserved eighteenth- and nineteenth-century houses with their dependencies. Some of these homes are architecturally impressive with names like Teardrops, Pilgrim's Rest, Heartsease, and Twin Chimneys. Most are modest structures that have sheltered Hillsborough's white, Black, and mixed-race families for generations. Just on the edge of town stand much larger homes once surrounded by fields and pastures such as Ayr Mount, Burnside, and Montrose that originally served as the residences of the town's planter elite.

A riverwalk offers ordinary folk opportunities for enjoying the lush landscape that follows the course of the Eno River through town.

The 1960s brought a renewed interest in the town's past and the need to come to grips with both the achievements of its former inhabitants and the profound tensions and ambiguities that thread their way through the town's history. Caught between the desire to celebrate themselves and an increasing awareness of the blind spots that hinder the telling of their story, those who concern themselves with such matters struggle to expand their understanding and presentation of their collective past. Preserving old houses, building the Occaneechi stockade down by the Eno, and cleaning up the "Old Slave Cemetery" on Margaret Lane were important first steps in complementing the historical signage that dots the town's landscape. Erasing "Confederate Library," carved in stone above the front door of the old library, was another. Researching and honoring the memory and accomplishments of the Black and mixed-race people who once resided within the town and its perimeters is yet another effort on the part of local historians, both white and Black, to expand the definition of who and what are to be considered historically significant and who gets to tell the story of this small southern town and its people.

ACKNOWLEDGMENTS

Producing this book has been very much a collaborative affair and in some ways a community project. My special thanks goes to the board and staff of the Burwell School, many of whom live in Hillsborough, who were extraordinarily generous with their enthusiasm for this project. They provided me with research material and knowledge of the town and directed me to resources that I would not necessarily have known about. Brooks Graebner, an Episcopal priest but the son of a historian, was always available to chat about the project and give me access to his own impressive research. Lucas Kelly's willingness to share his transcriptions of materials relating to Anna Kirkland saved me an immense amount of time. His help combined with that of Bobby Allen and Sarah Almond was invaluable to the completion of this endeavor as it related to the treatment of insanity in North Carolina. Carrie Curry's enthusiasm for this project and her impressive research and computer skills made collaboration with her a pleasure. She could find in minutes information it would have taken me hours to locate. Mark Chilton, the register of deeds in Orange County, not only alerted me to his work digitizing Orange County records but could be counted on to share his own research with me. He was always just an email away when I needed information or help clarifying details relating to Hillsborough's history. As he did his own archival research, he was always looking for material relating to this project. So it was always very exciting when I got an email from him with the heading "Look what I found!"

I would like to thank the Southern Historical Collection at the University of North Carolina in Chapel Hill, the David M. Rubenstein Rare Book and Manuscript Library at Duke University, the Burwell School Historic Site, Alamance Community College, Virginia Tech University, Library Special Collections at Western Kentucky University, and Dr. Graham Barden III for permission to quote from material in their collections.

I would also like to thank the editors of the *Journal of Southern History* and the *North Carolina Historical Review* for allowing me to republish some of the material that appeared in "Sophia Turner Devereux Turner and the Troubled Female Mind in the Late Nineteenth-Century South," *Journal of Southern History* 88 (2022): 681–706; "Anna Burwell and the Business of Being a Minister's Wife in North Carolina, 1835–1847," *North Carolina Historical Review* 96 (2019): 245–75; and "Earnest Efforts to Be Friends: Teacher-Student Relationships in Nineteenth-Century North Carolina," *Journal of Southern History* 84 (2018): 813–44.

I wish to thank Theda Perdue, Bill Andrews, Don Matthews, Reginald Hildebrand, Jan Irwin, Collette McCarty, and Jackie Lambertsen for their assistance and encouragement. Staff at the North Carolina State Archives, the Southern Historical Collection, the Orange County Historical Museum, and the Burwell School were exceptionally helpful in my efforts to collect the images to be used in this book. Finally, I thank my husband, Dick, who has been so immensely supportive over these many years.

A NOTE ON SOURCES

This book relies on a wide variety of sources to trace the role that gossip and rumor played in the lives of Hillsborough's inhabitants, how it influenced their interpersonal relations, how it affected household dynamics, how it impacted business ventures, and what it reveals about how they approached mental health issues. Diaries, letters, and memoirs are the most important sources for tracing what the people of Hillsborough were thinking and saying about each other. Such sources tend to privilege white voices over Black and mixed-race ones, partly because whites were more likely to be literate and partly because their written record was more likely to be preserved.

Rarely intended for public consumption, diaries like the one written by Anna Burwell provide insight into what and who she and her friends and relatives were talking about and the kind of judgments they made about those with whom they were concerned. Letters, often intended to be read aloud or shared, served a similar but somewhat more public purpose. Archibald Murphey's letters to Thomas Ruffin, for example, explicitly refer to gossip regarding Ruffin's treatment of his enslaved workers. Anna Burwell's letters to her daughter are full of domestic and local gossip. And Dr. Stribling's letters to the Kirkland/Cameron family not only satisfied their hunger for news about Anna Kirkland's health and state of mind but also provided them with the opportunity to satisfy the curiosity of their relatives, friends, and neighbors who could be counted on to speculate on and pass off their newly acquired information and opinions to others.

The published memoirs of Harriet Jacobs and Elizabeth Keckly as well as the family history of Pauli Murray are among the few sources that give us some insight into the role that gossip played in the Black and mixed-race community. Both Jacobs and Keckly made explicit references to the gossip that was prompted by their abuse and expressed belief that such gossip could help mitigate their situation. Pauli Murray similarly addresses the issue of gossip as it related to the Smith's treatment of her great-grandmother Harriet.

The value of journalism in the study of gossip depends entirely on the newspaper in question. The format and content of newspapers differed widely in the antebellum period. Those that covered local events tended to be more gossipy than those that did not. Take the *Raleigh Register*, for example. In order to justify the treatment that Allen Jones received at the hands of a Raleigh mob in October 1842, the editor of that paper engaged in character assassination when he passed on and gave credence to unsubstantiated gossip that characterized Jones as "obnoxious" and a "rabble rouser."

The format of the *Hillsborough Recorder* was very different. It did not often carry local news and is therefore less useful in providing insight into the way gossip functioned in Hillsborough. It began publication in 1820 under the editorship of Dennis Heartt. Every week for many years, he filled the paper's four pages with state and national political news, stories reprinted from other newspapers, poems and short stories, and an occasional political editorial. He did publish a local notice here and there, the results of local elections, and advertisements for local businesses, but other than that, one would be hard-pressed to find anything in the paper that had to do with what the people of Hillsborough were thinking or talking about. The *Recorder*'s value, then, is not so much as a source of gossip but rather as a lens on the economic and political landscape that characterized Hillsborough before the Civil War and provides the context for whatever gossip was circulating at the time. For example, it was partly through notices in the newspaper that James Strudwick Smith's creditors would have become aware of his financial circumstances and gossiped about it among themselves then began to make judgments about his creditworthiness, called in their loans, and forced him into bankruptcy.

Public records including court documents provide both context and information concerning the initiation, dissemination, and impact of gossip. Court records relating to the Anderson Mayo trial reveal that gossip about his treatment of his wife provided justification for the assumption that he was temperamentally capable of violence and provided a possible motive for her murder. Extrapolating information from public records relating to Henry Evans concerning the apprenticeship of free Black and mixed-race children tells us something about what was being said about his character and reputation as a businessman and the resources he was believed to have available to him as well as how word of opportunities for training in the skilled trades through apprenticeship made its way into the Black and mixed-race community. Census data provides context for understanding the role that gossip played in the community life of Hillsborough in the sense that it provides demographic information about such matters as the racial makeup of its population, the location of its households, and the way that its wealth was distributed.

Church records tell us a good deal not only about the value system that the people of Hillsborough used to make judgments about each other but also how consideration of a person's self-presentation and activities could influence their reputation. It was a critical factor in establishing Henry Evans's reputation for respectability. And it was equally important to someone like Job Berry, who was able to use it to establish a place for himself as a leader of Hillsborough's Black community following the Civil War, partly because of the religious training he received from William Mercer Green while studying for his confirmation. In the case of Robert Burwell, session records reveal what his congregation was saying about him in the 1840s, what they thought about the time he was spending administrating and teaching at the Burwell School, and how they resolved the reservations they had about his pastorship.

There are, of course, limits to what the available sources can tell us about the role that gossip played in Hillsborough's white, Black, and mixed-race communities. Gossiping in the town was and still is largely an oral exercise. So unless someone wrote about it and what they wrote appears in a document that someone went to the trouble to save, its content, its purpose, some notion of its audience, and how it was disseminated are simply lost to history.

Inaccessibility of extant sources is another problem. The state of Virginia is more generous in allowing access to records relating to concerns about and the care of the insane than the state of North Carolina, for example. Their collection of letters to and from Dr. Francis Stribling is particularly valuable for providing insight into how and what kind of information and opinions about the condition and care of patients in the Western State Hospital for the Insane in Staunton was distributed. Unfortunately, although the records of the North Carolina Insane Asylum in Raleigh (now known as Dorothea Dix Hospital) have been archived, they are essentially closed to researchers, thus making it impossible to do any sort of comparison.

Finally, collections of newspapers such as the *Hillsborough Recorder* are not always complete, a particularly frustrating situation when newspaper coverage of something like rumors about an impending slave rebellion in December 1830 would potentially offer insight into the origins of the rumor, the way it spread, and how it impacted the white, Black, and mixed-race inhabitants of the town.

NOTES

INTRODUCTION

1. Davis, "Great Trading Path," NCpedia; Fecher, "The Trading Path and North Carolina," 1, 5; Blackwelder, *Age of Orange*, 6; Hatfield, *Atlantic Virginia*, 27–28, 32–35; Rice, "Bacon's Rebellion in Indian Country," 738–40; Davis, "Occaneechi Indians," NCpedia; Hazel, "Occaneechi-Sapaoni Descendants"; Ward and Davis, *Indian Communities*, 411, 416, 427, 430–32, 441; Dickens et al., *Historic Occaneechi*, 4–7, 42, 47; Lawson, *New Voyage to Carolina*; Dunmore, "Orange County History," 5–9. The U.S. government has not yet recognized the Occaneechi as a tribe. But the state of North Carolina recognized the Haliwa Band of Saponi in 1965 and the Occaneechi Band of Saponi in 2002.
2. Rutman and Rutman, "The Village South," in *Small Worlds*, 231–72.
3. Darrett B. Rutman and Anita H. Rutman discuss the idea that a community is a network of relationships with reference to a specific location in "Community: A Sunny Little Dream," in *Small Worlds*, 291.
4. For county studies, see Rutman and Rutman, *A Place in Time*; Harris, *Plain Folk and Gentry*; Kenzer, *Kinship and Neighborhood*; Burton, *In My Father's House*. For the study of southern cities, see Goldfield, "Pursuing the American Dream"; Rogers, *Charleston*; Walter J. Fraser Jr., *Charleston! Charleston!*; Walter J. Fraser Jr., *Savannah in the Old South*; Clayton, *Antebellum Natchez*; Crenson, *Baltimore*; Powell, *Accidental City*. The literature on various aspects of plantation life is voluminous. A place to start might include Genovese, *Roll, Jordan, Roll*, and Fox-Genovese, *Within the Plantation Household*. For southern small-town studies, see Hendricks, *Backcountry Towns of Colonial Virginia*; Hofstra, *Planting of New Virginia*; Friend, *Along the Maysville Road*. In *A Place in Time*, Rutman and Rutman dedicate one chapter to the slow and tortuous founding and development of Urbanna as a county trading center (209–30).
5. Blodgett and Levering, *One Town, Many Voices*; Bonner, *Milledgeville*.
6. Tolbert, *Constructing Townscapes*.
7. For an analysis of these sources, see "A Note on Sources." For a recent discussion about the writing of microhistory, see Bell, "Peepholes, Eels, and Pickett's Charge."
8. Scholarly interest in gossip dates from the mid-twentieth century when Max Gluckman pointed out the ways that the propensity to circulate information about other peoples' private lives has influenced the formation of interpersonal relationships and the development of community life. See Gluckman, "Gossip and Scandal." For a good survey of the attention that scholars in such fields as philosophy, literary criticism, sociology, anthropology, and history have paid to gossip, see the introduction in Feeley

and Frost, *When Private Talk Goes Public*, 1–16. The sources I found most useful are found in the footnotes below.

9. Spacks, *Gossip*, 4, 5, 11, 33. In *Good Gossip*, editors Goodman and Ben-Ze'ev explore the tensions between gossip's value and its destructive power. See in particular Ben-Ze'ev's essay, "The Vindication of Gossip," 11–24. For a useful analyses of the social significance of gossip, see Bergmann, *Discreet Indiscretions*, 139–53, and Fine and Rosnow, "Gossip, Gossipers, Gossiping."

10. Nevo et al.'s research indicates that men and women engage in more or less the same amount of gossip, but the content of their gossip is often different. See Nevo et al., "Tendency to Gossip," 188.

11. My distinction between gossip and rumor is heavily influenced by the work of Luise White, *Speaking with Vampires*, 56–86, and Dowd, *Groundless*, 1–13.

12. For scattered references to the connection between gossip and reputation among the southern elite, see Wyatt-Brown, *Southern Honor*, 52, 196, 275, 186, 307, 309–10, 347–48, 446–47; Kierner, *Scandal at Bazaare*.

13. For explorations of the role that honor and shame played in southern men's lives, see Ayers, *Vengeance and Justice*; Stowe, *Intimacy and Power*; Greenburg, "The Nose, the Lie, and the Duel"; Greenburg, *Honor and Slavery*; Gorn, "Gouge and Bite."

14. Wyatt-Brown, *Southern Honor*, 14, 23, 34, 45, 56, 119, 122, 226–36.

15. Mary Walker, one of Duncan Cameron's most trusted enslaved servants, provides a perfect example of the advantages to be derived by nurturing such a reputation. See Nathans, *To Free a Family*.

16. U.S. Manuscript Census for 1800, Hillsborough, Orange County, North Carolina; Blackwelder, *Age of Orange*, 82.

17. Ryan, *Orange County Trio*, 19. For a discussion of the importance of market houses to small southern towns, see Friend, *Along the Maysville Road*, 137–40. The original Hillsborough Academy, which opened in 1785, had closed in 1790. Anderson, "Hillsborough Academy," NCpedia.

18. Belle Norwood to William Tillinghast, January 26, 1846, box 2, Folder: Correspondence, 1846–1847, Tillinghast Family Papers, Duke Library, Durham, North Carolina; Long, *High Time to Tell It*, 57.

19. Engstrom, "Hillsborough in 1775," 27.

20. Kenzer, *Kinship and Neighborhood*, 33.

21. Jean Bradley Anderson, *Piedmont Plantation*; Sanders, "Cameron, Duncan," NCpedia; Jean Bradley Anderson, *Kirklands of Ayr Mount*; Robinson with Deased, "Ruffin, Thomas," NCpedia; Engstrom, "Webb, James," NCpedia.

22. Hume and Dunaway, "Evolving Townscape," 9; Map 4, "Major Buildings and Properties," in Hume and Connor, *Hidden Hillsborough*, xvi–xvii; Blackwelder, *Age of Orange*, 149–50, 152. The Hillsborough Temperance Society was established in 1841. Rankin, *Ambivalent Churchmen and Evangelical Churchwomen*, 125–26. Sunday Schools existed as early as 1825. "Sunday School Society," *Hillsborough Recorder*, September 14, 1825, 3.

23. Long (a descendent of prominent Hillsborough doctor James Webb), *High Time to Tell It*, 58. Years ago, historian Frank Owsley noted the invisibility of what he called

"plain folk" in the historical narrative that comprised the history of the South despite their presence in church records and a wide variety of government documents. See Owsley, *Plain Folk of the Old South*, 6–7. David Dangerfield has expanded that discussion in his thesis titled "Plain People of Color."

24. For a more complete discussion on the role of memory in the construction of community, a good place to begin is Connerton, *How Societies Remember*, 13–21. For a similarly useful discussion of the role of memory in constructing historical sensibilities in the postbellum South, see Brundage, *Southern Past* and *Where These Memories Grow*, 1–28.
25. Strum, "The Misses Nash and Miss Kollock Select Boarding and Day School for Young Ladies," typescript, Burwell School Archives, Hillsborough, North Carolina.
26. An excellent discussion of that framing on an institutional level can be found in Handler and Gable's *New History of an Old Museum*.

CHAPTER 1

1. Maria L. Spear to Catharine Ruffin, May 20, 1831, box 1, folder 13, Ruffin-Roulhac-Hamilton Papers, no. 643, Southern Historical Collection, Louis Round Wilson Special Collections Library, University of North Carolina at Chapel Hill.
2. Mary was born in 1814. Her tombstone is in the Jones family cemetery.
3. The allegation that James Strudwick Smith was the illegitimate son of William F. Strudwick appears to be based on existing court minutes that say, "James Taylor is deemed sufficient security for William Strudwick to keep the parish indemnifiyd [sic] by reason of a child begotten on the body of [blank]." Orange County Court of Pleas and Quarter Session, book 4, p. 133, August 1788. The actual bond is missing. I would like to thank Mark Chilton, Orange County's register of deeds, for this information.
4. Jones with Southern, *Miss Mary's Money*, 16–68; Anderson, "Smith, James Strudwick," NCpedia.
5. Stowe, *Doctoring in the South*, 108, 112.
6. Hillsborough doctor James Webb trained many of the men in the Hillsborough medical community including William Webb, Edmund Strudwick, Henry Young Webb, Walter A. Norwood, James S. Smith, and Thomas H. Turner. Engstrom, "Webb, James," NCpedia. See Orange County censuses for men listing themselves as physicians.
7. Jones with Southern, *Miss Mary's Money*, 16–68, "puffing doctor" on 24; Anderson, "Smith, James Strudwick."
8. Francis Jones provided that all of his property in land and enslaved workers would be held in trust by James during Delia's lifetime. When she died, Price Creek plantation was to go to Mary, Jones Grove was to go to Mary's brother Frank, and Flower Place was to go to her other brother Sid. Jones with Southern, *Miss Mary's Money*, 14, 66; Spear to Ruffin, May 20, 1831. Delia joined the Chapel of the Cross [Episcopal] in Chapel Hill just before she died in 1854. *Hillsborough Recorder*, November 22, 1854, 3.
9. Spear to Ruffin, May 20, 1831.
10. Murray, *Proud Shoes*, 38.
11. According to the *Hillsborough Recorder*, in 1820 there were 419,000 white people,

205,017 enslaved workers, and 14,612 free Black people in Orange County. "Census for Orange County," *Hillsborough Recorder*, August 22, 1821, 2. That had not changed much by 1830. Green, "Slavery in Orange County," 96. For a broader perspective, see Smith, "I Was Raised Poor"; Fountain, "Broader Footprint."

12. For more on this issue, see Boles, *Masters and Slaves*.
13. Mathews, *Religion in the Old South*, 142–52.
14. For more on mortgaging the enslaved, see Martin, "Neighbor-to-Neighbor Capitalism."
15. "J. S. Smith," 1820 U.S. Census, *Orange, North Carolina*, NARA roll *M33_82*, 408, image no. *226*.
16. Francis Jones to Mary Ruffin Smith, February 25, 1824, Deed Book 21, 220, Office of the Orange County Clerk, Hillsborough, North Carolina.
17. "James S. Smith," 1830 U.S. Census, Orange, North Carolina, series *M19*, roll *123*, *250*, Family History Library film no. *0018089*. All Family History Library films are available at Ancestry.com.
18. Breeden, *Advice Among Masters*, 78–88.
19. Glymph, *Out of the House of Bondage*, 48.
20. Glymph, *Out of the House of Bondage*, 6, 32–62, quotation on page 37.
21. Maria's birth and baptism dates as well as her parents' names appear in *London, England, Church of England Baptisms, Marriages and Burials, 1538–1812*; Cornelia Phillips Spencer, "Obituary [of Maria Louisa Spear]," *Church Messenger*, January 27, 1881, [3].
22. Falk, "Warrenton Female Academy," 281–98; Anderson, "Warrenton Female Academy," NCpedia.
23. Jones with Southern, *Miss Mary's Money*, 37. Maria and her sister Mary Ann were both teaching at an academy in Wadesborough. *Carolina Observer and Fayetteville Gazette*, March 20, 1823, 1.
24. Long, *Son of Carolina*, 32; Cornelia Phillips Spencer, "Obituary [of Maria Louisa Spear]," [3]. Her name as well as that of her mother, her aunt, Mary Ann, and William are listed in the "List of Communicants," St. Matthew's Church Records, Hillsborough, North Carolina, 37, 38. In a letter, Maria affectionately refers to her brother "Charles," saying that he was "as frolicsome as ever" and had begun attending the Bingham School in Hillsborough. Maria L. Spear to Catharine Ruffin, July 27, 1829, folder 10, Ruffin-Roulhac-Hamilton Papers. Phebe Kirkland to Eliza M. Johnston, November 9, 1835, folder 14, Eliza Mary Bond Weissinger Papers, no. 4443, Southern Historical Collection, and Coon, *North Carolina Schools and Academies* (308) refer to Elizabeth. The deed was registered in 1839. John Norwood to Susan Baker, October 15, 1839, Deed Book 28, 488, County Clerk's Office, Hillsborough, North Carolina. There is no evidence that the Spearses purchased any enslaved workers, but three are listed in the 1840 census as part of Susan Baker's household. 1840 U.S. Manuscript Census, Northern Division, Orange County, North Carolina, roll 367, p. 212, Family History Library film no. 0018096.
25. Spear to Ruffin, May 20, 1831.

26. Summer Examination Report of Mary Ruffin Smith, folder 3, Mary Ruffin Smith Papers, no. 3879, Southern Historical Collection.
27. Spear to Ruffin, May 20, 1831. For more on their friendship, see Hoffert, "Earnest Efforts to Be Friends."
28. It is commonly accepted among historians that women in the nineteenth century routinely formed intense, loving, sometimes passionately intimate, and often long-lasting bonds with each other during this period. While they disagree about the degree to which these so-called romantic friendships included an erotic or sexual component, they agree that until the end of the nineteenth century, as long as such relationships did not interfere with conventional heterosexual arrangements, did not undermine conventional definitions of respectability, posed no threat to the transfer of property, and caused no perceivable harm, they were casually and widely accepted. The literature on this subject is vast. See, for example, Smith-Rosenberg, "Female World of Love and Ritual"; Sahli, "Smashing"; Rupp, "Imagine My Surprise"; Lasser, "Let Us Be Sisters Forever."
29. Spear to Ruffin, May 20, 1831.
30. Spear to Ruffin, May 20, 1831.
31. Spacks, *Gossip*, 4–6; Erikson, *Wayward Puritans*, 3–29.
32. Session Books 1 and 2 (typescripts), Hillsborough Presbyterian Church Archives, Hillsborough, North Carolina.
33. Gluckman, "Gossip and Scandal"; Merry, "Rethinking Gossip and Scandal"; Stirling, "Some Psychological Mechanisms."
34. Oates, *Fires of Jubilee*, 48; Eaton, "Dangerous Pamphlet," 324, 330–31; Hinks, *To Awaken My Afflicted Brethren*, 137.
35. Taylor, "Slave Conspiracies in North Carolina," 29–30.
36. Charles L. Pettigrew to his father, December 29, 1830, box 34, folder 663, Pettigrew Family Papers, no. 592, Southern Historical Collection.
37. Pettigrew to father, December 29, 1830; Joseph B. Hinton to John Gray Blout of New Bern quoted in Hinks, *To Awaken My Afflicted Brethren*, 143; Eaton, "Dangerous Pamphlet," 333.
38. Charles L. Pettigrew to his father, December 20, 1830, December 29, 1830, box 2, folder 36, Pettigrew Family Papers; Alexander M. Kirkland to Catherine Ruffin, January 10, 1831, quoted in Jean Bradley Anderson, *Kirklands of Ayr Mount*, 51.
39. Kraditor, *Means and Ends*, 3.
40. Stirling, "Psychological Mechanisms," 265.
41. William Kell to James Smith, September 30, 1834, Deed Book 31, 401, County Clerk's Office, Orange County, North Carolina.
42. "William Full [Kell]," 1830 manuscript census, North District, Orange, North Carolina, series M19, roll 123, 344, Family History Library film no. 00118089; "William Kell," 1840 manuscript census, Marion, Tennessee, roll 528, 276, Family History Library film no. 0024547.
43. Murray, *Proud Shoes*, 38. Unless otherwise noted, information about Harriet comes from this source.

44. On courtship and marriage among the enslaved, see Griffin, "Goin' Back Over There"; Fraser, *Courtship and Love*, 8–95; Hunter, *Bound in Wedlock*, 43–50, 92–101; O'Neil, "Bosses and Broomsticks"; West, *Chains of Love*, 19–79. A "Reuben Day" appears in every Orange County census from 1820 to 1870. Sometimes there is more than one entry. For a discussion of Reuben Day, see Kim Smith, "Book of Harriet," 55n133.
45. Murray, *Proud Shoes*, 40.
46. Deborah Gray White, *Ar'n't I a Woman?*, 111–12; Kennedy, *Born Southern*, 61, 66–68; McMillen, *Motherhood in the Old South*, 17–23.
47. Murray, *Proud Shoes*, 39–40.
48. When James purchased Harriet in 1834, Frank, born in 1816, was eighteen, and Sid, born in 1819, was fifteen. Jones with Southern, *Miss Mary's Money*, 88, 69; quotation from Murray, *Proud Shoes*, 40.
49. Jones with Southern, *Miss Mary's Money*, 21.
50. Jones with Southern, *Miss Mary's Money*, 69; Murray, *Proud Shoes*, 40.
51. Murray, *Proud Shoes*, 41–43.
52. Hartman, *Scenes of Subjugation*, 79–95.
53. Block, *Rape and Sexual Power*, 12.
54. Deborah Gray White, *Ar'n't I a Woman*, 27–46. See also Hartman, *Scenes of Subjugation*, 86–88. For a discussion of the vulnerability of enslaved women to the sexual exploitation of slave traders, see Baptist, "Cuffy."
55. Clinton, "Southern Dishonor," 60; Murray, *Proud Shoes*, 40–47, quotations on 41, 42, 43, 45.
56. Murray, *Proud Shoes*, 46.
57. Stevenson, "What's Love Got to Do with It?," esp. 108, 114–15.
58. Murray, *Proud Shoes*, 46–47; Jones with Southern, *Miss Mary's Money*, 90.
59. Murray, *Proud Shoes*, 47.
60. The most complete description of James Smith's complicated business dealings can be found in Jones with Southern, *Miss Mary's Money*, 53–62. For a discussion of the transfer of Price Creek to James Smith, see Jones with Southern, *Miss Mary's Money*, 14.
61. "Bacon and Leather," *Hillsborough Recorder*, July 10, 1845, 3.
62. Jones with Southern, *Miss Mary's Money*, 59. Lawyers made a great deal of money acting as agents for their indebted clients. Skeel, *Debt's Dominion*, 34.
63. Jones with Southern, *Miss Mary's Money*, 57; deeds, August 25, 1845, box 1, folder 9, and November 21, 1845, box 1, folder 7, Mary Ruffin Smith Papers; James Smith to Mary Smith, August 5, 1845, Deed Book 31, 329; James Smith to Delia Smith, September 27, 1845, Deed Book 31, 400; James Smith to Frank Smith, November 21, 1845, Deed Book 31, 369.
64. "Sale of Valuable Property," August 21, 1845, *Hillsborough Recorder*, 3; "Mills and Tan Yard Still for Sale," October 2–November 13, 1845, *Hillsborough Recorder*, 3.
65. Jones with Southern, *Miss Mary's Money*, 59–62.
66. Sellers, *Market Revolution*, 238.
67. Balleisen, *Navigating Failure*, 3; Sandage, *Born Losers*, 7.

68. For a discussion of the impact of bankruptcy on gender identity, see Ditz, "Shipwrecked."
69. Jones with Southern, *Miss Mary's Money*, 63.
70. [Margaret] Anna Burwell to Mary A. Kirkland, January 17, 1846, Anna Burwell Letters, Burwell School Archives, Hillsborough, North Carolina (hereafter Burwell Letters). Margaret Anna Burwell is referred to as Anna throughout the text and notes.
71. Jones with Southern, *Miss Mary's Money*, 14, 65, 67, 90; Inflation figures are based on data for 2023 and come from https://westegg.com/inflation/.
72. Jones with Southern, *Miss Mary's Money*, 106–7.
73. Murray, *Proud Shoes*, 53–54.
74. Murray, *Proud Shoes*, 54.
75. Charles P. Mallett to Charles B. Mallett, April 25, 1865, Charles B. Mallett Papers, no. 3165, Southern Historical Collection.
76. Murray, *Proud Shoes*, 162–63; Charles P. Mallett to Charles B. Mallett, April 18–19, 25, and 29, 1865.
77. Murray, *Proud Shoes*, 164. Despite losing all of her enslaved workers through emancipation, Mary claimed to own twenty thousand in real estate and one thousand in personal property in 1870. Manuscript Census Returns, Ninth Census of the United States, 1870, Chapel Hill, Orange County, North Carolina, roll M593_1153, 171A, Family History Library film no. 552652. For more on post–Civil War negotiations between freed women and their former mistresses, see Glymph, *Out of the House of Bondage*, 137–203.
78. On the isolation of plantation mistresses, see Clinton, *Plantation Mistress*, 164–66.
79. Jones with Southern, *Miss Mary's Money*, 84; Maria L. Spear to Maggie Mallett, May 13, 1867, and Maria L. Spear to Carrie Mallett, May 13, 1867, folder 19, Mallett Papers; Cornelia Phillips Spencer, "Obituary [of Maria Louisa Spear]," [3]; Manuscript Census Returns, Ninth Census of the United States, 1870, Chapel Hill, Orange County, North Carolina.
80. Maria L. Spear to Carrie Mallett, August 26, 1867, March 22, 1869; Maria L. Spear to Maggie Mallett, May 1, 1869, all in folder 19, box 2, Mallett Papers.
81. For a description of the storm, see Spear to Carrie Mallett, August 26 and Spear to Maggie Mallett, August 27, 1872, both in folder 19, box 2, Mallett Papers.
82. Murray, *Proud Shoes*, 165. For more on the lives of her children, see Kim Smith, "Book of Harriet."
83. Maria L. Spear to Carrie Mallett, December 29, 1875, and March 7, 1877, box 2, folder 19, Mallett Papers.
84. Jones with Southern, *Miss Mary's Money*, 94–95.
85. Maria L. Spear to Carrie Mallett, March 7, 1877, box 2, folder 19, Mallett Papers.
86. Mary Ruffin Smith's will dated April 27, 1877, Orange County Wills, 1753–1968, North Carolina State Archives, Raleigh, North Carolina.
87. Maria L. Spear to Alice Mallet, April 12, 1880, box 2, folder 19, Mallett Papers.
88. Cornelia Phillips Spencer, "Obituary [of Maria Louisa Spear]," [3]; Murray, *Proud Shoes*, 233.

89. Cornelia Phillips Spencer, "Obituary [of Maria Louisa Spear]," [3]. See also "Chapel Hill in Brief," *Orange County Observer*, January 15, 1881, 2. Maria's tombstone records her death date as January 6.
90. Mary Ruffin Smith to Carrie Mallett, January 20, 1881, folder 19, box 2, Mallett Papers.
91. Mary Ruffin Smith died on November 13, 1885. "Chapel Hill--Chapel of the Cross [Obituary of Mary Ruffin Smith]," *Church Messenger*, November 19, 1885, 3. The little family cemetery is adjacent to Galloway Ridge, a retirement community in Chatham County.
92. Murray, *Proud Shoes*, 41.
93. Murray, *Proud Shoes*, 42–43.
94. Cornelia Phillips Spencer, "A Notable Woman North Carolina Has Produced," *State Chronicle* (Raleigh), February 1886.

CHAPTER 2
1. Blackwlder, *Age of Orange*, 33.
2. Milteer, *North Carolina's Free People of Color*, 8, 9, 16, 19, 23–25. Throughout the South, there was an even wider variety of terms used to describe free people of color. See Milteer, *Beyond Slavery's Shadow*, 8–10; Myers, *Forging Freedom*, 13; Marks, *Black Freedom*, 1–2.
3. By 1860 there were only 250,000 free people of color as opposed to four million enslaved individuals in the South. Johnson and Roark, "Strategies of Survival," 89. In 1860 they comprised only 30,463 out of a total population of 992,622 in North Carolina. Milteer, *North Carolina's Free People of Color*, 6.
4. Wood, *"When the Roll Is Called Up Yonder,"* 7; Milteer, *North Carolina's Free People of Color*, 7.
5. Since the statistics available account for the number of free people of color in the county, it is impossible to determine how many of them lived and worked in Hillsborough.
6. Census data from 1800, 1810, 1820, 1850, and 1860 in Moore, *Impact of Slavery*, 234–35, 237–38, 245–47; 1850 and 1860 U.S. Manuscript Census, Orange County, North Carolina. William Chavis, a resident of Granville County, was a tavern/innkeeper and slave owner who died owning hundreds of acres of land. Milteer, *North Carolina's Free People of Color*, 31–32, 42–43. His first appearance in the public records of Orange County seems to have been as early as 1755 when he purchased 320 acres of land. William Chavis, no. 12 under Chavis Family at "Free African Americans in Colonial Virginia, North Carolina, and South Carolina," available at Free African Americans in Colonial Virginia, North Carolina, South Carolina, Maryland and Delaware, https://freeafricanamericans.com/Virginia-NC.htm.
7. Franklin, *Free Negro in North Carolina*, 68–101.
8. von Daacke, *Freedom Has a Face*.
9. Johnson and Roark, "Strategies of Survival," 88–93; Berlin, *Slaves Without Masters*; Franklin, *Free Negro in North Carolina*; Milteer, *North Carolina's Free People of Color*, 87–114. For a larger discussion of white dependence on the labor of free people of color throughout the South, see Milteer, *Beyond Slavery's Shadow*, 127–35.
10. Toplin, "Between Black and White"; Marshall and Leimenstoll, *Thomas Day*, 20–21; Andrews, *Slavery and Class*, 230.

11. Chesnut, *Mary Chestnut's Civil War*, 29.
12. Fanny Evans's name first appears in 1820 U.S. Manuscript Census, Orange County, North Carolina, 408, NARA roll M33_82, image 226. She was born sometime around 1785. For her birth date see "Henry Evans," 1850 U.S. Manuscript Census, Hillsborough, Orange County, North Carolina, roll 639, 172B.
13. "Delilah Evans," North Carolina, Marriage Index, 1741–2004; "A Semi-Centennial Anniversary," *Oberlin Weekly News*, August 19, 1881; "Henry Evans," 1850 U.S. Manuscript Census, Hillsborough, Orange County, North Carolina, roll 639, 172B; John Wilson to Jane and Henry Evans, May 7, 1822, Orange County Deed Book 21, 233, Recorder of Deeds Office, Hillsborough, North Carolina; "Wilson Evans," 1850 U.S. Manuscript Census, Hillsborough, Orange County, North Carolina, roll 639, 176A.
14. Lebsock, *Free Women of Petersburg*, 104; Schweninger, "Property Owning Free African-American Women," 24. Emily West documents the case of Percy Ann Martin, a free woman of color from Davidson County, North Carolina, who was so concerned about being separated from her husband that she petitioned to be enslaved by his owner. West, *In Family or Freedom*, 117.
15. "John Wilson," 1820 U.S. Manuscript Census, Caswell County, North Carolina, NARA Roll M33_81, p. 94, image 64. Wilson's marital status is unclear. The 1820 census lists only the number of females organized in age groups in his household. Wilson to Jane and Henry Evans, May 7, 1822.
16. Delilah, Henry, and Wilson were listed as literate in the 1850 census. "Deborah [Delilah] Copeland," 1850 U.S. Manuscript Census, Russia, Lorain County, Ohio; roll 705, 258B; "Henry Evans," 1850 U.S. Manuscript Census, Hillsborough, Orange County, North Carolina, roll 639, 172B; "Wilson Evans," 1850 U.S. Manuscript Census, Hillsborough, Orange County, North Carolina, roll 639, 176A.
17. Franklin, *Free Negro in North Carolina*, 123–29; *Acts Passed by the General Assembly of North Carolina at Its Session on the 25th of December 1826* (Raleigh: Lawrence & Lemay, 1827), 15, available at https://digital.ncdcr.gov/Documents/Detail/acts-passed-by-the-general-assembly-of-the-state-of-north-carolina-1826/1955749. For a discussion of the apprenticeship of craftsmen of color in New Bern, North Carolina, see Bishir, *Crafting Lives*, 121–25.
18. Berlin, *Slaves Without Masters*, 226–27.
19. Susannah Revill, August 1812, Orange County Apprenticeship Bonds, Orange County Court of Pleas and Quarter Session, Minute Book 8, 397, and November 1826, Minute Book 12, 3, North Carolina State Archives, Raleigh, North Carolina. The details for this case may be found in familysearch.com apprenticeship bonds, images 663, 665, 667–670, 692. My thanks to Orange County Register of Deeds Mark Chilton for references to this case.
20. On Thomas Day, see Wood, "When the Roll Is Called Up Yonder," 7–8; Marshall and Leimenstoll, *Thomas Day*, 9–16; "Thomas Day, Cabinetmaker," *Hillsborough Recorder*, April 6, 1825, 1.
21. "Furniture at Public Sale," *Hillsborough Recorder*, August 13, 1828, 3.
22. "Cabinet-Maker," *Hillsborough Recorder*, September 16, 1829, 3; October 7 and 14, 1829, 1. Since Hillsborough was such a small town at the time, everyone in town would have known who to go to if they needed furniture repaired or wanted to buy new

furnishings for their home. Therefore, it is not surprising that Marshall apparently decided to place no more ads in the paper. The name Joseph Marshall appears twice in the 1830 census for Orange County but no occupations are listed.

23. There is no record of a court-appointed apprenticeship for him in Caswell County.
24. Marshall and Leimenstoll, *Thomas Day*, 11–12.
25. Johnson and Roark, *Black Master*, 97–98.
26. Henry Evans, 1840 U.S. Manuscript Census, Orange County, North Carolina, roll 367, 265, Family History Library film 0018096. In this census Fanny Evans is listed as the head of a household in which three members were identified as being employed in manufacture and trade.
27. William Anderson to Henry Evans, August 24, 1838, Orange County Deed Book 28, 197B. This property transfer was recorded twice. See William Anderson to Henry Evans, May 8, 1840, Orange County Deed Book 29, 240A. The first extant advertisement entitled "Cabinet Making" appears in the *Hillsborough Recorder*, February 18, 1841, 4.
28. There are two John Wilsons listed in the 1840 census for Caswell County. One was engaged in agriculture, the other in commerce and industry.
29. Lloyd and Lloyd, *History of the Churches of Hillsborough*, 18, 79, 98–99, 126; L. J. Phipps, "Churches of Orange County," 292–93, 295, 297, 301. The Baptists did not organize their congregation until 1853.
30. Boles, introduction to *Masters and Slaves*, 10.
31. Hillsborough Presbyterian Session Records, Hillsborough Presbyterian Church, Hillsborough, North Carolina.
32. St. Matthew's Parish Records, St. Matthew's Episcopal Church, Hillsborough, North Carolina. My thanks to Brooks Graebner, former rector of St. Matthew's, for bringing Henry Evans to my attention.
33. Introduction to the Moses Ashley Curtis Papers, no. 199, Southern Historical Collection, Louis Round Wilson Special Collections Library, University of North Carolina at Chapel Hill.
34. Moses Ashley Curtis Diary, after September 24, 1831, folder 111, Moses Ashley Curtis Papers.
35. Graebner, "Episcopal Church and Race," 92.
36. St. Matthew's Parish Records. There is no evidence that Henry's wife Henrietta joined the church, but it appears that she had been baptized in Fayetteville before her marriage since she stood as sponsor at the baptism of their daughter on April 18, 1847.
37. John's origins are unclear. His father may have been freed when Eli and William Copeland of Hertford County asked permission from the North Carolina state legislature to emancipate one of their enslaved workers. See a reference to this in Cecil-Fronsman, *Common Whites*, 88. Or as Lasser and Kornblith assert, he may have been the son of his owner, who freed him in his will. See *Elusive Utopia*, 42.
38. "Delilah Evans," North Carolina, Marriage Index, 1741–2004; "A Semi-centennial Anniversary," *Oberlin Weekly News*, August 19, 1881; "A Historic Character Passes Away," *Oberlin News*, January 11, 1894, 5; Ronald Hendrikson and Nancy Hendrikson,

"History of the Hiram A. Pease Property," https://www2.oberlin.edu/external/EOG/Copeland/Copelandmain.htm.

39. Marshall and Leimenstoll, *Thomas Day*, 25; Howard, "Tar Heels at Harper's Ferry," NCpedia; "A Historic Character Passes Away," *Oberlin News*.

40. Andrews, *Slavery and Class*, 190–92; Cecil-Fronsman, *Common Whites*, 77, 86–87; David W. Stone to Thomas Ruffin, May 3, 1842, in *Papers of Thomas Ruffin*, 2:205–6.

41. "Allen Jones," 1840 U.S. Manuscript Census, Wake County, North Carolina, roll 374, 124, Family History Library film no. 0018098. Jones is listed as enslaving two adult slaves, one male and one female, who presumably were among his enslaved relatives. Franklin, *Free Negro in North Carolina*, 27. On free people of color who enslaved others, see Johnson and Roark, "Strategies for Survival," 94–101; Franklin, *Free Negro in North Carolina*, 27, 159–61. On the increasing pressure on free people of color in North Carolina during this period, see Bishir, *Crafting Lives*, 98–145. On the cost of freeing an enslaved person, see Bashir, *Crafting Lives*, 115; Lasser and Kornblith, *Elusive Utopia*, 41–42, 74; "Disgraceful Outrage," *Raleigh Register*, October 18, 1842, 3; "Town Meeting" and "Meeting of the Board of Commissioners," *Raleigh Register*, October 21, 1842, 3.

42. Lasser and Kornblith, *Elusive Utopia*, 42–43; "A Semi-Centennial Anniversary," *Oberlin Weekly News*, August 19, 1881, [3]. John Lane is not listed in the 1840 census. Crowell, *Images of America*, 8, 17, 31; "A Historic Character Passes Away," *Oberlin News*, January 11, 1894, 5; Hendrikson and Hendrikson, "History of the Hiram A. Pease Property"; "John Copeland," 1850 U.S. Manuscript Census, Russia, Lorain County, Ohio, roll 705, 258B. Allen Jones set up a blacksmithing business in the same town. "Allin Jones," 1850 U.S. Manuscript Census, Russia, Lorain County, Ohio, roll 705, 248AA. There are two towns called New Richmond in the Midwest. One is in Indiana, the other in Ohio. It seems likely that once the party arrived in Ohio, they would have had no reason to travel farther west into Indiana and therefore settled temporarily in New Richmond, Ohio. John Lane served as one of seven delegates from Lorain County to the Mass Convention of the Colored Citizens of Ohio held in Columbus in January 1849. John Lane and John Copeland voted in the 1855 Ohio elections for governor, judges, and state legislators. See Lasser and Kornblith, *Elusive Utopia*, 47, 71.

43. "Henry Evans," North Carolina, *Index to Marriage Bonds*, 1741–1868; "Matthew Leary," 1850 U.S. Manuscript Census, Fayetteville, Cumberland County, North Carolina, roll 627; Page: 114A. Leary enslaved two adult men and a 14-year-old girl. "Matthew Leary," 1850 U.S. Federal Census--Slave Schedules, Fayetteville, Cumberland County, North Carolina.

44. "Henry Evans," 1850 U.S. Manuscript Census, Hillsborough, Orange County, North Carolina, roll 639, 172B. By that time, Wilson had left his brother's increasingly crowded house on Churton Street and was living in a boardinghouse. "Wilson Evans," 1850 U.S. Manuscript Census, Hillsborough, Orange County, North Carolina, roll 639, 176A.

45. "Cabinet-Making," *Hillsborough Recorder*, February 18, 1841, 4. Like many artisans, Henry did not usually sign his name to the furniture he made. One example of his signed work, however, is held by the Museum of Early Southern Decorative Arts in

Winston-Salem, North Carolina, shown at https://mesda.org/item/object/table-dining/4168/.

46. The congregation of St. Matthew's relies on oral tradition to substantiate their claim that Evans made the chairs and balcony panels in their possession.
47. February 1851, Orange County Court of Pleas and Quarter Session Minute Book 17, 620, North Carolina State Archives, Raleigh, North Carolina. The court paid him $3.50 for his services. My thanks to Mark Chilton for this reference.
48. Marshall and Leimenstoll, *Thomas Day*, 35–36.
49. William Mayho, May 1843, Apprenticeship Bonds, Orange County Court of Pleas and Quarter Session Minute Book 15, 359. The family name Mayho also appears in the public record as Mayo and Mayhoe.
50. William Mayo, May 1847, Apprenticeship Bonds, Orange County Court of Pleas and Quarter Session Minute Book 16, 326; "John Lyon," 1850 U.S. Manuscript Census, Orange County, North Carolina, roll 639, 230a. Since neither Melinda nor Simmons appears in the 1840 census, it is impossible to tell if they were William's parents or if those two apprenticeship bonds apply to the same William Mayo.
51. "John B. Mitchell," U.S. Manuscript Census, District 1, Orange County, North Carolina, roll 639, 230a; William Mitchell, March 1851, Apprenticeship Bonds, Orange County Court of Pleas and Quarter Session Minute Book 17, 611; "Adaline Mitchell," 1850 U. S. Manuscript Census, Orange County, North Carolina, roll 639, 163b. She lists no occupation. In February 1855 the court bound out Adaline's nine-year-old daughter Mary to Thomas Webb, a Hillsborough lawyer, to learn to be a domestic servant. Mary Mitchell, February 1855, Apprenticeship Bonds, Orange County Court of Pleas and Quarter Session Minute Book 18, 298. Her apprenticeship bond provided that at the end of her apprenticeship, she would receive fifty dollars and "a fine suit of clothes."
52. "James Allison," 1850 U.S. Manuscript Census, Hillsborough, Orange County, North Carolina, roll 639, 176A.
53. "Accommodation for Travelers," Hillsborough Recorder, September 20, 1848, 4; "Cabinet Ware-house," *Hillsborough Recorder*, July 10, 1850, 4; Suzanne E. Smith, *To Serve the Living*, 33–35.
54. *State v. Evans Chaves*, August 1845, Orange County Court of Pleas and Quarter Session Minute Book 16, 24; "[Eavins Chasom, Eavins Chavous, Evin Chavous]," 1840 U.S. Manuscript Census, Granville, Granville County, North Carolina, roll 360, 155, Family History Library film no. 0018094; "Evans Chavers [Chavis]," 1850 U.S. Manuscript Census, Country Line, Granville County, North Carolina, roll 631, 178b; apprenticeship bond for Samuel Benton [Barton], November 1845, Orange County Court of Pleas and Quarter Session Minute Book 16, 74; "James M. Palmer," 1850 U.S. Manuscript Census, Hillsborough, Orange County, North Carolina, roll 639, 173b.
55. *Henry Evans vs. John R. Minnis and James Jackson*, May 1847, Orange County Court of Pleas and Quarter Session Minute Book 16, [348]; "John R. Minnis," 1850 U.S. Manuscript Census, District 1, Orange County, North Carolina, roll 639, 181a. The 1840 census for Orange County lists three heads of farming households named James Jackson. The 1850 census for Orange County lists one.

56. October 10, 1843, Hillsborough Board of Commissioners Minute Book, 1843–54, Town Clerk's Office, Hillsborough, North Carolina. My thanks to Mark Chilton, register of deeds, for this information.
57. "Henry Evans," 1850 U.S. Manuscript Census, Hillsborough, Orange County, North Carolina, roll 639, 176A.
58. "Wilson Evans," May 24, 1853, North Carolina, *Index to Marriage Bonds*, 1741–1868; "Land for Sale," *Hillsborough Recorder*, January 5, 1853, 3; "Cabinet Shop and Furniture for Sale," *Hillsborough Recorder*, November 23, 1853, 3; Henry Evans to Thomas and James Webb, November 29, 1853, Orange County Deed Book 34, 337.
59. Greene, *Leary-Evans*, 46–47. Of the people accompanying the Evanses, only the boy Lee Chavers is not listed in the 1850 census for Orange County.
60. "Henry Evans," 1860 U.S. Manuscript Census, Oberlin, Lorain County, Ohio, 209, Family History Library film no. 805002; "Wilson Evans," 1860 U.S. Manuscript Census, Oberlin, Lorain County, Ohio, 203.
61. McPherson, *Battle Cry of Freedom*, 78–80; Bordewich, *America's Great Debate*, 225–26; Morris, *Free Men All*, 145–46.
62. Morris, *Free Men All*, 42–58. For a thorough analysis of Ohio's legislative response to the presence of Black people within its borders, see Masur, *Until Justice Be Done*, 15–18, 83–118, 183–224.
63. Lasser and Kornblith, *Elusive Utopia*, 93; "History of Oberlin," City of Oberlin website, https://www.cityofoberlin.com/for-visitors/history-of-oberlin/.
64. Lasser and Kornblith, *Elusive Utopia*, 94–102; "Wellington Rescue Case," *Cleveland Daily Herald*, December 7 and 9, 1858; Fletcher, *History of Oberlin College*, 1:401–16; Howard, "Tar Heels at Harper's Ferry"; Brandt, *Town That Started the Civil War*.
65. Lasser and Kornblith, *Elusive Utopia*, 104–5; Lubet, *The "Colored Hero" of Harper's Ferry*; Howard, "Tar Heels at Harper's Ferry"; Hendrikson and Hendrikson, "History of the Hiram A. Pease Property."
66. Lasser and Kornblith, *Elusive Utopia*, 115, 119.
67. Hendrikson and Hendrikson, "History of the Hiram A. Pease Property," claim that Henry signed up to fight with the First Kansas Volunteers, but I could find no evidence to confirm that. "Henry Evans," 1870, U.S. Manuscript Census, Oberlin, Lorain, Ohio, roll M593_1235, 637A, Family History Library film no. 552734.
68. Henry Evans grave site, Westwood Cemetery, Oberlin, Ohio, https://www.oberlin-westwood.org/omeka/items/show/52259.
69. McPherson, *Battle Cry of Freedom*, 563.
70. U.S. Civil War Soldier Records and Profiles, 1861–1865; Ohio, Soldier Grave Registrations, 1804–1958; "Wilson B. Evans," 1870 U.S. Manuscript Census, Oberlin, Lorain County, Ohio, roll M593_1235, 637A, Family History Library film no. 552734.
71. Anderson Mayhoe married Jesse Tatum on July 25, 1828. Marriage Bond, July 25, 1828, Orange County Marriage Book M, 42, Orange County Register of Deeds Office, Hillsborough, North Carolina.
72. Engstrom, "Witherspoon, John Knox," NCpedia.
73. Mason, "American Silk Industry," 41.

74. Witherspoon had ten enslaved workers living on his plantation in 1840. John Knox Witherspoon, 1840 U.S. Manuscript Census, Southern Division, Orange County, North Carolina, roll 367, 221, Family History Library film no. 0018096; "A Report to the Board of Trustees of Davidson College on the Importance of Silk Culture in the Western Parts of North and South Carolina," *Hillsborough Recorder,* January 17, 1839, 1; "Reasons for Making Silk," *Hillsborough Recorder,* March 25, 1841, 1; "Silk and Silkworms," *Hillsborough Recorder,* June 13, 1844, 1.
75. Marsh, "Republic's New Clothes," 207–8, 211, 221.
76. Unless otherwise stated, the information that follows comes from *State v. Anderson Mayo, a free negro,* September Term, Superior Court, Orange County, North Carolina, 1841, in Criminal Action Records, Orange County, North Carolina, boxes 41 and 42, North Carolina State Archives, Raleigh, North Carolina; Minutes of the Superior Court of North Carolina, September Term, 1841, vol. 3, North Carolina State Archives. It should be noted that the white clerk of the court did not always identify correctly members of the Tatum, Strudwick, and Mayo families, all of whom were free.
77. Anderson Mayho, 1840 U.S. Manuscript Census, Southern Division, Orange County, North Carolina, roll 367, 255, Family History Library film no. 0018096; Apprenticeship of James Mayhoe, May 1849, Orange County Pleas and Quarter Sessions, Book 17, 344. Catherine Mayo appears to have been misidentified in the court records as Catherine Strudwick. In her testimony she identified herself as Jesse and Anderson Mayo's daughter.
78. It appears to have been acceptable in Orange County for the enslaved to testify in court against nonwhites as long as they were sponsored by their enslavers.
79. Apprenticeship bond of James Mayhoe, May 1849, Orange County Pleas and Quarter Sessions, Book 17, 344. According to the census, there was more than one Henry Crabtree living in Orange County in 1850. Both are listed as laborers. The guarantors were James M. Palmer, an Orange County farmer and slave owner, and Levi McCollum, listed in the census as a laborer. "James M. Palmer," 1850 U.S. Manuscript Census, Hillsborough, Orange County, North Carolina, roll 639, 173b; "Levi McCollum," 1850 U.S. Manuscript Census, Hillsborough, Orange County, North Carolina, roll 639, 178b.
80. Blackwelder, *Age of Orange,* 95; *James Mayho v. William H. Whitsman and Abner Peace,* May 1854, Orange County Court of Pleas and Quarter Session, Book 18, 202, Recorder of Deeds Office. Court records provide more than one spelling for the two petitioners' names. My thanks to Mark Chilton, Orange County register of deeds, for this information.
81. Bernie D. Jones, *Fathers of Conscience,* 1–8.
82. Will of Absolum Tatum, December 17, 1802, Orange County Will Book D, 94, and May 1803, Orange County Court of Pleas and Quarter Sessions, Book 6, 411, Register of Deeds Office.
83. Kimball, "African, American, Virginian," 69.
84. *James Mayho v. William H. Whitsman and Abner Peace,* May 1854, and *James Mayo v. Wm. H. Whitson and Abner Pearce,* 47 N.C. 231 (N.C. 1855), https://casetext.com/case/mayo-v-whitson.

85. Margaret Lane Cemetery brochure, Town of Hillsborough, https://assets.hillsboroughnc.gov/media/documents/public/margaret-lane-cemetery-brochure.pdf.

CHAPTER 3

1. In a letter to her mother, Eliza A. Murphy, July 15, 1848, Mary B. Murphy mentions having bread and butter for both breakfast and supper. Murphy letters, private collection of Eleanor Saunders Morris, copies in the Burwell School Archives, Hillsborough, North Carolina.
2. William Norwood to William Tillinghast, May 9, 1850, box 3, Folder--Correspondence, 1848–50, Tillinghast Family Papers, David M. Rubenstein Rare Book and Manuscript Library, Duke University, Durham, North Carolina. For more on the lives of clerks in small southern towns, see Tolbert, *Constructing Townscapes*, 153–58.
3. Stowe, "Not-So-Cloistered Academy," 92–98; Elder, *Sacred Mirror*, 90–93.
4. James Webb, "Bill of Mortality," *Hillsborough Recorder*, January 6, 1842, 3. The 1840 census listed 6,463 children between the ages of five and twenty in Orange County. Of those, fewer than five hundred were in school. Blackwelder, *Age of Orange*, 146.
5. Bell Norwood to William Tillinghast, January 18, 1847, box 2, Folder--Correspondence, 1846–47, Tillinghast Family Papers.
6. Lizzie Hobbs Keckly, discussed in the next chapter, probably learned to read and write from her literate but enslaved parents. Apprenticeship bonds can be found in the Orange County Court of Pleas and Quarter Session Minute Books, North Carolina State Archives, Raleigh.
7. Knight, "Education in Orange County," 131–32.
8. Knight, "Education in Orange County," 136–37; Coon, *North Carolina Schools*, 310–14; Blackwelder, *Age of Orange*, 137.
9. "Privaet [sic] Boarding School," *Hillsborough Recorder*, April 15, 1841, 3.
10. Bell Norwood to William Tillinghast, January 18, 1847; Anna M. Kirkland to [Duncan Cameron], October 25, 1847, box 43, folder 1019, December 15, 1847, box 43, folder 1022, and July 6, 1848, box 44, folder 1036, Cameron Family Papers, no. 133, Southern Historical Collection, Louis Round Wilson Special Collections Library, University of North Carolina at Chapel Hill; "Female School," *Hillsborough Recorder*, January 27, 1848, 3.
11. Sketches of the Burwell School, the Hillsborough Academy, the Bingham School, and the Caldwell Institute can be found in NCpedia. For information on the Hillsborough Female Academy, see Hoffert, "Earnest Efforts to Be Friends," 818–21.
12. Cashin, "Decidedly Opposed to the Union"; Jabour, "It Will Never Do"; Jabour, *Scarlett's Sisters*, 80–92; Carter, *Southern Single Blessedness*; O'Brien, *Evening When Alone*; Fox-Genovese, *Within the Plantation Household*, 46, 258.
13. Nash, "Means of Honorable Support"; Tolley, "Music Teachers."
14. Engstrom, "Webb, James," NCpedia; Engstrom, *Book of Burwell Students*, 218–19.
15. Session meeting, November 25, 1835, Hillsborough Presbyterian Church Session Records typescript, book 1, 21, Hillsborough Presbyterian Church Archives, Hillsbor-

ough, North Carolina; John Bott Burwell, "Record of the Descendants of the Rev. Robert Burwell, D. D. and Margaret Anna Robertson, Married December 22nd, 1831," 2, Burwell School Archives. Accounting for inflation, $400 a year would have amounted to $12,300 in 2023. Mary (Molly) Susan Burwell was born in 1832, John Bott Burwell in 1834, and Ann[a] (Nannie) Robertson Burwell in 1836. Engstrom, *Book of Burwell Students*, 58, 61.

16. Hoffert, "Anna Burwell," 245–50.
17. Van Zandt, *"Elect Lady,"* 152. For more on ministers' wives, see Boyd, "Presbyterian Ministers' Wives."
18. Morey, "Lamentations for the Minister's Wife."
19. [Beecher], *Dawn to Daylight*, 54.
20. Cutler, *Jottings from Life*, 87, 41–42.
21. Engstrom, *Book of Burwell Students*, 218–19, 80.
22. Farnham, *Education of the Southern Belle*, 2.
23. The Burwells eventually had twelve children.
24. Anna Burwell to Mary A. Kirkland, January 17, 1846, Burwell Letters.
25. "Umstead Mayo," 1850 U.S. Manuscript Census, Hillsborough, Orange County, North Carolina, roll 639, 173b. For mention of Umstead and Eliza, see Burwell Diary, February 19 and 26, March 28, April 12 and 17, and December 10, 1855, and January 5, 1856, Burwell School Archives (hereafter Burwell Diary).
26. The Burwells listed enslaved workers living in their household in the census, but they had little money to invest in them and there is no record of them having done so.
27. "Confectionaries, &c.," *Hillsborough Recorder*, November 24, 1842, 3; "Fall and Winter Goods," *Hillsborough Recorder*, January 20, 1842, 4; "Millinery and Mantua-making," *North Carolina Democrat*, May 16, 1849, 3.
28. Lizzie Glass to her mother [Margret Graham Kerr Glass Scott], April 18, 1856, Scott Family Collection, Alamance Community College, Graham, North Carolina; "Julia Miner," 1850 U.S. Manuscript Census, Hillsborough, Orange County, North Carolina, roll 639, 178A.
29. Engstrom, *Book of Burwell Students*, 111–13; Anna Burwell to Mary Burwell, August 17, 1855, Burwell Letters.
30. Engstrom, "Burwell, Robert Armistead," NCpedia; John Bott Burwell, "Record of the Descendants," 4.
31. Ann Strudwick Nash, *Ladies in the Making*, 12.
32. Burwell, "Record of the Descendants," 4.
33. Burwell, "Record of the Descendants," 2.
34. North Carolina did not pass a married women's property act changing this situation until after the Civil War. Warbasse, *Changing Legal Rights*, 167.
35. For examples of the ads, see Coon, *North Carolina Schools*, 320–22; *Hillsborough Recorder*, June 21, 1848, 3; *North Carolina Standard* (Raleigh, NC), June 14, 1848, 4; Burwell Diary, December 10, 1855.
36. Anna Burwell to Fanny Burwell, November 27, 1855, Burwell Letters.
37. Hoffert, "Anna Burwell," 257–59.

38. Anna Burwell to Fanny Burwell, March 10, 1856, Burwell Letters.
39. Burwell Diary, May 15, October 2 and 23, 1855.
40. Anna Burwell to Fanny Burwell, January 19, 1856, Burwell Letters.
41. Anna Burwell to Fanny Burwell, February 4, 1856, Burwell Letters.
42. Farnham, *Education of the Southern Belle*, 123; Long, *High Time to Tell It*, 89–90. For examples of such language among Burwell students, see Mary B. Murphy and Susan Murphy to their mother [Eliza A. Murphy], July 15, 1848, copy in the Burwell School Archives.
43. Anna Burwell to Fanny Burwell, February 8, 1856, Burwell Letters. Mary Cameron Jones was the daughter of Dr. Pride Jones of Hillsborough. Engstrom, *Book of Burwell Students*, 117.
44. *North Carolina Standard* (Raleigh), June 24, 1846, 1.
45. Anna Burwell to Fanny Burwell, December 29, 1855, Burwell Letters.
46. Anna Burwell to Fanny Burwell, December 29, 1855.
47. Anna Burwell to Fanny Burwell, February 8, 1856, Burwell Letters.
48. Mary B. and Susan M. Murphy to their mother [Eliza A. Murphy], July 15, 1848, copy in Burwell School archives.
49. Susan Murphy to her mother, April 1849, copy in Burwell School archives.
50. Ann H. Kerr to half-sister Margaret Scott, February 25, 1854, Scott Collection.
51. Lizzie Glass to her mother [Margaret Scott], September 18, 1854, Scott Collection.
52. The curricula of the Hillsborough Female Academy and the Burwell School were similar. *Hillsborough Recorder* advertisement for the Hillsborough Female Academy, July 13, 1825, 3; Green, "A Tabular View of the Order and Distribution of Studies," *Circular and Catalogue of Mr. and Mrs. Burwell's Female School*.
53. Tolley, "Significance of the 'French School,'" 137, 142–44; Kilbride, *American Aristocracy*, 55–56.
54. Bell Norwood to William Tillinghast, January 26, 1846, box 2, folder--Correspondence, 1846–47; Bell Norwood to William Tillinghast, October 10, 1845, box 2, folder—Correspondence, 1843–45, both in Tillinghast Family Papers.
55. Bell Norwood to William Tillinghast, October 10, 1845; Margaret Isabella Walker, "Reminiscences," in Engstrom, *Book of Burwell Students*, 209.
56. Bell Norwood to William Tillinghast, October 9, 1845, box 3, folder--Correspondence, 1848–50, Tillinghast Family Papers; quotation in Anna Burwell to Fannie Burwell, February 8, 1856, Burwell Letters.
57. Mary Pearce to William Tillinghast, November 1, 1851, in Engstrom, *Book of Burwell Students*, 177.
58. Mary B. Murphy to her mother, July 15, 1848, copy in Burwell School Archives; Lizzie Glass to her mother, September 18, 1854, Scott Collection.
59. Bell Norwood to William Tillinghast, June 14, 1847, in Engstrom, *Book of Burwell Students*, 158. See also Bell Norwood to William Tillinghast, October 10, 1845; Burwell Diary, June 6, 1855; Annabella Norwood to William Tillinghast, undated [Christmas season, 1849] in Engstrom, *Book of Burwell Students*, 159.

60. Mary B. Murphy to her mother, July 15, 1848.
61. Kate to Lizzie Roberson, October 1, 1850, Burwell School Archives.
62. Kate to Lizzie Roberson, October 1, 1850.
63. Susan Murphy to Pa, April 1849, Burwell School Archives.
64. Sarah Ray to John Tillinghast, February 28, 1852, in Engstrom, *Book of Burwell Students*, 184.
65. Burwell Diary, October and 11, 1855. A student, Lizzie Glass, reported his dismissal in a letter to her mother but did not explain why. Lizzie Glass to Margaret Scott, October 12, 1855, Scott Collection. Vampill threatened to sue Robert, presumably for breach of contract, but they ultimately came to an agreement without hiring lawyers and going to court. Burwell Diary, October 14 and 17, 1855.
66. Jabour, *Scarlett's Sisters*, 39–43.
67. Burwell Diary, January 26, September 2, 1855.
68. See specific references to appropriate dress in the 1861 catalog of the Charlotte Female Institute where Anna served as matron. *Catalogue of the Charlotte Female Institute*, 13.
69. Elizabeth Coit to her sister, April 10, 1852, in Engstrom, *Book of Burwell Students*, 70.
70. Lizzie Glass to Margaret Scott, October 12, 1855.
71. Sarah Kollock to Thomas Bout Littlejohn, 1841, in Engstrom, *Book of Burwell Students*, 123–24. Engstrom's identification of Shepard Kollock as Sarah's grandfather is incorrect.
72. Susan Murphy to Ma, n.d., Burwell School Archives.
73. Mary Easley's Account, July 1852, in Engstrom, *Book of Burwell Students*, 86; Susan Murphy to Ma, n.d., Burwell School Archives; Lizzie Glass to her mother, April 18, 1856, Scott Collection.
74. Lizzie Glass to Margaret Scott, April 18, 1856. A spencer was originally a short jacket worn over a high-waisted Regency-style dress in the early nineteenth century.
75. Bell Norwood to William Tillinghast, January 18, 1847, box 2, folder: Correspondence, 1846–47, Tillinghast Family Papers. The 1850 U.S. Manuscript Census, Hillsborough, Orange County, North Carolina, lists Haynes Waddell, age fifty-five, as having no occupation. He lived with his wife Mary, age forty-three, and five children ranging in ages from five to eighteen.
76. William Norwood to William Tillinghast, May 9, 1850, box 3, folder: Correspondence, 1848–50, Tillinghast Family Papers.
77. Anna Burwell to Fanny Burwell, February 20, 1856. See also Anna Burwell to Fanny Burwell, March 15, 1856, both in Burwell Letters.
78. *Catalogue of the Charlotte Female Institute*.
79. Engstrom, "Burwell, Robert Armistead," NCpedia.
80. Mary B. Murphy to her mother, July 15, 1848, Burwell School archives; quotation in Kate to Lizzie Roberson, October 1, 1850, Burwell School Archives.
81. In 1855 Anna wrote to her daughter Mary, "The girls are all good & give no trouble." Anna Burwell to Mary Burwell Strudwick, August 17, 1855, Burwell Letters.
82. Anna Burwell to Fanny Burwell, January 25, 1856, Burwell Letters.

83. Burwell Diary, September 29, November 12, 1855.
84. Green, "Tabular View," [3].
85. Glenn, "School Discipline and Punishment"; Neem, *Democracy's Schools*, 101, 129, 137; Greenough, "Forgive Us Our Transgressions"; Greven, *Protestant Temperament*, 276–81; Censer, *North Carolina Planters*, 40.
86. For discussions of southerners' propensity to use violence to respond to perceived insults and settle conflicts, see Wyatt-Brown, *Southern Honor*; Bruce, *Violence and Culture*; Hindus, *Prison and Plantation*; Ayers, *Vengeance and Justice*, 9–33.
87. *Catalogue of the Trustees, Faculty, and Students of the Caldwell Institute*, 9–10.
88. John Bott Burwell, "Record of the Descendants," 5.
89. Steelman, "Bingham, William," NCpedia; Curtis, "Bingham School," 331–32, 335–36; James Barry Bingham, *Descendants of James Bingham*, 8–10; Robert Bingham, "William Bingham"; Williamson, "Bingham School."
90. Battle, *History of the University of North Carolina*, 1:200–218; Novak, *Rights of Youth*, 22–23. For general discussions of violence at the university level during this period, see Allmendinger, *Paupers and Scholars*, 114–26; Mullins, "Honorable Violence"; Bledstein, *Culture of Professionalism*, 223–47; Kett, *Rites of Passage*, 51–61; Tomlinson and Windham, "Northern Piety and Southern Honor," 6; Glover, "Let Us Manufacture Men," 29; Glover, *Southern Sons*, 33, 64–83.
91. Steelman, "Bingham, William James," NCpedia; Anderson, "Hillsborough Academy," NCpedia; Jones with Southern, *Miss Mary's Money*, 37; Coon, *North Carolina Schools*, 281–82.
92. Anderson, "Bingham School," NCpedia; Troxler and Vincent, *Shuttle and Plow*, 338–40; Allmendinger, "Dangers of Antebellum Student Life," 79–80.
93. Greven, *Spare the Child*, 6, 46–54.
94. Quoted in Blackwelder, *Age of Orange*, 123. James Claiborne, who went to a private school in Virginia, remembered a teacher who "never lost his temper--but with great grace and good humor could plant a birch" on the backside of his male students. Claiborne, *Seventy-Five Years in Old Virginia*, 28.
95. Wagoner, "Honor and Dishonor," 160–62; Wakelyn, "Antebellum College Life."
96. Steelman, "Bingham, William James"; James Barry Bingham, *Descendants of James Bingham*, 35–38; Curtis, "Bingham School," 338–45; Robert Bingham, "William James Bingham," 69; Williamson, "Bingham School," 372; *Hillsborough Recorder*, June 22, 1825, 3; Coon, *North Carolina Schools*, 286–95.
97. Censer, *North Carolina Planters*, 47; McMillin, *Schoolmaker*, 23.
98. Ebenezer Pettigrew to William James Bingham, January 5, 1842, in *The Pettigrew Papers*, ed. Sarah McCulloch Lemon, vol. 2: 1819–1843 (Raleigh: State Department of Archives and History, 1988, 501–2.
99. Ebenezer Pettigrew to William James Bingham, January 22, 1842, in *Pettigrew Papers*, 2:506.
100. Ebenezer Pettigrew to James Johnston Pettigrew, July 16, 1838, *Pettigrew Papers*, 2:375.
101. William James Bingham to Ebenezer Pettigrew, July 1, 1839, in *Pettigrew Papers*, 2:410–11.

102. Ebenezer Pettigrew to James Johnston Pettigrew, September 2, 1839, in *Pettigrew Papers,* 2:414.
103. Hessinger, "Most Powerful Instrument," 247–48.
104. "The Trustees of Hillsborough Academy [to the Parents of Academy Students]," September 16, 1839, box 4, folder 76, Pettigrew Family Papers no. 592, Southern Historical Collection.
105. William James Bingham to Ebenezer Pettigrew, November 4, 1839, in *Pettigrew Papers,* 2:417.
106. William James Bingham to Ebenezer Pettigrew, December 1, 1841, in *Pettigrew Papers,* 2:493. Moses Ashley Curtis, who eventually lived in Hillsborough, used similar tactics to control his students in Wilmington, North Carolina. Moses Ashley Curtis Diary, September 30, October 21 and 29, [1831], folder 111, vol. 6, Moses Ashley Curtis Papers no. 199, Southern Historical Collection.
107. William James Bingham to Ebenezer Pettigrew, March 8, 1842, in *Pettigrew Papers,* 2:507; Steelman, "Bingham, William James"; Curtis, "Bingham School," 345. There is some disagreement about when he opened his school at the Oaks. Steelman, "Bingham, William James," says 1845. Curtis, "Bingham School" (345) and Anderson, "Bingham School," say 1844. Williamson, "Bingham School" (371) says 1843.
108. William Bingham to Samuel Tillinghast, January 23, 1846, box 2, folder--Correspondence, 1846–47, Tillinghast Family Papers. $2,000 would have been worth about $66,500 in 2023.
109. James Barry Bingham, *Descendants of James Bingham,* 35.
110. McMillin, *Schoolmaker,* 20, 22–23.
111. Ellis, *Robert Worth Bingham,* 4–5; Curtis, "Bingham School," 351–54; James Barry Bingham, *Descendants of James Bingham,* 42.
112. North Carolina Hospital for the Insane, Admissions Ledger, 1:1856–1911, North Carolina Department of Cultural Resources, Division of Archives and Records, Raleigh, North Carolina. These records are available through the Odum Institute for Research in the Social Sciences, Davis Library, University of North Carolina, Chapel Hill.
113. Steelman, "Bingham, William James"; "The Late Wm J. Bingham," *Raleigh Sentinel,* March 1, 1866, 2; "W. J. Bingham," *Daily Journal* (Wilmington, NC), March 6, 1866, 2.
114. Ellis, *Robert Worth Bingham,* 8.
115. Curtis, "Bingham School," 362–64; Page, *The Southerner,* x, 41; Barringer, *Natural Bent,* 156–57.
116. Curtis, "Bingham School," 374; Ellis, *Robert Worth Bingham,* 11. See a testimonial/promotional pamphlet by F. B. Arendell, "Bingham School: 1793–1897," n.d. [1897], 2, 9, North Carolina Collection, Louis Round Wilson Special Collections Library, https://archive.org/details/binghamschool17900aren/page/8. Bingham's new approach to discipline mirrored that instituted by colleges, which had made honor codes and student courts the center of their disciplinary regimen. Leloudis, *Schooling in the Old South,* 59–60.
117. Andrew, *Long Gray Lines,* 118; Curtis, "Bingham School," 375.
118. See the profiles of Burwell students at https://www.burwellschool.org/people-of-the-past-burwell-school-students.

119. Junk, "To Become a Power," 40–41.
120. "Susan A. Webb," https://www.burwellschool.org/people-of-the-past-burwell-school-students.
121. Engstrom, "Nash, Sally (Sarah) Jane and Maria Jane Nash," NCpedia.
122. "Mrs. Huske's School," *Hillsborough Recorder*, January 29, 1864, 3.
123. Bass, "Robertson, Lucy Henderson Owen," NCpedia.
124. Anderson, "Strudwick, Edmund Charles," NCpedia.
125. Moore, "Burgwin, Nathaniel Hill," NCpedia; Powell, "Tillinghast, John Huske," NCpedia.
126. Cooper, "Page, Walter Hines," NCpedia.
127. Hodgson, "Webb, William Robert (Sawney)," NCpedia.

CHAPTER 4
1. Tolbert, *Constructing Townscapes*, 205–6.
2. Jacobs, *Incidents*, 29, 33, 35.
3. "Robert Burwell," 1840 U.S. Manuscript Census, Southern Division, Orange County, North Carolina, roll 367, 213, image 441; "Robert [Berrwell]," 1850 Manuscript Census--Slave Schedules, 1st District, Orange County, North Carolina. In 1860 he listed six enslaved workers in his household in Charlotte. 1860 U.S. Manuscript Census—Slave Schedules, Mecklenburg County, North Carolina, M653. Anna Burwell's diary in 1846, 1855, and 1856 mentions thirty or so enslaved workers and free people of color who worked at the school. For a list of all the people, enslaved and free, who could be identified as working for the Burwells over the twenty years they lived in Hillsborough, see Morris and Eidenier, *Antebellum Hillsborough*, 10–22.
4. Keckley, *Behind the Scenes*, 32. For critiques of that memoir, see Sheila Smith McKoy's two-volume *Elizabeth Keckly Reader*. Although her name is frequently spelled Keckley, she signed her name without an e, and that spelling is adopted here. Those who knew her also shortened her first name to either Lizzie or Lizzy. I have chosen the former.
5. When North Carolina Supreme Court justice Thomas Ruffin declared in *State v. Mann (1829)* that "the power of the master must be absolute to render the submission of the slave perfect," he granted legal and moral justification for the unlimited use of corporal punishment as a means of disciplining those held in bondage. *State v. Mann*, 13 NC 263 (1829); Yanuck, "Thomas Ruffin and North Carolina Slave Law"; Tushnet, *Slave Law*; Hadden, "Judging Slavery."
6. Keckley, *Behind the Scenes*, 31–42, quotations on 32, 33, 38, 42.
7. Jean Bradley Anderson, *Kirklands of Ayr Mount*, 15–22, 31–32, 77, 93–101, genealogical chart.
8. Hine, "Rape," 38.
9. "Robert Burwell," 1840 U.S. Federal Census, Southern Division, Orange County, North Carolina.
10. Keckley, *Behind the Scenes*, 39–90; Fleischner, *Mrs. Lincoln and Mrs. Keckly*; Hoffert, "Emancipation of Elizabeth Hobbs Keckly"; Hoffert, "Mary Lincoln." Keckly named

her son George Kirkland and listed Alexander Kirkland as her son's father in her 1863 pension application. Elizabeth Keckly pension application, National Archives, Washington, DC.
11. Andrews, *Slavery and Class,* 318–21.
12. Burwell Diary, January 5, 6, 13, 24, 31, and February 10, 1846.
13. Burwell Diary, February 9, 16, 17, 1846.
14. Burwell Diary, April 28, 1855.
15. Robert Burwell to Thomas Webb, July 16, 1850, Orange County Deed Book, 33:486–487, County Clerk's Office, Hillsborough, North Carolina.
16. Martin, "Neighbor-to-Neighbor Capitalism."
17. Burwell Diary, February 13, March 1, April 9, 1855.
18. Anna Burwell to Fanny Burwell, November 27, 1855, Burwell Letters.
19. Anna Burwell to Fanny Burwell, December 10, 1855, Burwell Letters.
20. Burwell Diary, December 12, 13, 14, 1855.
21. "O. F. Long," 1860 U.S. Manuscript Census, South Side of the NC Railroad, Orange County, North Carolina, 549, Family History Library film no. 803908.
22. Burwell, *Record of the Burwell Family,* 16–17; Stowe, "Obstetrics," 550.
23. Schwartz, *Birthing a Slave,* 1–6.
24. Anna Burwell to Fanny Burwell, December 29, 1855, January 19, 1856; Burwell Diary, December 29, 1855.
25. Burwell Diary, October 13, 1868.
26. Morris and Eidenier, *Antebellum Hillsborough,* 14.
27. Burwell Diary, February 14, 1846.
28. Stampp, *Peculiar Institution,* 103–4.
29. Burwell Diary, February 26, 27, 28, March 1, 2, 3, 4, 27, 29, 30, 31, April 2, 5, 1855.
30. Mary Ann was also sick. Burwell Diary, April 30, May 1, 3, 4, 6, 1855.
31. Burwell Diary, June 25 and 26, 1855.
32. Burwell Diary, August 28, 1855.
33. Burwell Diary, October 7, 8, 10, 1855.
34. Burwell Diary, October 31, 1855.
35. Anna Burwell to Fanny Burwell, November 27, 1855, Burwell Letters.
36. Anna Burwell to Fanny Burwell, December 10, 1855, Burwell Letters. Eliza Chavois is listed in both the 1850 and 1860 U.S. Manuscript censuses.
37. If Hannah was on loan from the Virginia Burwells, Anna or Robert would also have written to them to convince them that this was the best course of action and to get permission to make the arrangements necessary.
38. Burwell Diary, December 11 and 12, 1855. James Bridges, a farmer, lived twelve miles from Richmond in Lee, Virginia. See 1850 U.S. Manuscript Census.
39. Anna Burwell to Fanny Burwell, December 29, 1855, Burwell Letters. See also Anna Burwell to Fanny Burwell, January 12, 1856.
40. Anna Burwell to Fanny Burwell, January 25, 1856. For a reference to Anna's satisfaction with Julia's work, see Burwell Diary, January 23, 1856.

41. Anna Burwell to Fanny Burwell, February 8, 1856.
42. Anna Burwell to Fanny Burwell, March 15, 1856.
43. Anna Burwell to Edmund Burwell, February 16, 1865, quoted in Silkenat, "In Good Hands," 57.
44. Reid, "Jesse Ruffin and Rebecca Norwood Ruffin," 29. The Orange County Deed Books record this transfer of property twice. Jesse, male age thirteen, Thomas Hunt to Thomas Ruffin, by sheriff and Deed Book 21, p. 53, December 2, 1823, and Jesse, male age thirteen, Thomas Hunt to Thomas Ruffin, by sheriff, Deed Book 21, p. 54, October 27, 1823, Orange County Clerk's Office, Hillsborough, North Carolina. Orange County NC Slave Records, February 20, 2018, http://ocncslaverecords.blogspot.com/2018/02/what-follows-is-index-by-name-of-over.html?m=1. Thomas Hunt had five enslaved workers in 1820. Thomas Hunt, 1820 U.S. Manuscript Census, Orange County, North Carolina, NARA roll M33_82, p. 332, image 188.
45. Robinson with Deased, "Ruffin, Thomas," NCpedia.
46. "Thomas Ruffin," 1810 U.S. Manuscript Census, Hillsborough, Orange County, North Carolina, roll 41, 932, image 00308, Family History Library film no. 0337914; "Thomas Ruffin," 1820 U.S. Manuscript Census, Orange County, North Carolina, NARA roll M33_82, p. 302, image 175.
47. Reid, "Jesse Ruffin and Rebecca Norwood Ruffin," 30.
48. Muller, "Judging Thomas Ruffin," 780.
49. Blassingame, *Slave Community*, 271–73, 276–77.
50. Archibald Murphey to Thomas Ruffin, June 3, 1824, Thomas Ruffin Papers, no. 641, box 11, folder 148, Southern Historical Collection, Wilson Library, University of North Carolina, Chapel Hill.
51. Fede, "Legitimized Violent Slave Abuse," 147.
52. Murphey to Ruffin, June 3, 1824.
53. Reid, "Jesse Ruffin and Rebecca Norwood Ruffin," 29; "Jesse and Becky Ruffin," married 1828, Orange County Marriage Records, in Barbara McGhee White, *Somebody Knows My Name*, 2:655.
54. O'Neil, "Bosses and Broomsticks," 33–34.
55. Rebecca J. Fraser, *Courtship and Love*, 89, 92, 95; Raboteau, *Slave Religion*, 228–29.
56. Muller, "Judging Thomas Ruffin," 785–91. For a more extensive discussion of slave trading, see Doyle, *Carry Me Back*; Joshua D. Rothman, *The Ledger and the Chain*.
57. William Hooper to Thomas Ruffin, July 11, 1838, Thomas Ruffin Papers, quoted in Muller, "Judging Thomas Ruffin," 794–95. No enslaved individual named November is listed in the Orange County slave records.
58. Jones, "Murphey, Archibald DeBow," NCpedia.
59. Reid, "Jesse Ruffin and Rebecca Norwood Ruffin," 29, 30.
60. For a reference to Jesse carrying a message and transporting a guest between the Kirklands at Ayr Mount and the Ruffins at the Hermitage, see Jean Bradley Anderson, *Kirklands of Ayr Mount*, 125. See also Camp, *Closer to Freedom*, 16, 28.
61. For a discussion of this issue and Thomas Ruffin's legal opinion regarding it, see Lichtenstein, "That Disposition to Theft," 432.

62. Bridget, female, age not given, Archibald D. Murphey to Thomas Ruffin, December 24, 1829, Orange County Deed Book 24, 157; Thomas Ruffin, 1830 U.S. Census, Slave Schedules, Orange, North Carolina, series M19, roll 123, 252, Family History Library film no. 0018089.
63. Thomas Ruffin to Archibald Murphey, October 29, 1831, box 17, folder 245, Ruffin Papers.
64. Ruffin to Murphey, October 29, 1831.
65. Weithoff, *Insolent Slave*, 1–9.
66. Sanders, "Cameron, Paul Carrington," NCpedia.
67. Reid, "Jesse Ruffin and Rebecca Norwood Ruffin," 29, 30.
68. Faucette, *Slave Narratives*, 304.
69. Engstrom, "Norwood, William," NCpedia; Engstrom, "Norwood, John Wall," NCpedia.
70. Faucette, *Slave Narratives*, 304.
71. Schwartz, "At Noon, Oh How I Run," 243, 245, 250.
72. Shaw, "Mothering Under Slavery," 250–53; King, "Suffer with Them till Death," 147, 152–59.
73. Faucette, *Slave Narratives*, 303.
74. "Robina (Rob) Norwood," in Engstrom, *Book of Burwell Students*, 165; Reid, "Jesse Ruffin and Rebecca Norwood Ruffin," 31; "Dinah," J. W. Norwood to Robina Webb, June 23, 1859, Orange County Deed Book 36, 136, Recorder of Deeds Office, Hillsborough, North Carolina.
75. "Beecy, Benenah, Jepe, Julia, and Willie," J. W. Norwood to Anna B. Hanks, December 25, 1862, Orange County Deed Book 37, 72.
76. Jean Bradley Anderson, *Piedmont Plantation*, 60–61, 115–16.
77. Faucette, *Slave Narratives*, 305.
78. Reid, "Jesse Ruffin and Rebecca Norwood Ruffin," 32.
79. Isaac Porter served as assistant sub-assistant commissioner of the Freedmen's Bureau in Hillsborough from May 1866 to September 1867. Records of the Field Offices for the State of North Carolina, Bureau of Refugees, Freedmen, and Abandoned Lands, 10.
80. The court clerk was required to maintain a record book for this purpose and to receive twenty-five cents per entry for his service. In section 6, chapter 40 of the act, it was a misdemeanor if "negroes" did not record their marriage by September 1866. "North Carolina Cohabitation Records," Family Search, last updated August 12, 2024, https://www.familysearch.org/wiki/en/North_Carolina_Cohabitation_Records.
81. Reid, "Jesse Ruffin and Rebecca Norwood Ruffin," 29; "Jesse and Becky Ruffin," in White, *Somebody Knows My Name*, 2:655. For the Camerons and the one Norwood couple, see White, *Somebody Knows My Name*, 644, 652.
82. McPherson, *Battle Cry of Freedom*, 841–42.
83. Litwack, *Been in the Storm So Long*, 399–408.
84. Paul Cameron to Thomas Ruffin, May 11, 1865, *Papers of Thomas Ruffin*, 3:451–52.
85. "Thomas Ruffin," 1860 U.S. Manuscript Census, Slave Schedules, Orange County, North Carolina.

86. John Norwood to Thomas Ruffin, August 6, 1865, *Papers of Thomas Ruffin*, 3:463.
87. Neither she nor Jesse is listed in the 1870 U.S. Manuscript Census, so it is unclear where they lived.
88. Jesse Ruffin to Thomas Ruffin, December 15, 1865, *Papers of Thomas Ruffin*, 4:48.
89. Long, *High Time to Tell It*, 124–25.
90. Reid, "Jesse Ruffin and Rebecca Norwood Ruffin," 32.
91. "William Faucette and Lindsay Faucette," 1870 U.S. Manuscript Census, Hillsborough, Orange County, North Carolina, roll M593_1153, 241A, Family History Library film no. 552652; "William Faucette," 1880 U.S. Manuscript Census, Hillsborough, Orange County, North Carolina, roll 975, 8C, Enumeration District 189; "Lindsay Faucette [Linsey Fossett]," 1900 U.S. Manuscript Census, Durham, Durham County, North Carolina, 24, Enumeration District 0026, Family History Library film no. 1241193; Faucette, *Slave Narratives*, 305; Reid, "Jesse Ruffin and Rebecca Norwood Ruffin," 29.
92. "Jesse Ruffin," 1880 U.S. Manuscript Census, Hillsborough, Orange County, North Carolina, roll 975, 8C, Enumeration District 189.
93. "Jesse Ruffin," 1900 U.S. Manuscript Census, Durham, Durham County, North Carolina, 25, Enumeration District 0031, Family History Library film no. 1241193.
94. Reid, "Jesse Ruffin and Rebecca Norwood Ruffin," 29.
95. My thanks to Betty Eidenier for sharing her research on Job Berry.
96. "Job Benny," 1870 U.S. Manuscript Census, Hillsborough, Orange, North Carolina, roll M593_1153, 253B, Family History Library film no. 552652; St. Matthew's Parish Records, Hillsborough, North Carolina.
97. Moore, "Burgwin [Burgwyn], Nathaniel Hill," NCpedia.
98. Graebner, "Remarks."
99. St. Matthew's Parish Records.
100. Reed, "Nash, Francis," NCpedia; Moore, "Burgwin, George William Bush," NCpedia.
101. Sarah (Sally) Moore is listed as living with the Francis Waddell family in the 1850 U.S. Manuscript Census, District 1, Orange County, North Carolina, roll 639, 205b. For the sale of Job, see F. N. Waddell to Stephen Moore, September 1, 1839, Orange County Deed Book 28, 426, and Stephen Moore to Hugh Waddell, July 23, 1841, Orange County Deed Book 30, 286, County Clerk's Office, Hillsborough, North Carolina; "From Old Job's Sermon," *Orange County Observer*, April 29, 1909, 5.
102. "Job Benny," 1870 U.S. Manuscript Census, Hillsborough, Orange County, North Carolina, roll M593_1153, 253B, Family History Library film no. 552652; "Richard Berry," 1900 U.S. Manuscript Census, Hillsboro, Orange County, North Carolina, 12, Enumeration District 0069, Family History Library film no. 1241210. Rebecca Nash is listed as Job's wife on her daughter Alice E. Berry's death certificate. North Carolina Death Certificates, North Carolina State Archives, Raleigh, North Carolina.
103. Dunaway, *Hillsborough, N.C.*, 137.
104. Burwell Diary, March 8, 1855.
105. Faucette, *Slave Narratives*, 303.
106. Raboteau, *Slave Religion*, 212–13.
107. Keckley, *Behind the Scenes*, 57, 60.

108. "Job Benny," *1870 U.S. Manuscript Census, 253B*.
109. "Notice," *Hillsborough Recorder*, September 20, 1865, 3.
110. James Anderson, *Education of Blacks*, 4–32.
111. Dunaway, *Hillsborough, N.C.*, 282–84, 519–21. In 1886 the Quakers conveyed the property to the trustees of the AME church for eight hundred dollars.
112. Murray, *Proud Shoes*, 71, 87, 130–31, 191–92.
113. W. Roulhac to "Arthur," January 26, 1867, quoted in Kenzer, *Kinship and Neighborhood*, 109.
114. Murray, *Proud Shoes*, 192–94; "Howard [Heywood] Beverly," 1870 U.S. Manuscript Census, Hillsborough, Orange County, North Carolina, *251B*. On the treatment of freedmen's school teachers, see Jacqueline Jones, *Soldiers of Light and Love*, 81–83; Morton, "Yankee Teacher." Robert Fitzgerald eventually married Cornelia Smith, Harriet and Sydney Smith's daughter. For a comment on the ostracism of white women who taught in Hillsborough's freedmen's school, see Long, *High Time to Tell It*, 81.
115. Dunaway, *Hillsborough, N.C.*, 125, 135.
116. *Minutes of the South Carolina Annual Conference of the African M. E. Church*, 13. My thanks to Brooks Graebner for this reference.
117. Hildebrand, *Times Were Strange and Stirring*, 12–13, 18, 31, 33, 46–48, 67, 77.
118. Lloyd and Lloyd, *History of the Churches of Hillsborough* (52) make this claim, but there is no reliable documentary evidence to substantiate it, and they incorrectly list the second and third pastors as Reverends Wilson and Jordan rather than Henry K. Polke and S. B. Williams.
119. "Letter from Bishop Wayman," *Christian Recorder*, November 14, 1868.
120. S. B. Williams to Governor William W. Holden, September 16, 1869, William Holden Papers, North Carolina Division of Archives and History, Raleigh, North Carolina, reproduced at https://ldhi.library.cofc.edu/exhibits/show/after_slavery_educator/unit_nine_documents/a—m—e—pastor-s—b—williams.
121. S. B. Williams is not listed in the 1870 census for Orange County.
122. "Orange County," *Carolina Era* (Raleigh, NC), April 11, 1872, 3.
123. "De B. Waddell [De Bernier Waddell]," 1910 U.S. Manuscript Census, Meridian, Ward 2, Lauderdale County, Mississippi, roll T624_746, 2A, Enumeration District 0042; Family History Library film no. 1374759.
124. "From Old Job's Sermon," *Orange County Observer*, April 29, 1909, 5.
125. Reference to these ceremonies can be found in Betty Eidenier, "Rev. Job Berry's Legacy Rooted in Faith, Marriage, Education," *News of Orange*, March 25, 2022. The list was compiled by Mark Chilton, register of deeds, Orange County, North Carolina. The records can be found in Orange County Marriage Books, Register of Deeds Office, Hillsborough, North Carolina.
126. "Susan Berry," August 24, 1887, North Carolina Marriage Index, 1741–2011.

CHAPTER 5

1. Alexander Kirkland to Catherine Ruffin, January 10, 1831, box 1, folder 13, Ruffin-Roulhac-Hamilton Papers, no. 643, Southern Historical Collection.

2. Blackwelder, *Age of Orange*, 96.
3. On the treatment of the insane in the South, see Hughes, "Madness of Separate Spheres"; Thielman, "Southern Madness"; McCandless, *Moonlight, Magnolias, and Madness*.
4. North Carolina Hospital for the Insane, Admissions Ledger, vol. 1: 1856–1911, North Carolina Department of Natural and Cultural Resources, Division of Archives and Records, Raleigh, North Carolina. These records can be accessed through the Odum Institute for Research in the Social Sciences, Davis Library, University of North Carolina--Chapel Hill. My thanks to Robert Allen at the University of North Carolina for access to this information.
5. Hughes, "Madness of Separate Spheres," 56.
6. Duncan Cameron of Stagville and Hillsborough also began suffering from bouts of depression beginning in the 1820s. Anderson, *Piedmont Plantation*, 46–47; Jean Bradley Anderson, *Kirklands of Ayr Mount*, 122–24; Nathans, *To Free a Family*, 18–20, 27; Sanders, "Cameron, Duncan," NCpedia.
7. On addiction, see Kandall, *Substance and Shadow*; Courtwright, "Female Opiate Addict"; Courtwright, "Hidden Epidemic"; Hickman, "Mania Americana"; Aurin, "Chasing the Dragon."
8. Those in the field of disability studies have pointed out that the belief in women's predisposition to mental impairment effectively reinforced the patriarchal structure of society while it bolstered doctors' authority to identify, diagnose, and treat mental illness. See Kudlick, "Disability History"; Neilson, "Historical Thinking and Disability History."
9. Quotation in Smith-Rosenberg, "Puberty to Menopause," 183. For a discussion of this attitude, see Ann Douglas Wood, "Fashionable Diseases"; Smith-Rosenberg, "Hysterical Woman"; Smith-Rosenberg and Rosenberg, "Female Animal"; Welter, "Female Complaints."
10. Hoffert, *Private Matters*, 112–16; McMillen, *Motherhood in the Old South*, 92–93.
11. Smith-Rosenberg, "Puberty to Menopause," 188–92.
12. Discussion of and quotations concerning Phebe's case can be found in Jean Bradley Anderson, *Kirklands of Ayr Mount*, 68–71, 85–88.
13. Nelson sent Maggie to live at Ayr Mount with her relatives after her mother's death. She grew up in Hillsborough and attended the Burwell School and then the Charlotte Female Academy when the Burwells moved there in 1857. Having lost her inheritance, which had been invested in Confederate bonds, Maggie McLester worked at the Nash-Kollock School and as a housekeeper for a number of Hillsborough families after the Civil War. She died on August 1, 1921, at the age of seventy-nine and is buried at Ayr Mount. Engstrom, *Book of Burwell Students*, 135–36.
14. "Hugh Lenox Hodge, 1796–1873," Penn Libraries University Archives and Records Center, https://archives.upenn.edu/exhibits/penn-people/biography/hugh-lenox-hodge; Thoms, "Hugh Lenox Hodge."
15. David J. Rothman, *Discovery of the Asylum*; Dwyer, *Homes for the Mad*; Tomes, *Generous Confidence*; Grob, *The State and the Mentally Ill*; McCulloch, "Founding the North Carolina Asylum"; O'Rorke, *Haven on a Hill*; Zwelling, *Quest for a Cure*; Dain,

Disordered Minds; Alice Davis Wood, *Dr. Francis Stribling;* Goodheart, *Mad Yankees;* McCandless, *Moonlight, Magnolias, and Madness;* Gonaver, *Peculiar Institution.*

16. Unless otherwise noted, information about Mary and her family comes from Engstrom, *Book of Burwell Students,* 231–32, and Engstrom, "Witherspoon, John Knox," NCpedia.
17. John Witherspoon to Susan K. McDowall, July 9, 1846, box 1, folder 9, Witherspoon-McDowall Papers, no. 799, Southern Historical Collection.
18. Mary Witherspoon and Susan Witherspoon to Susan McDowall, August 6, [1846], box 1, folder 9, Witherspoon-McDowall Papers.
19. Susan Witherspoon to Susan McDowall, [September 21, 1846], box 1, folder 9, Witherspoon-McDowall Papers. It is not clear which asylum they had in mind. The North Carolina Hospital for the Insane did not open until 1856 in Raleigh. "Samuel Jackson, 1787–1872," Penn Libraries University Archives and Records Center, https://archives.upenn.edu/exhibits/penn-people/biography/samuel-jackson.
20. Elizabeth M. Rice to Susan McDowall, October 7, 1846, box 1, folder 9, Witherspoon-McDowall Papers.
21. Susan Witherspoon to Susan McDowall, November [1846], box 1, folder 9, Witherspoon-McDowall Papers.
22. Susan Witherspoon to Susan McDowall, April 2, 1847, box 1, folder 10, Witherspoon-McDowall Papers.
23. Susan Witherspoon to Susan McDowall, [May 12] and May 31, [1847], box 1, folder 10, Witherspoon-McDowall Papers.
24. Mary and Susan Witherspoon to Susan McDowall, June 15, 1847, and June 1847, box 1, folder 10, Witherspoon-McDowall Papers, quotations in both letters.
25. Susan Witherspoon to Susan McDowall, [July 8] and [July 17, 1847], Mary and Susan Witherspoon to Susan McDowall, August 22, 1847, box 1, folder 10, Witherspoon-McDowall Papers.
26. John Witherspoon and Susan Witherspoon to Susan McDowall, July 7, 1850, box 1, folder 11, Witherspoon-McDowall Papers.
27. Susan Witherspoon to Susan McDowall, February, April, July 1852, and John Witherspoon to Susan McDowall, December 1 and 14, 1852, box 1, folder 11, John Witherspoon to Susan McDowall, January 27, [1853], box 1, folder 12, Witherspoon-McDowall Papers.
28. John and Susan Witherspoon to Susan McDowall, August 19 [1853], box 1, folder 12, Witherspoon-McDowall Papers.
29. John and Susan Witherspoon to Susan McDowall, August 19, [1853], box 1, folder 12, and Susan McDowall to her son, August 25, [no year], box 1, folder 13, Witherspoon-McDowall Papers.
30. M. G. Nash to Susan McDowall, April 5, 1854, box 1, folder 12, Witherspoon-McDowall Papers; Engstrom, "Witherspoon, John Knox," NCpedia. M. G. Nash's relationship to the Witherspoon-McDowalls is unclear. Engstrom claims that after Susan Witherspoon's death, two of Mary's aunts tried to have her committed. Engstrom, "Mary Nash Witherspoon," *Book of Burwell Students,* 232. I could find no evidence to support this contention.

31. They married on November 24, 1857. "Mary Witherspoon," North Carolina, *Index to Marriage Bonds*.
32. "Mary Bowers," 1860 U.S. Manuscript Census, Chapel Hill, Orange County, North Carolina, 526, Family History Library film no. 803908; "Green W. Bowers," Civil War Soldier Records and Profiles, 1861–1865; "Mary N. Bowers," 1870 U.S. Manuscript Census, Chapel Hill, Orange County, North Carolina, roll M593_1153, 166A, Family History Library film no. 552652; "Mary Bowers," 1900 U.S. Manuscript Census, Hickory Mountain, Chatham County, North Carolina, 13, Enumeration District 0010, Family History Library film no. 1241188; U.S. Southern Claims Commission, Disallowed and Barred Claims, 1871–1880, National Archives, Washington, D.C.
33. Jean Bradley Anderson, *Piedmont Plantation*, chart 1; Anne Cameron to [Francis T. Stribling], [1846], box 25, Superintendent's Correspondence Files, 1825–1942, Western Lunatic Asylum Collection; Anna M. Kirkland to [Duncan Cameron], [June 23,] 1846, box 42, folder 987, and Anna M. Kirkland to [Margaret Cameron], April 14–15, 1850, box 45, folder 1075, Cameron Family Papers, no. 133, Southern Historical Collection.
34. Anne Cameron to [Francis T. Stribling], [1846]; Peterson, "Brain Fever," 447–50.
35. Jean Bradley Anderson, *Kirklands of Ayr Mount*, 56–59, 93–96; Anne Cameron to [Francis T. Stribling], [1846]; Margaret Cameron to sister, February 4, [1835], box 77, folder 1835, and Anne Owen Cameron to [Duncan Cameron], March 4, 1835, box 34, folder 746, Cameron Family Papers.
36. Catherine Ruffin to [Anne K. Ruffin], March 24, 1836, box 2, folder 23, Ruffin-Roulhac-Hamilton Papers.
37. Jean Bradley Anderson, *Kirklands of Ayr Mount*, "The Kirklands of Ayr Mount" genealogy, end page.
38. Anne Cameron to [Francis T. Stribling], [1846].
39. Catherine Ruffin Rouhlac to Joseph Rouhlac, September 30, 1839, box 3, folder 30, Ruffin-Roulhac-Hamilton Papers.
40. Anna M. Kirkland to [Duncan Cameron], [June 23], 1846, box 42, folder 987, Cameron Family Papers.
41. Anna M. Kirkland to [Duncan Cameron], [June 23], 1846. For another example of a woman institutionalized for obsessing over religious matters, see Tomes, "Devils in the Heart."
42. Anna M. Kirkland to [Duncan Cameron], [June 23], 1846, and Anne Cameron to [Duncan Cameron], n.d. [December 1845 or January 1846], box 74, folder 1764, Cameron Family Papers.
43. Anne Cameron to [Duncan Cameron], January 8, [1846?], box 74, folder 1763, and Anne Cameron to Duncan Cameron, January 22, [1846?], box 74, folder 1762, Cameron Family Papers.
44. Anne Owen Cameron to [Duncan Cameron], December 28, 1845, box 42, folder 975, Cameron Family Papers.
45. Anna Burwell to Mary A. Kirkland, January 17, 1846, Burwell Letters.
46. Jean Bradley Anderson, *Kirklands of Ayr Mount*, 102.
47. [Thomas Ruffin] to Anne [K. Ruffin], January 21, 1846, box 22, folder 329, Thomas

Ruffin Papers no. 641, Southern Historical Collection; Anne Cameron to [Francis T. Stribling], [1846].
48. Anna M. Kirkland to Margaret Mordecai, n.d., box 9, folder 133, Mordecai Family Papers, Southern Historical Collection.
49. "Historical Information," *Guide to the Records of Western State Hospital, 1825 –2000,* Library of Virginia, Richmond, http://ead.lib.virginia.edu/vivaxtf/view?docId=lva/vi00937.xml; Thielman, "Southern Madness," 272.
50. Alice Davis Wood, *Dr. Francis Stribling,* 15–26.
51. Gonaver, *Peculiar Institution,* 82–86.
52. "Anna Kirkland," Admission Ledger, 1828–1941, Western Lunatic Asylum Collection; J[ean].M. Syme to [Duncan Cameron], February 7, 1846, box 42, folder 978, Cameron Family Papers.
53. Alice Davis Wood, *Dr. Francis Stribling,* 124; "Anna Kirkland," Western State Hospital Casebook I, 273:272, 294, Western Lunatic Asylum, Record Group 38.
54. Francis T. Stribling to [William Cameron or John Cameron], February 18, 1846, box 42, folder 979, Cameron Family Papers.
55. Anna M. Kirkland to [Duncan Cameron], [June 23], 1846, box 42, folder 987, Cameron Family Papers.
56. Francis T. Stribling to Anne Cameron, October 13, 1846, box 42, folder 994, Cameron Family Papers.
57. "Anna Kirkland," Admission Ledger, 1828–1941, Western Asylum Papers.
58. Anne Cameron to [Duncan Cameron], January 1, 1847, box 43, folder 1000, Cameron Family Papers.
59. Anna M. Kirkland to [Francis Stribling], February 9, 1847, box 25, Superintendent's Correspondence Files.
60. Anne's property was held in trust. See Duncan Cameron to Alexander Kirkland and William Cameron, December 12, 1837, Deed Book 28, 148–50, and Anne Cameron to William Edmunds, May 6, 1844, Deed Book 30, 359–60, Orange County Clerk's Office, Hillsborough, North Carolina.
61. Anna M. Kirkland to [Duncan Cameron], April 20, 1847, box 43, folder 1007, Cameron Family Papers; Anna M. Kirkland et al. to William Edmunds, August 11, 1847, Deed Book 33, 336–37, and Anne Cameron to Anna Kirkland, August 11, 1847, Deed Book 32, 443–44, Orange County Clerk's Office.
62. Anna M. Kirkland to [Duncan Cameron], October 25, 1847, box 43, folder 1019, December 15, 1847, box 43, folder 1022, and July 6, 1848, box 44, folder 1036, Cameron Family Papers; "Female School," *Hillsborough Recorder,* January 27–March 8, 1848.
63. Anna M. Kirkland to Duncan Cameron, July 6, 1848, box 44, folder 1036, August 15, 1848, box 44, folder 1038, Cameron Family Papers, quotation from August 15 letter.
64. Anne Cameron to [Duncan Cameron], December 25, [1849], box 74, folder 1764, Cameron Family Papers.
65. William Cameron to [Francis T. Stribling], February 3, 1850, box 25, Superintendent's Correspondence Files; Francis T. Stribling to Duncan Cameron, February 2, 1850, box 45, folder 1073, Cameron Family Papers; William Cameron to [Francis T. Stribling], March 7, 1850, box 25, Superintendent's Correspondence Files.

66. William Cameron to [Francis T. Stribling], March 7, 1850.
67. Anna M. Kirkland to Margaret Cameron, April 14–15, 1850, box 45, folder 1075, Cameron Family Papers; "Anna Kirkland," Admission Ledger, 1828–1941, Western Insane Asylum.
68. "Anna Kirkland," Western State Hospital Casebook II, 274:172, 216, Western Insane Asylum, Record Group 38.
69. Engstrom, "Norwood, John Wall," NCpedia; Engstrom, *Book of Burwell Students*, 157; Robina Norwood to Tom Tillinghast, February 2, 1846, box 2, folder: Correspondence, 1846–47, Tillinghast Family Papers.
70. William Tillinghast and Grandma Robina Norwood to Jane Tillinghast, October 10, 1841, box 2, folder: Correspondence, 1841–42, Tillinghast Family Papers.
71. Robina Norwood to Samuel Tillinghast, May 23, 1846, box 2, folder: Correspondence, 1846–47, Tillinghast Family Papers.
72. Bell Norwood to Cousin [William Tillinghast], January 18, 1847, box 2, folder: Correspondence, 1846–47, Tillinghast Family Papers.
73. Mary Witherspoon and Susan Waddell were both seeking treatment from Hodge in Philadelphia in the summer of 1847. Susan Witherspoon to Susan McDowall, [July 17, 1847], box 1, folder 10, Witherspoon-McDowall Papers. In 1844 Mildred Cameron developed symptoms similar to those of Mary Witherspoon. She too sought treatment in Philadelphia under the direction of Hugh Hodge in the late 1840s. Nathans, *To Free a Family*, 23, 25–27, 41, 95, 97, 161; Anna M. Kirkland to [Margaret Cameron] in care of Dr. Hodge of Philadelphia, April 14–15, 1850, box 45, folder 1075, Cameron Family Papers, no. 133, Southern Historical Collection.
74. Bell Norwood to Cousin [William Tillinghast], August 12, 1847, box 2, folder: Correspondence, 1846–47, Tillinghast Family Papers.
75. Bell Norwood to Cousin [William Tillinghast], October 30, 1847, box 2, folder: Correspondence, 1846–47, Tillinghast Family Papers.
76. Bell Norwood to Cousin [William Tillinghast], December 12, 1848, box 3, folder: Correspondence, 1848–50, Tillinghast Family Papers.
77. Bell Norwood to Cousin [William Tillinghast], May 18, 1849, box 3, folder: Correspondence, 1848–50, Tillinghast Family Papers.
78. Bell Norwood to Cousin [William Tillinghast], July 25, 1849, box 3, folder: Correspondence, 1848–50, Tillinghast Family Papers.
79. "Anna Kirkland" and "Annabella Norwood," Admissions Ledger, 1828–1941, Western Lunatic Asylum Collection.
80. Robina Norwood Bingham to Cousin, March 3, 1852, box 3, folder: Correspondence, 1852, Tillinghast Family Papers. Engstrom, *Book of Burwell Students*, 157.
81. Anne Cameron to Margaret [Mordecai], November 30, 1854, box 48, folder 1135, Cameron Family Papers.
82. Anna M. Kirkland to unknown, November 18, 1855, box 48, folder 1148; M[ary]. M[cLean]. L. Bryant to Margaret Mordecai, December 21, 1855, box 48, folder 1149; and George Mordecai to Margaret Mordecai, February 12, 1856, box 49, folder 1153, Cameron Family Papers.
83. Anna M. Kirkland by guardian, O[smund]. F. Long to C. M. Latimer and Israel Turner,

February 7, 1859, Deed Book 36, 205, Orange County Clerk's Office. Anna's mother died in June 1856. Genealogy, end page, Jean Bradley Anderson, *Piedmont Plantation*; "Valuable Property for Sale," *Semi-Weekly Standard*, June 21, 1856, 3; *Hillsborough Recorder*, July 16, 1856, 3; *Weekly Raleigh Register*, August 6, 1856, 4; *Weekly Standard*, July 2, 1856.

84. O'Rorke, *Haven on the Hill*, xi, 4, 5–7. For reference to grated windows, see M[ary]. M[cLean]. L. Bryant to Margaret Mordecai, December 21, 1855.
85. Francis T. Stribling to Duncan Cameron, February 2, 1850, box 45, folder 1073, Cameron Family Papers.
86. George Mordecai to Margaret Mordecai, March 2, 1856, box 49, folder 1156, Cameron Family Papers.
87. Anna M. Kirkland to [Margaret Mordecai], August 19, 1857, box 6, folder 86, and Anna M. Kirkland to George Mordecai, December 29, 1858, box 6, folder 86, Mordecai Family Papers, no. 847, Southern Historical Collection; Anna M. Kirkland to Susan Webb, December 18, 1860, box 1, folder 8, Webb Family Papers no. 1900, Southern Historical Collection.
88. Anna M. Kirkland to Eliza C. Edmunds, September 14, 1859, box 1, folder 10, Edmunds Family Papers, MSS443, Manuscript and Folklore Archives, Western Kentucky University, Bowling Green, Kentucky.
89. Anna M. Kirkland to Eliza C. Edmunds, March 16, 1859, box 1, folder 10, Edmunds Family Papers.
90. O'Rorke, *Haven on a Hill*, 25; quotations in Nan Smith to Mattie [Herring], November 22, 1889, and December 11, box 1, folder 2, Herring Family Papers, no. 478, Southern Historical Collection.
91. Anna M. Kirkland to Eliza C. Edmunds, August 3 and September 14, 1859, box 1, folder 10, Edmunds Family Papers.
92. Anna M. Kirkland to Eliza C. Edmunds, March 13, 1872, box 1, folder 12, Edmunds Family Papers.
93. Anna M. Kirkland to Mary Read Edmunds, July 18, 1861, box 1, folder 9, Edmunds Family Papers.
94. Reiss, *Theaters of Madness*, 13–14, quotation on 13; Dwyer, *Homes for the Mad*, 26; McCandless, *Moonlight, Magnolias, and Madness*, 108–10.
95. Miron, *Prisons, Asylums, and the Public*, 5–7, 34–55, 68, 119, 136.
96. Long, *High Time to Tell It*, 5, quotation on 205.
97. Paul Cameron to Pauline Cameron, February 12, 1890, box 73, folder 1717, Cameron Family Papers; "Anna Kirkland Obituary," *Orange County Observer* (Hillsborough, NC), February 15, 1890, 4.
98. O'Rorke, *Haven on a Hill*, 16. In 1880 the state opened an insane asylum in Goldsboro to serve the African American community. Anthony and Homrighaus, "Psychiatric Hospitals," NCpedia. For a more complete discussion of the experiences of people of color in insane asylums such as the Eastern Lunatic Asylum in Williamsburg, Virginia, and the connection between race and the treatment of the insane, see Gonaver, *Peculiar Institution*.
99. Hoffert, *"Grief of a Mind Giving Way,"* 37.

CONCLUSION

1. Jean Bradley Anderson, *Kirklands of Ayr Mount*, 53.
2. "African Candor," *Weekly Standard* (Raleigh, NC), November 5, 1845, 1; reprinted in the *Biblical Reporter* (Raleigh, NC), November 29, 1845, 4.
3. Quotation in Connor, *History of North Carolina*, vol. 1: *The Colonial and Revolutionary Periods*, 179. For a more detailed description of those who settled the southern backcountry, see Tillson, "Southern Backcountry."
4. For a brief discussion of standards of behavior in late eighteenth-century America, see Kasson, *Rudeness and Civility*, 13–18.
5. The best discussions of these adjustments in gender expectations are found in Faust, *Mothers of Invention*, and Edwards, *Gendered Strife and Confusion*, 107–44.
6. For a description of Hillsborough in the 1870s, see William Henry Bailey, "A Visit to the Athens of North Carolina," box 2, folder 29, John Lancaster Bailey Papers, Southern Historical Collection.
7. John Norwood to Thomas Ruffin, August 6, 1865, *Papers of Thomas Ruffin*, 3:463.
8. Kenzer, *Kinship and Neighborhood*, 114–26.
9. Page, "Study of an Old Southern Borough," 652.
10. Davis, *Folklore Study of West Hillsborough*, 1–2. For a general discussion of this transition, see Hall et al., *Like a Family*.

BIBLIOGRAPHY

Government Documents
Hillsborough Board of Commissioners Minute Book, 1843–1854, Town Clerk's Office, Hillsborough, N.C.
An Index to Marriage Bonds Filed in the North Carolina Archives. North Carolina Division of Archives and History, 1977.
London, England, Church of England Baptisms, Marriages and Burials, 1538–1812 (database on Ancestry.com).
Minutes of the Superior Court of North Carolina, North Carolina State Archives, Raleigh.
North Carolina Death Certificates, North Carolina State Archives, Raleigh.
North Carolina Marriage Index, 1741–2011 (database on Ancestry.com).
Ohio, Soldier Grave Registrations, 1804–1958 (database on Ancestry.com).
Orange County Apprenticeship Bonds, Orange County Court of Pleas and Quarter Session, Minute Books, North Carolina State Archives, Raleigh.
Orange County Court of Pleas and Quarter Session Minute Books, North Carolina State Archives, Raleigh.
Orange County Criminal Action Records, North Carolina State Archives, Raleigh.
Orange County Deed Books, Orange County Register of Deeds Office, Hillsborough, N.C.
Orange County Marriage Books, Orange County Register of Deeds Office, Hillsborough, N.C.
Orange County Will Books, North Carolina State Archives, Raleigh.
Records of the Field Offices for the State of North Carolina, Bureau of Refugees, Freedmen, and Abandoned Lands, 1865–1972, M1909, National Archives and Records Administration, 2004.
State v. Mann, 13 NC263 (1829).
U.S. Civil War Soldier Records and Profiles, 1861–1865 (database on Ancestry.com).
U.S. Manuscript Census for 1800–1900 (database on Ancestry.com).
U.S. Manuscript Census—Slave Schedules, 1830, 1850, 1860 (database on Ancestry.com).
U.S. Southern Claims Commission, Disallowed and Barred Claims, 1871–1880, National Archives, Washington, D.C. (database on Ancestry.com).

Church Records
Hillsborough Presbyterian Church Session Records, Hillsborough, N.C.
Minutes of the South Carolina Annual Conference of the African M. E. Church for 1865, 66, and 67. Record Printing House, 1867.
St. Matthew's Parish Records, St. Matthew's Episcopal Church, Hillsborough, N.C.

Archival Materials
Alamance Community College, Graham, North Carolina
Scott Family Collection

Burwell School Archives, Hillsborough, North Carolina
Burwell, John Bott. "Record of the Descendants of the Rev. Robert Burwell, D. D. and Margaret Anna Robertson, Married December 22nd, 1831," typescript.
Burwell, Margaret Anna. Letters.
Burwell, Margaret Anna. Diaries, multiple volumes.
Murphy Family Letters.
Strum, Nan Doub. "The Misses Nash and Miss Kollock Select Boarding and Day School for Young Ladies," typescript.

Library of Virginia, Richmond
Western Lunatic Asylum in Staunton, Virginia, record group 38, accession no. 41253, Records of the Western State Hospital, 1825–2000.
Admission Registers, 1828–1941
Western State Hospital Casebook I, vol. 273 and Casebook II, vol. 274.

Manuscript and Folklore Archives, Library Special Collections, Western Kentucky University, Bowling Green
Edmunds Family Papers

North Carolina Division of Archives and History, Raleigh
William Holden Papers
North Carolina Hospital for the Insane, Admissions Ledgers [available through the Odum Institute for Research in the Social Sciences, Davis Library, University of North Carolina, Chapel Hill.]

David M. Rubenstein Rare Book and Manuscript Library, Duke Library, Durham, North Carolina
Tillinghast Family Papers

Southern Historical Collection, Louis Round Wilson Special Collections Library, University of North Carolina at Chapel Hill
John Lancaster Bailey Papers
Cameron Family Papers
Moses Ashley Curtis Papers
Herring Family Papers
Charles B. Mallett Papers
Mordecai Family Papers
Pettigrew Family Papers
Thomas Ruffin Papers
Ruffin-Roulhac-Hamilton Papers
Mary Ruffin Smith Papers
Webb Family Papers
Eliza Mary Bond Weissinger Papers
Witherspoon and McDowall Family Papers

Western Lunatic Asylum Collection, Ms2016-021, Special Collections and University Archives, Virginia Tech University, Blacksburg
Superintendent's Correspondence Files, 1825–1942

Periodicals
Biblical Reporter
Carolina Era
Carolina Observer and Fayetteville Gazette
Christian Recorder
Church Messenger
Cleveland Daily Herald
Daily Journal
Hillsborough Recorder
News of Orange
North Carolina Democrat
North Carolina Standard
Oberlin News
Oberlin Weekly News
Orange County Observer
Raleigh Register
Raleigh Sentinel
State Chronicle
Weekly Standard
Semi-Weekly Standard
Weekly Raleigh Register

NCpedia
[Electronic version of William S. Powell, ed. *Dictionary of North Carolina Biography*, 6 vols. University of North Carolina Press, 1979–1996.]
Anderson, Jean B. "Bingham School." 2006. https://www.ncpedia.org/bingham-school.
———. "Hillsborough Academy." 2006. https://www.ncpedia.org/biography/hillsborough-academy.
———. "Smith, James Strudwick." 1994. https://www.ncpedia.org/biography/smith-james-strudwick.
———. "Strudwick, Edmund Charles." 1994. https://www.ncpedia.org/biography/strudwick-edmund-charles.
———. "Warrenton Female Academy." 2006. https://www.ncpedia.org/warrenton-female-academy.
Anthony, Robert G., Jr., and Ruth Homrighaus. "Psychiatric Hospitals." 2006. https://www.ncpedia.org/psychiatric-hospitals.
Bass, Anna Jeanette. "Robertson, Lucy Henderson Owen." 1994. https://www.ncpedia.org/biography/robertson-lucy-henderson.
Cooper, John M. "Page, Walter Hines." 1994. https://www.ncpedia.org/biography/page-walter-hines.
Davis, R. P. Stephen, Jr. "Great Trading Path." 2006. https://www.ncpedia.org/great-trading-path.
———. "Occaneechi Indians." 2006. https://www.ncpedia.org/occaneechi-indians.
Engstrom, Mary Claire. "Burwell, Robert Armistead." 1979. https://ncpedia.org/biography/burwell-robert-armistead.
———. "Nash, Sally (Sarah) Jane and Maria Jane Nash." n.d. https://www.ncpedia.org/biography/nash-sarah-maria.

———. "Norwood, John Wall." 1991. https://www.ncpedia.org/biography/norwood-john-wall.
———. "Norwood, William." 1991. https://www.ncpedia.org/biography/norwood-william.
———. "Webb, James." 1996. https://www.ncpedia.org/biography/webb-james.
———. "Witherspoon, John Knox." 1996. https://www.ncpedia.org/biography/witherspoon-john-knox.
Hodgson, Matthew. "Webb, William Robert (Sawney)." 1996. https://www.ncpedia.org/biography/webb-william-robert.
Howard, Joshua. "Tar Heels at Harper's Ferry, October 16–18, 1859: Lewis S. Leary." 2011. https://www.ncpedia.org/leary-lewis-s.
Jones, H. G. "Murphey, Archibald DeBow." 1991. https://www.ncpedia.org/biography/murphey-archibald-debow.
Moore, James Elliott. "Burgwin, George William Bush." 1979. https://www.ncpedia.org/biography/burgwin-george-william.
———. "Burgwin [Burgwyn], Nathaniel Hill." 1979. https://www.ncpedia.org/biography/burgwin-nathaniel-hill.
Powell, William S. "Tillinghast, John Huske." 1996. https://www.ncpedia.org/biography/tillinghast-john-huske.
Reed, John F. "Nash, Francis." 1991. https://www.ncpedia.org/biography/nash-francis.
Robinson, Blackwell P. "Ruffin, Thomas." 1994, revised by Jared Deased in 2023. https://www.ncpedia.org/biography/ruffin-thomas.
Sanders, Charles Richard. "Cameron, Duncan." 1979. https://www.ncpedia.org/biography/cameron-duncan.
Steelman, Bennett L. "Bingham, William." 1979. https://ncpedia.org/biography/bingham-william.
———. "Bingham, William James." 1979. https://www.ncpedia.org/biography/bingham-william-james.

Other Internet Sources

Acts Passed by the General Assembly of North Carolina at Its Session on the 25th of December 1826 (Raleigh: Lawrence and Lemay, 1827). https://digital.ncdcr.gov/digital/collection/p249901coll22/id/161280.
Arendell, F. B. "Bingham School: 1793–1897" (N.P.: n.p., [1897], North Carolina Collection, Louis Round Wilson Special Collections Library. https://archive.org/details/binghamschool17900aren/page/8.
Burwell School Student Profiles. https://www.burwellschool.org/research/pCategory.php?id=2
City of Oberlin. https://www.cityofoberlin.com/for-visitors/history-of-oberlin/.
Fecher, Rebecca Taft. "The Trading Path and North Carolina," *Journal of Backcountry Studies*, (2008). https://libjournal.uncg.edu/index.php/jbc/article/viewFile/26/15.
Heinegg, Paul. "Free African Americans of North Carolina, Virginia, and South Carolina from the Colonial Period to about 1820." https://freeafricanamericans.com/.
Henrikson, Ronald and Nancy Henrikson, "History of the Hiram A. Pease Property, Including 46785 West Hamilton Street, the Home of John A. and Delilah E. Copeland, Lorain County, Ohio," Copeland—Oberlin College. https://www2.oberlin.edu/external/EOG/Copeland/Copelandmain.htm.
Henry Evans dining table, Museum of Early Southern Decorative Arts, Winston-Salem, North Carolina. https://mesda.org/item/object/table-dining/5012/.

"Historical Information," *Guide to the Records of Western State Hospital*, 1825–2000, Library of Virginia, Richmond, Virginia. http://ead.lib.virginia.edu/vivaxtf /view?docId=lva/vi00937.xml

"Hugh Lenox Hodge, 1796–1873." https://archives.upenn.edu/exhibits/penn-people /biography/hugh-lenox-hodge.

Inflation calculator. https://westegg.com/inflation/infl.cgi?money=11500&first=1854&final=2022.

Margaret Lane Cemetery. https://assets.hillsboroughnc.gov/media/documents/public /margaret-lane-cemetery-brochure.pdf

James Mayho v. William H. Whitsman and Abner Peace, May, 1854, and *James Mayo v. Wm. H. Whitson and Abner Pearce*, 47 N. C. 231 (N.C. 1855). https://casetext.com /case/mayo-v-whitson.

Neilson, Kim E. "Historical Thinking and Disability History," *Disability Studies Quarterly* 28, no. 3 (Summer 2008). https://dsq-sds.org/index.php/dsq/article/view/107/107.

North Carolina Cohabitation Records. https://www.familysearch.org/wiki/en /North_Carolina_Cohabitation_Records

Queen's University of Charlotte, NC. www.queens.edu/about/history.html

Records of those Enslaved in Orange County, NC. http://ocncslaverecords.blogspot .com/2018/02/what-follows-is-index-by-name-of-over.html?m=1

"Samuel Jackson, 1787–1872." https://archives.upenn.edu/exhibits/penn-people /biography/samuel-jackson

"Susan A. Webb." https://www.burwellschool.org/research/pPerson.php?id=678

Westwood Cemetery, Oberlin, Ohio. https://www.oberlinwestwood.org/omeka/items /show/52259

U. S. Southern Claims Commission, Disallowed and Barred Claims, 1871–1880, National Archives, Washington. DC. https://www.ancestry.com/imageviewer/collections/1218 /images/rhusa1871_102831__0003-00125?treeid=&personid=&rc=&usePUB=true& _phsrc=kqK1468&_phstart=successSource&pId=121387

Secondary and Printed Primary Sources

Allmendinger, David F., Jr. "The Dangers of Antebellum Student Life." *Journal of Social History* 7, no. 1 (1973): 75–85.

———. *Paupers and Scholars: The Transformation of Student Life in Nineteenth-Century New England*. St. Martin's Press, 1975.

Anderson, James. *The Education of Blacks in the South, 1860–1935*. University of North Carolina Press, 1988.

Anderson, Jean Bradley. *The Kirklands of Ayr Mount*. University of North Carolina Press, 1991.

———. *Piedmont Plantation: The Bennehan-Cameron Family and Lands in North Carolina*. Historic Preservation Society of Durham, 1985.

Andrew, Rod, Jr. *Long Gray Lines: The Southern Military School Tradition, 1839–1915*. University of North Carolina Press, 2001.

Andrews, William L. *Slavery and Class in the American South: A Generation of Slave Narrative Testimony, 1840–1865*. Oxford University Press, 2019.

Aurin, Marcus. "Chasing the Dragon: The Cultural Metamorphosis of Opium in the United States, 1825–1935." *Medical Anthropology Quarterly* 14, no. 3 (2000): 414–41.

Ayers, Edward L. *Vengeance and Justice: Crime and Punishment in the 19th Century American South*. Oxford University Press, 1984.

Balleisen, Edward J. *Navigating Failure: Bankruptcy and Commercial Society in Antebellum America*. University of North Carolina Press, 2001.
Baptist, Edward E. "'Cuffy,' 'Fancy Maids,' and the 'One-Eyed Man': Rape, Commodification, and the Domestic Slave Trade in the United States." *American Historical Review* 106, no. 5 (2001): 1619–50.
Barringer, Paul B. *The Natural Bent: The Memoirs of Dr. Paul B. Barringer*. University of North Carolina Press, 1949.
Battle, Kemp P. *History of the University of North Carolina*. 2 vols. Edwards & Broughton, 1907–12.
[Beecher, Eunice White Bullard]. *Dawn to Daylight; or, The Simple Story of a Western Home by a Minister's Wife*. Derby & Jackson, 1859.
Bell, Richard. "Peepholes, Eels, and Pickett's Charge: Doing Microhistory Then and Now." *Journal of the Civil War Era* 12, no. 3 (2022): 362–87.
Bergmann, Jorg R. *Discreet Indiscretions: The Social Origins of Gossip*. Translated by John Bedharz Jr. Aldine de Gruyter, 1993.
Berlin, Ira. *Slaves Without Masters: The Free Negro in the American South*. Vintage, 1974.
Bingham, James Barry, comp. *Descendants of James Bingham of County Down, Northern Ireland*. Gateway Press, 1980.
Bingham, Robert. "William Bingham." In *Biographical History of North Carolina from Colonial Times to the Present*, edited by Samuel Ashe, Stephen B. Weeks, and Charles L. Van Noppen, 65–68. Charles L. Van Noppen, 1905–17.
———. "William James Bingham." In *Biographical History of North Carolina from Colonial Times to the Present*, edited by Samuel Ashe, Stephen B. Weeks, and Charles L. Van Noppen, 69–70. Charles L. Van Noppen, 1905–17.
Bishir, Catherine. *Crafting Lives: African American Artisans in New Bern, North Carolina*. University of North Carolina Press, 2013.
Blackwelder, Ruth. *The Age of Orange: Political and Intellectual Leadership in North Carolina, 1752–1861*. William Loftin, 1961.
Blassingame, John W. *The Slave Community: Plantation Life in the Antebellum South*. Oxford University Press, 1979.
Bledstein, Burton J. *The Culture of Professionalism: The Middle Class and the Development of Higher Education in America*. W. W. Norton, 1976.
Block, Sharon. *Rape and Sexual Power in Early America*. University of North Carolina Press, 2006.
Blodgett, Jan, and Ralph B. Levering. *One Town, Many Voices: A History of Davidson, North Carolina*. Davidson Historical Society, 2012.
Boles, John B., ed. *Masters and Slaves in the House of the Lord: Race and Religion in the American South, 1740–1870*. University Press of Kentucky, 1988.
Bonner, James C. *Milledgeville: Georgia's Antebellum Capital*. University of Georgia Press, 1978.
Bordewich, Fergus M. *America's Great Debate: Henry Clay, Stephen A. Douglas, and the Compromise That Preserved the Union*. Simon & Schuster, 2012.
Boyd, Lois A. "Presbyterian Ministers' Wives: A Nineteenth-Century Portrait." *Journal of Presbyterian History* 59, no. 1 (1981): 3–17.
Brandt, Nat. *The Town That Started the Civil War*. Syracuse University Press, 1990.
Breeden, James O., ed. *Advice Among Masters: The Ideal of Slave Management in the Old South*. Greenwood, 1980.

Bruce, Dickson D., Jr. *Violence and Culture in the Antebellum South*. University of Texas Press, 1979.
Brundage, W. Fitzhugh. *The Southern Past: A Clash of Race and Memory*. Harvard University Press, 2005.
———, ed. *Where These Memories Grow: History, Memory, and Southern Identity*. University of North Carolina Press, 2000.
Burton, Orville. *In My Father's House Are Many Mansions: Family and Community in Edgefield, South Carolina*. University of North Carolina Press, 1985.
Burwell, George H. *Record of the Burwell Family Copied in Part from the Manuscript. By the Rev. Robert Burwell*. Whittet & Shepperson, 1908.
Camp, Stephanie M. H. *Closer to Freedom: Enslaved Women and Everyday Resistance in the Plantation South*. University of North Carolina Press, 2004.
Carter, Christine Jacobson. *Southern Single Blessedness: Unmarried Women in the Urban South, 1800–1865*. University of Illinois Press, 2006.
Cashin, Joan. "'Decidedly Opposed to the Union': Women's Culture, Marriage, and Politics in Antebellum South Carolina." *Georgia Historical Quarterly* 78, no. 4 (1994): 735–59.
Catalogue of the Charlotte Female Institute, Charlotte, N.C., for the Session 1860–61. W. W. Holden, 1861.
Catalogue of the Trustees, Faculty, and Students of the Caldwell Institute: Hillsborough, NC, 1848–49. Dennis Heartt, 1849.
Cecil-Fronsman, Bill. *Common Whites: Class and Culture in Antebellum North Carolina*. University Press of Kentucky, 1992.
Censer, Jane Turner. *North Carolina Planters and Their Children, 1800–1860*. Louisiana State University Press, 1984.
Chesnut, Mary Boykin. *Mary Chestnut's Civil War*, edited by C. Vann Woodward. Yale University Press, 1981.
Circular and Catalogue of Mr. and Mrs. Burwell's Female School, Hillsboro, N. C., Term 1848–1851. N.C. Institute for the Deaf, Dumb and Blind, 1851.
Claiborne, James Herbert. *Seventy-Five Years in Old Virginia*. Neale, 1904.
Clayton, James D. *Antebellum Natchez*. Louisiana State University Press, 1968.
Clinton, Catherine. *The Plantation Mistress: Woman's World in the Old South*. Pantheon, 1982.
———. "'Southern Dishonor': Flesh, Blood, Race, and Bondage." In *In Joy and in Sorrow: Women, Family, and Marriage in the Victorian South, 1830–1900*, edited by Carol Blesser, 52–68. Oxford University Press, 1991.
Connerton, Paul. *How Societies Remember*. Cambridge University Press, 1989.
Connor, R. D. W. *The History of North Carolina*. Vol. 1: *The Colonial and Revolutionary Periods, 1584–1783*. Lewis, 1919.
Coon, Charles L., ed. *North Carolina Schools and Academies, 1789–1840: A Documentary History*. Edwards & Broughton, 1915.
Courtwright, David T. "The Female Opiate Addict in Nineteenth-Century America." *Essays in Arts and Sciences* 10, no. 2 (1982): 161–71.
———. "The Hidden Epidemic: Opiate Addiction and Cocaine Use in the South, 1860–1920." *Journal of Southern History* 49, no. 1 (1983): 57–72.
Crenson, Matthew A. *Baltimore: A Political History*. Johns Hopkins University Press, 2017.
Crowell, Cheryl. *Images of America: New Richmond* [Ohio]. Arcadia, 2012.

Curtis, Robert I. "The Bingham School and Classical Education in North Carolina, 1793–1873." *North Carolina Historical Review* 73, no. 3 (1996): 328–77.

Cutler, Helen R. *Jottings from Life; or, Passages from the Diary of an Itinerant's Wife*. Poe & Hitchcock, 1864.

Dain, Norman. *Disordered Minds: The First Century of Eastern State Hospital in Williamsburg, Virginia, 1766–1866*. University Press of Virginia, [1971].

Dangerfield, David. "Plain People of Color: Rural Free People of Color in the Antebellum Charleston District." MA thesis, Graduate School of the College of Charleston and the Citadel, 2009.

Davis, Bryant Kenneth. *A Folklore Study of West Hillsborough, North Carolina, Including Local Legends and Games*. [Hillsborough, N.C.]: P. P., 1986.

Dickens, Roy S., Jr., H. Trawick Ward, and R. P. Stephen Davis Jr. *The Historic Occaneechi: An Archeological Investigation of Culture Change: Preliminary Report of 1984 Investigations*. Research Laboratories of Anthropology, University of North Carolina, 1984.

Ditz, Toby. "Shipwrecked; or, Masculinity Imperiled: Mercantile Representations of Failure and the Gendered Self in Eighteenth-Century Philadelphia." *Journal of American History* 81, no. 1 (1994): 51–80.

Dowd, Gregory Evan. *Groundless: Rumors, Legends, and Hoaxes on the Early American Frontier*. Johns Hopkins University Press, 2015.

Doyle, Steven. *Carry Me Back: The Domestic Slave Trade in American Life*. Oxford University Press, 2005.

Dunaway, Stewart E., comp. *Hillsborough, N.C.: History of Town Lots*. [Hillsborough, N.C.]: P. P., 2012.

Dunmore, Lawrence A., III. "The Orange County History of the Occaneechi Band of the Saponi Nation." *Eno Journal* 10, no. 1 (2021): 5–13.

Dwyer, Ellen. *Homes for the Mad: Life Inside Two Nineteenth-Century Asylums*. Rutgers University Press, 1987.

Eaton, Clement. "A Dangerous Pamphlet in the Old South." *Journal of Southern History* 2, no. 3 (1936): 324–34.

Edwards, Laura F. *Gendered Strife and Confusion: The Political Culture of Reconstruction*. University of Illinois Press, 1997.

Eidenier, Betty. "Rev. Job Berry's Legacy Rooted in Faith, Marriage, Education." *News of Orange*, March 25, 2022.

Elder, Robert. *The Sacred Mirror: Evangelicalism, Honor, and Masculinity in the Deep South, 1790–1860*. University of North Carolina Press, 2016.

Ellis, William E. *Robert Worth Bingham and the Southern Mystique: From the Old South to the New South and Beyond*. Kent State University Press, 1997.

Engstrom, Mary Claire. *The Book of Burwell Students: Lives of Educated Women in the Antebellum South*. Historic Hillsborough Commission, 1979.

———. "Hillsborough in 1775." *Historical Society of Hillsborough Journal* 1, no. 1 (1998): 25–32.

Erikson, Kai T. *Wayward Puritans: A Study on the Sociology of Deviance*, rev. ed. John Wiley, 1966.

Falk, Stanley L. "The Warrenton Female Academy of Jacob Mordecai, 1809–1818." *North Carolina Historical Review* 35, no. 3 (1958): 281–98.

Farnham, Christie Ann. *The Education of the Southern Belle: Higher Education and Student Socialization in the Antebellum South*. New York University Press, 1994.

Faucette, Lindsay. *Slave Narratives: A Folk History of Slavery in the United States from Interviews with Former Slaves.* Vol. 11, *North Carolina Narratives,* Part 1. [U.S. Government Printing Office], 1941.
Faust, Drew Gilpin. *Mothers of Invention: Women of the Slaveholding South in the American Civil War.* University of North Carolina Press, 1996.
Fede, Andrew. "Legitimized Violent Slave Abuse in the American South, 1619-1865." *American Journal of Legal History* 29, no. 2 (1985): 93-150.
Feeley, Kathleen A., and Jennifer Frost, eds. *When Private Talk Goes Public: Gossip in American History.* Palgrave Macmillan, 2014.
Fine, Gary Alan, and Ralph L. Rosnow. "Gossip, Gossipers, Gossiping." *Personality and Social Psychology* 4, no. 1 (1978): 161-68.
Fleischner, Jennifer. *Mrs. Lincoln and Mrs. Keckly: The Remarkable Story of the Friendship Between a First Lady and a Former Slave.* Broadway Books, 2003.
Fletcher, Robert S. *A History of Oberlin College from Its Foundation Through the Civil War.* 2 vols. Oberlin College, 1943.
Fountain, Daniel L. "A Broader Footprint: Slavery and Slaveholding Households in Antebellum Piedmont North Carolina." *North Carolina Historical Review* 91, no. 4 (2014): 407-44.
Fox-Genovese, Elizabeth. *Within the Plantation Household: Black and White Women of the Old South.* University of North Carolina Press, 1988.
Franklin, John Hope. *The Free Negro in North Carolina, 1790-1860.* University of North Carolina Press, 1995.
Fraser, Rebecca J. *Courtship and Love Among the Enslaved in North Carolina.* University Press of Mississippi, 2007.
Fraser, Walter J., Jr. *Charleston! Charleston!: The Story of a Southern City.* University of South Carolina Press, 1989.
———. *Savannah in the Old South.* University of Georgia Press, 2005.
Friend, Craig. *Along the Maysville Road: The Early Republic in the Trans-Appalachian West.* University of Tennessee Press, 1999.
Genovese, Eugene. *Roll, Jordan, Roll: The World the Slaves Made.* Vintage, 1976.
Glenn, Myra C. "School Discipline and Punishment in Antebellum America." *Journal of the Early Republic* 1, no. 4 (1981): 395-408.
Glover, Lori. "'Let Us Manufacture Men': Educating Elite Boys in the Early National South." In *Southern Manhood: Perspectives on Masculinity in the Old South,* edited by Craig Thompson Friend and Lori Glover, 22-48. University of Georgia Press, 2004.
———. *Southern Sons: Becoming Men in the New Nation.* Johns Hopkins University Press, 2007.
Gluckman, Max. "Gossip and Scandal." *Current Anthropology* 4, no. 3 (1963): 307-16.
Glymph, Thavolia. *Out of the House of Bondage: The Transformation of the Plantation Household.* Cambridge University Press, 2008.
Goldfield, David R. "Pursuing the American Dream: Cities in the Old South." In *The City in Southern History: The Growth of Urban Civilization in the South,* edited by Blaine A. Brownell and David R. Goldfield, 52-91. Kennikat Press, 1977.
Gonaver, Wendy. *The Peculiar Institution and the Making of Modern Psychiatry, 1840-1880.* University of North Carolina Press, 2018.
Goodheart, Lawrence. *Mad Yankees: The Hartford Retreat for the Insane and Nineteenth-Century Psychiatry.* University of Massachusetts Press, 2003.

Goodman, Robert F., and Arron Ben-Ze'ev, eds. *Good Gossip*. University of Kansas Press, 1994.
Gorn, Elliot J. "'Gouge and Bite, Pull Hair and Scratch': The Social Significance of Fighting in the Southern Backcountry." *American Historical Review* 90, no. 1 (1985): 18–43.
Graebner, N. Brooks. "The Episcopal Church and Race in Nineteenth-Century North Carolina." *Anglican and Episcopal History* 78, no. 1 (2009): 85–93.
———. "Remarks on the Divergent Pilgrimages of Job Berry and Henry Evans After Leaving St. Matthew's." Lecture, Burwell School Historic Site, February 21, 2021, Hillsborough, North Carolina.
Green, Fletcher M. "Slavery in Orange County." In *Orange County, 1752–1952*, edited by Hugh Lefler and Paul Wager, 95–106. [Chapel Hill, N.C.]: P. P., 1953.
Green, W. M. "A Tabular View of the Order and Distribution of Studies Observed in the Respective Classes of the Hillsborough Female Seminary, 1826." Hillsborough, N.C.: P. P., 1826.
Greenburg, Kenneth S. *Honor and Slavery*. Princeton University Press, 1996.
———. "The Nose, the Lie, and the Duel in the Antebellum South." *American Historical Review* 95, no. 1 (1990): 57–74.
Greene, Robert Ewell. *The Leary-Evans, Ohio's Free People of Color*. Keitt, 1979.
Greenough, Jan Price. "Forgive Us Our Transgressions: Rule and Misrule in Antebellum Southern Schools." *Southern Historian* 21, no. 1 (2000): 5–24.
Greven, Philip. *The Protestant Temperament: Patterns of Child-Rearing, Religious Experience, and the Self in Early America*. New American Library, 1977.
———. *Spare the Child: The Religious Roots of Punishment and the Psychological Impact of Physical Abuse*. Alfred A. Knopf, 1991.
Griffin, Rebecca J. "'Goin' Back Over There to See That Girl': Competing Spaces in the Social World of the Enslaved in Antebellum North Carolina." *Slavery and Abolition* 25, no. 1 (2004): 94–113.
Grob, Gerald N. *The State and the Mentally Ill: A History of Worcester State Hospital in Massachusetts, 1830–1920*. University of North Carolina Press, 1966.
Hadden, Sally. "Judging Slavery: Thomas Ruffin and State v. Mann." In *Local Matters: Race, Crime, and Justice in the Nineteenth-Century South*, edited by Christopher Waldrep and Donald G. Neiman, 1–28. University of Georgia Press, 2001.
Hall, Jacquelyn Dowd, James L. Leloudis, Robert Korstad, Mary Murphy, Lu Ann Jones, and Christopher B. Daly. *Like a Family: The Making of a Southern Cotton Mill World*. University of North Carolina Press, 1987.
Hamilton, J. G. de Roulhac, ed. *The Papers of Thomas Ruffin*, 4 vols. Edwards and Broughton, 1918–1920.
Handler, Richard, and Eric Gable. *The New History of an Old Museum: Creating the Past at Colonial Williamsburg*. Duke University Press, 1997.
Harris, J. William. *Plain Folk and Gentry in a Slave Society: White Liberty and Black Slavery in Augusta's Hinterlands*. Wesleyan University Press, 1985.
Hartman, Saidiya V. *Scenes of Subjugation: Terror, Slavery, and Self-Making in Nineteenth-Century America*. Oxford University Press, 1997.
Hatfield, April. *Atlantic Virginia: Intercolonial Relations in the Seventeenth Century*. University of Pennsylvania Press, 2004.
Hazel, Forest. "Occaneechi-Sapaoni Descendants in the North Carolina Piedmont: The

Texas Community" [Little Texas, Pleasant Grove Township, Alamance County, North Carolina]. *Southern Indian Studies* 40 (1991): 3–29.

Hendricks, Christopher E. *The Backcountry Towns of Colonial Virginia*. University of Tennessee Press, 2006.

Hessinger, Rodney. "'The Most Powerful Instrument of College Discipline': Student Disorder and the Growth of Meritocracy in the Colleges of the Early Republic." *History of Education Quarterly* 39, no. 3 (1999): 237–62.

Hickman, Timothy A. "'Mania Americana': Narcotic Addiction and Modernity in the United States, 1870–1920." *Journal of American History* 90, no. 4 (2004): 1269–94.

Hildebrand, Reginald. *The Times Were Strange and Stirring: Methodist Preachers and the Crisis of Emancipation*. Duke University Press, 1995.

Hindus, Michael Stephen. *Prison and Plantation: Crime, Justice, and Authority in Massachusetts and South Carolina, 1767–1878*. University of North Carolina Press, 1980.

Hine, Darlene Clark. "Rape and the Inner Lives of Black Women: Thoughts on the Culture of Dissemblance." In *In Hine Sight: Black Women and the Re-construction of American History*, edited by Darlene Clark Hine, 37–47. Indiana University Press, 1994.

Hinks, Peter P. *To Awaken My Afflicted Brethren: David Walker and the Problem of Antebellum Slave Resistance*. Pennsylvania State University Press, 1997.

Hoffert, Sylvia D. "Anna Burwell and the Business of Being a Presbyterian Minister's Wife in North Carolina, 1835–1857." *North Carolina Historical Review* 96, no. 3 (2019): 245–75.

———. "Earnest Efforts to Be Friends: Teacher Student Relationships in the Nineteenth-Century South." *Journal of Southern History* 84, no. 4 (2018): 813–44.

———. "The Emancipation of Elizabeth Hobbs Keckly: St. Louis, 1847–1860." *Missouri Historical Review* 112, no. 4 (2018): 243–59.

———, ed. *"The Grief of a Mind Giving Way": Sophia Turner's Poems from the North Carolina Asylum for the Insane, 1878–1880*. North Carolina Office of Archives and History, 2023.

———. "Mary Lincoln, Elizabeth Keckly, and the Perils of White House Friendship." In *Southern First Ladies: Culture and Place in White House History*, edited by Katherine A. S. Sibley, 113–32. University of Kansas Press, 2020.

———. *Private Matters: American Attitudes toward Childbearing and Infant Nurture in the Urban North, 1800–1860*. University of Illinois Press, 1989.

Hofstra, Warren R. *The Planting of New Virginia: Settlement and Landscape in the Shenandoah Valley*. Johns Hopkins University Press, 2004.

Hughes, John Starrett. "The Madness of Separate Spheres: Insanity and Masculinity in Victorian Alabama." In *Meanings for Manhood: Constructions of Masculinity in Victorian America*, edited by Mark C. Carnes and Clyde Griffin, 53–66. University of Chicago Press, 1990.

Hume, Barbara, and Callie Connor, eds. *Hidden Hillsborough: Historic Dependencies and Landscapes in a Small Southern Town*. Eno, 2017.

Hume, Barbara, and Stewart Dunaway. "Evolving Townscape: The Location and Early Importance of Hillsborough." In Hume and Connor, *Hidden Hillsborough*, 5–18.

Hunter, Tera W. *Bound in Wedlock: Slave and Free Black Marriage in the Nineteenth Century*. Harvard University Press, 2017.

Jabour, Anya. "'It Will Never Do for Me to Be Married': The Life of Laura Wirt Randall, 1803-1833." *Journal of the Early Republic* 17, no. 2 (1997): 193-236.

———. *Scarlett's Sisters: Young Women in the Old South*. University of North Carolina Press, 2007.

Jacobs, Harriet A. *Incidents in the Life of a Slave Girl*, edited by Jean Fagan Yellin. Harvard University Press, 1987.

Johnson, Michael P., and James L. Roark. *Black Master: A Free Family of Color in the Old South*. W. W. Norton, 1984.

———. "Strategies of Survival: Free Negro Families and the Problem of Slavery." In *In Joy and In Sorrow: Women, Family, and Marriage in the Victorian South, 1830-1900*, edited by Carol Blesser, 88-102. Oxford University Press, 1991.

Jones, Bernie D. *Fathers of Conscience: Mixed-Race Inheritance in the Antebellum South*. University of Georgia Press, 2011.

Jones, H. G., with David Southern. *Miss Mary's Money: Fortune and Misfortune in a North Carolina Plantation Family, 1760-1924*. McFarland, 2015.

Jones, Jacqueline. *Soldiers of Light and Love: Northern Teachers and Georgia Blacks, 1865-1873*. University of North Carolina Press, 1980.

Junk, Cheryl F. "'To Become a Power in the Land': The Burwell School and Women's Education in North Carolina, 1837-1857." *Hillsborough Historical Society Journal* 2, no. 1 (1999): 13-47.

Kandall, Stephen R. *Substance and Shadow: Women and Addiction in the United States*. Harvard University Press, 1996.

Kasson, John F. *Rudeness and Civility: Manners in Nineteenth-Century Urban America*. Hill & Wang, 1990.

Keckley, Elizabeth. *Behind the Scenes, or, Thirty Years a Slave, and Four Years in the White House*. G. W. Carleton, 1868.

Kennedy, V. Lynn. *Born Southern: Childbirth, Motherhood, and Social Networks in the Old South*. Johns Hopkins University Press, 2010.

Kenzer, Robert C. *Kinship and Neighborhood in a Southern Community: Orange County, North Carolina, 1849-1881*. University of Tennessee Press, 1987.

Kett, Joseph F. *Rites of Passage: Adolescence, 1790 to the Present*. Basic Books, 1977.

Kierner, Cynthia A. *Scandal at Bazaare: Rumor and Reputation in Jefferson's America*. Palgrave, 2004.

Kilbride, Daniel. *An American Aristocracy: Southern Planters in Antebellum Philadelphia*. University of South Carolina Press, 2006.

Kimball, Gregg D. "African, American, Virginian: The Shaping of Black Memory in Antebellum Virginia, 1790-1860." In *Where These Memories Grow: History, Memory, and Southern Identity*, edited by W. Fitzhugh Brundage, 57-77. University of North Carolina Press, 2002.

King, Wilma. "'Suffer with Them Till Death': Slave Women and Their Children in Nineteenth-Century America." In *More Than Chattel: Black Women and Slavery in the Americas*, edited by Darlene Clark Hine and David Barry Gaspar, 147-68. Indiana University Press, 1996.

Knight, Edgar W. "Education in Orange County." In *Orange County, 1752-1952*, edited by Hugh Lefler and Paul Wager, 130-46. Orange Print Shop, 1953.

Kraditor, Aileen S. *Means and Ends in American Abolitionism: Garrison and His Critics on Strategy and Tactics, 1834–1850*. Ivan R. Dee, 1989.
Kudlick, Catherine J. "Disability History: Why We Need Another 'Other.'" *American Historical Review* 108, no. 3 (2003): 763–93.
Lasser, Carol. "'Let Us Be Sisters Forever': The Sororal Model of Nineteenth-Century Female Friendship." *Signs* 14, no. 1 (1988): 158–81.
Lasser, Carol, and Gary J. Kornblith. *Elusive Utopia: The Struggle for Racial Equality in Oberlin, Ohio*. Louisiana State University Press, 2018.
Lawson, John. *A New Voyage to Carolina*, edited by Hugh Talmage Lefler. University of North Carolina Press, 1967.
Lebsock, Suzanne. *The Free Women of Petersburg: Status and Culture in a Southern Town, 1784–1860*. W. W. Norton, 1985.
Leloudis, James L. *Schooling in the Old South: Pedagogy, Self, and Society in North Carolina*. University of North Carolina Press, 1996.
Lemon, Sarah McCulloch, ed. *The Pettigrew Papers*, 2 Vols. State Department of Archives and History, 1971–88.
Lichtenstein, Alex. "'That Disposition to Theft with Which They Have Been Branded': Moral Economy, Slave Management, and the Law." *Journal of Social History* 21, no. 3 (1988): 413–40.
Litwack, Leon F. *Been in the Storm So Long: The Aftermath of Slavery*. Vintage, 1979.
Lloyd, Pauline O., and Allen A. Lloyd. *History of the Churches of Hillsborough, N.C., ca. 1766–1962*. [Hillsborough, 1962 or 1963].
Long, Augustus White. *Son of Carolina*. Duke University Press, 1939.
Long, Mary Alves. *High Time to Tell It*. Duke University Press, 1950.
Lubet, Steven. *The "Colored Hero" of Harper's Ferry: John Anthony Copeland and the War Against Slavery*. Cambridge University Press, 2015.
Marks, John Garrison. *Black Freedom in the Age of Slavery: Race, Status, and Identity in the Urban Americas*. University of South Carolina Press, 2020.
Marsh, Ben. "The Republic's New Clothes: Making Silk in the Antebellum United States." *Agricultural History* 86, no. 4 (2012): 206–34.
Marshall, Patricia Phillips, and Jo Ramsey Leimenstoll. *Thomas Day: Master Craftsman and Free Man of Color*. University of North Carolina Press, 2010.
Martin, Bonnie. "Neighbor-to-Neighbor Capitalism: Local Credit Networks and the Mortgaging of Slaves." In *Slavery's Capitalism: A New History of American Economic Development*, edited by Sven Beckert and Seth Rockman, 107–21. University of Pennsylvania Press, 2016.
Mason, Frank. "The American Silk Industry and the Tariff." *American Economic Association Quarterly* 11, no. 4 (1910): 1–82.
Masur, Kate. *Until Justice Be Done: America's First Civil Rights Movement from the Revolution to Reconstruction*. W. W. Norton, 2021.
Mathews, Donald G. *Religion in the Old South*. University of Chicago Press, 1977.
McCandless, Peter. *Moonlight, Magnolias, and Madness: Insanity in South Carolina from the Colonial Period to the Progressive Era*. University of North Carolina Press, 1996.
McCulloch, Margaret Callender. "Founding the North Carolina Asylum for the Insane." *North Carolina Historical Review* 13, no. 3 (1936): 185–201.
McKoy, Sheila Smith. *The Elizabeth Keckly Reader*. 2 vols. Eno, 2016, 2017.

McMillen, Sally G. *Motherhood in the Old South: Pregnancy, Childbirth, and Infant Rearing*. Louisiana State University Press, 1990.
McMillin, Laurence. *The Schoolmaker: Sawney Webb and the Bell Buckle Story*. University of North Carolina Press, 1971.
McPherson, James M. *Battle Cry of Freedom: The Civil War Era*. Ballantine, 1988.
Merry, Sally Engle. "Rethinking Gossip and Scandal." In *Toward a General Theory of Social Control. Vol. 1: Fundamentals*, edited by Donald J. Black, 271–302. Academic Press, 1984.
Milteer, Warren Eugene, Jr. *Beyond Slavery's Shadow: Free People of Color in the South*. University of North Carolina Press, 2021.
———. *North Carolina's Free People of Color, 1715–1885*. Louisiana State University Press, 2020.
Miron, Janet. *Prisons, Asylums, and the Public: Institutional Visiting in the Nineteenth Century*. University of Toronto Press, 2011.
Moore, Rosetta Austin. *The Impact of Slavery on the Education of Blacks in Orange County, North Carolina, 1619–1970*. [Hillsborough, N.C.]: P. P., 2015.
Morey, Ann-Janine. "Lamentations for the Minister's Wife, by Herself." *Women's Studies* 19, nos. 3–4 (1991): 327–40.
Morris, Janie, and Betty Eidenier, comp. *Antebellum Hillsborough, Slavery, and Enslaved and Free People of Color Who Worked at the Burwell School, 1837–1857*. Burwell Historic Site, 2019.
Morris, Thomas D. *Free Men All: The Personal Liberty Laws of the North, 1780–1861*. Johns Hopkins University Press, 1974.
Morton, Richard L., ed. "A 'Yankee Teacher' in North Carolina." *North Carolina Historical Review* 30, no. 4 (1953): 564–82.
Muller, Eric L. "Judging Thomas Ruffin and the Hindsight Defense." *North Carolina Law Review* 87, no. 3 (2009): 757–98.
Mullins, Jeffrey A. "Honorable Violence: Youth Culture, Masculinity, and Contested Authority in Liberal Education in the Early Republic." *American Transcendental Quarterly* 17, no. 3 (2003): 161–79.
Murray, Pauli. *Proud Shoes: The Story of an American Family*. Beacon Press, 1999.
Myers, Amrita Chakrabarti. *Forging Freedom: Black Women and the Pursuit of Liberty in Antebellum Charleston*. University of North Carolina Press, 2011.
Nash, Ann Strudwick. *Ladies in the Making (also a Few Gentlemen) at the Select Boarding and Day School of the Misses Nash and Miss Kollock, 1859–1890, Hillsborough, North Carolina*. [Hillsborough, N.C.]: P. P., 1964.
Nash, Margaret A. "A Means of Honorable Support: Art and Music in Women's Education in the Mid-Nineteenth Century." *History of Education Quarterly* 53, no. 1 (2013): 45–63.
Nathans, Sydney. *To Free a Family: The Journey of Mary Walker*. Harvard University Press, 2012.
Neem, Johann. *Democracy's Schools: The Rise of Public Education in America*. Johns Hopkins University Press, 2017.
Nevo, Ofra, Baruch Nevo, and Anat Derech-Zehavi. "The Tendency to Gossip as a Psychological Disposition: Constructing a Measure and Validating It." In *Good Gossip*, edited by Robert F. Goodman and Arron Ben-Ze'ev, 180–89. University of Kansas Press, 1994.

Novak, Stephen J. *The Rights of Youth: American Colleges and Student Revolt, 1798–1815*. Harvard University Press, 1977.
Oates, Stephen B. *The Fires of Jubilee: Nat Turner's Fierce Rebellion*. Harper & Row, 1975.
O'Brien, Michael, ed. *An Evening When Alone: Four Journals of Single Women in the South, 1827–67*. University Press of Virginia, 1993.
O'Neil, Patrick W. "Bosses and Broomsticks: Ritual and Authority in Antebellum Slave Weddings." *Journal of Southern History* 75, no. 1 (2009): 29–48.
O'Rorke, Marjorie. *Haven on a Hill: A History of North Carolina's Dorothea Dix Hospital*. Office of Archives and History, North Carolina Department of Cultural Resources, 2010.
Owsley, Frank Lawrence. *Plain Folk of the Old South*. Quadrangle Books, 1965.
Page, Walter Hines. *The Southerner*. University of South Carolina Press, 2008.
———. "Study of an Old Southern Borough." *Atlantic Monthly*, May 1881, 648–58.
Peterson, Audrey C. "Brain Fever in Nineteenth-Century Literature: Fact and Fiction." *Victorian Studies* 19, no. 4 (1976): 445–64.
Pettigrew, Ebenezer. *The Pettigrew Papers*. Edited by Sarah McCulloch Lemon. 2 vols. North Carolina State Department of Archives and History, 1971–88.
Phipps, L. J. "The Churches of Orange County." In *Orange County, 1752–1952*, edited by Hugh Lefler and Paul Wager, 288–321. Orange Print Shop, 1953.
Powell, Lawrence N. *The Accidental City: Improvising New Orleans*. Harvard University Press, 2012.
Raboteau, Albert J. *Slave Religion: The "Invisible Institution" in the Antebellum South*. Oxford University Press, 1978.
Rankin, Richard. *Ambivalent Churchmen and Evangelical Churchwomen: The Religion of the Episcopal Elite in North Carolina, 1800–1860*. University of South Carolina Press, 1993.
Reid, Holly. "Jesse Ruffin and Rebecca Norwood Ruffin, Contemporaries of Elizabeth Keckly." In Morris and Eidenier, *Antebellum Hillsborough*, 29–34.
Reiss, Benjamin. *Theaters of Madness: Insane Asylums and Nineteenth-Century American Culture*. University of Chicago Press, 2008.
Rice, James. "Bacon's Rebellion in Indian Country." *Journal of American History* 101, no. 3 (2014): 726–50.
Rogers, George C. *Charleston in the Age of the Pinckneys*. University of Oklahoma Press, 1969.
Rothman, David J. *The Discovery of the Asylum: Social Order and Disorder in the New Republic*. Little, Brown, 1971.
Rothman, Joshua D. *The Ledger and the Chain: How Domestic Slave Traders Shaped America*. Basic Books, 2021.
Ruffin, Thomas. *The Papers of Thomas Ruffin*. Edited by J. G. de Roulhac Hamilton. 4 vols. Edwards & Broughton, 1918–20.
Rupp, Leila J. "'Imagine My Surprise': Women's Relationships in Historical Perspective." *Frontiers: A Journal of Women's Studies* 5, no. 3 (1980): 61–70.
Rutman, Darrett B., and Anita H. Rutman. *A Place in Time: Middlesex County, Virginia, 1650–1750*. W. W. Norton, 1984.
———, eds. *Small Worlds, Large Questions: Explorations in Early American Social History, 1660–1850*. University Press of Virginia, 1994.

Ryan, Elizabeth Shreve. *Orange County Trio: Hillsborough, Chapel Hill, and Carrboro, North Carolina*. Chapel Hill Press, 2004.

Sahli, Nancy. "Smashing: Women's Relationships Before the Fall." *Chrysalis* 8, no. 1 (1979): 17–27.

Sandage, Scott. *Born Losers: A History of Failure in America*. Harvard University Press, 2006.

Schwartz, Marie Jenkins. "'At Noon, Oh How I Run': Breastfeeding and Weaning on Plantation and Farm in Antebellum Virginia and Alabama." In *Discovering the Women in Slavery: Emancipating Perspectives on the American Past*, edited by Patricia Morton, 241–59. University of Georgia Press, 1996.

———. *Birthing a Slave: Motherhood and Medicine in the Antebellum South*. Harvard University Press, 2006.

Schweninger, Loren. "Property Owning Free African-American Women in the South, 1800–1870." *Journal of Women's History* 1, no. 3 (1990): 13–44.

Sellers, Charles. *The Market Revolution: Jacksonian America, 1815–1846*. Oxford University Press, 1991.

Shaw, Stephanie J. "Mothering Under Slavery in the Antebellum South." In *Mothering: Ideology, Experience, and Agency*, edited by Evelyn Nakano Glenn, Grace Chang, and Linda Rennie Forcey, 237–58. Routledge, 1994.

Silkenat, David. "'In Good Hands, in a Safe Place': Female Academies in Confederate North Carolina." *North Carolina Historical Review* 88, no. 1 (2011): 40–71.

Skeel, David A., Jr. *Debt's Dominion: A History of Bankruptcy Law in America*. Princeton University Press, 2001.

Smith, John David. "'I Was Raised Poor and Hard as Any Slave': African American Slavery in Piedmont North Carolina." *North Carolina Historical Review* 90, no. 1 (2013): 1–25.

Smith, Kim. "The Book of Harriet: The Disambiguation of Five North Carolinian Siblings, 1840–1941." MA thesis, Duke University, 2016.

Smith, Suzanne E. *To Serve the Living: Funeral Directors and the African-American Way of Death*. Belknap Press, 2010.

Smith-Rosenberg, Carroll. "The Female World of Love and Ritual: Relations Between Women in Nineteenth-Century America." *Signs* 1, no. 1 (1975): 1–29.

———. "The Hysterical Woman: Sex Roles and Role Conflict in 19th-Century America." In *Disorderly Conduct: Visions of Gender in Victorian America*, edited by Carroll Smith-Rosenberg, 197–216. Oxford University Press, 1985.

———. "Puberty to Menopause: The Cycle of Femininity in Nineteenth-Century America." In *Disorderly Conduct: Visions of Gender in Victorian America*, edited by Carroll Smith-Rosenberg, 182–96. Oxford University Press, 1985.

Smith-Rosenberg, Carroll, and Charles Rosenberg. "The Female Animal: Medical and Biological Views of Women and Her Role in Nineteenth-Century America." *Journal of American History* 60, no. 2 (1973): 332–56.

Spacks, Patricia Meyer. *Gossip*. Alfred A. Knopf, 1985.

Spenser, Cornelia Phillips. "A Notable Woman North Carolina Has Produced," *State Chronicle* (Raleigh), February, 1886.

———"Obituary [of Maria Louisa Spear]." *Church Messenger*, January 27, 1881, [3].

Stampp, Kenneth M. *The Peculiar Institution: Slavery in the Ante-bellum South*. Vintage, 1956.

Stevenson, Brenda E. "What's Love Got to Do with It?: Concubinage and Enslaved Women

and Girls in the Antebellum South." *Journal of African American History* 98, no. 1 (2013): 99–125.
Stirling, Rebecca Birch. "Some Psychological Mechanisms Operative in Gossip." *Social Forces* 34, no. 3 (1956): 262–67.
Stowe, Steven M. *Doctoring in the South: Southern Physicians and Everyday Medicine in the Mid-Nineteenth Century*. University of North Carolina Press, 2004.
———. *Intimacy and Power in the Old South: Ritual in the Lives of the Planters*. Johns Hopkins University Press, 1987.
———. "The Not-So-Cloistered Academy: Elite Women's Education and Family Feeling in the Old South." In *The Web of Social Relations: Women, Family, and Education*, edited by Walter J. Fraser Jr., R. Frank Saunders Jr., and Jon L. Wakelyn, 90–106. University of Georgia Press, 1986.
———. "Obstetrics and the Work of Doctoring in the Mid-Nineteenth-Century American South." *Bulletin of the History of Medicine* 64, no. 4 (1990): 540–66.
Taylor, R. H. "Slave Conspiracies in North Carolina." *North Carolina Historical Review* 5, no. 1 (1928): 20–34.
Thielman, Samuel B. "Southern Madness: The Shape of Mental Health Care in the Old South." In *Science and Medicine in the Old South*, edited by Ronald L. Numbers and Todd L. Savitt, 256–75. Louisiana State University Press, 1989.
Thoms, Herbert. "Hugh Lenox Hodge: A Master Mind in Obstetrical Science." *American Journal of Obstetrics and Gynecology* 33, no. 5 (1937): 886–92.
Tillson, Albert H. "The Southern Backcountry: A Survey of Current Research." *Virginia Magazine of History and Biography* 98, no. 3 (1990): 387–442.
Tolbert, Lisa. *Constructing Townscapes: Space and Society in Antebellum Tennessee*. University of North Carolina Press, 1999.
Tolley, Kim. "Music Teachers in the North Carolina Education Market, 1800–1840: How Mrs. Sambourne Earned a 'Comfortable Living for Herself and Her Children.'" *Social Science History* 32, no. 1 (2008): 75–106.
———. "The Significance of the 'French School' in Early National Female Education." In *The Founding Fathers, Education and "the Great Contest": The American Philosophical Society Prize of 1797*, edited by Benjamin Justice, 135–54. Palgrave Macmillan, 2013.
Tomes, Nancy. "Devils in the Heart: A Nineteenth-Century Perspective on Women and Depression." *Transactions and Studies of the College of Physicians of Philadelphia* 13, no. 4 (1991): 363–86.
———. *A Generous Confidence: Thomas Story Kirkbride and the Art of Asylum Keeping, 1840–1883*. Cambridge University Press, 1984.
Tomlinson, Stephen, and Kevin Windham. "Northern Piety and Southern Honor: Alva Woods and the Problem of Discipline at the University of Alabama, 1831–1837." *Perspectives on the History of Higher Education* 25, no. 1 (2006): 1–42.
Toplin, Robert Brent. "Between Black and White: Attitudes Toward Southern Mulattoes, 1830–1861." *Journal of Southern History* 45, no. 2 (1979): 185–200.
Troxler, Carole Watterson, and William Murray Vincent, ed. *Shuttle and Plow: A History of Alamance County, North Carolina*. Alamance County Historical Association, 1999.
Tushnet, Mark V. *Slave Law in the American South: State v. Mann in History and Literature*. University Press of Kansas, 2003.
Van Zandt, A[braham] B[rooks]. *"The Elect Lady": A Memoir of Mrs. Susan Catharine Bott of Petersburg, Va*. Presbyterian Board of Publication, 1857.

von Daacke, Kirt. *Freedom Has a Face: Race, Identity and Community in Jefferson's Virginia*. University of Virginia Press, 2012.

Wagoner, Jennings L., Jr. "Honor and Dishonor at Mr. Jefferson's University: The Antebellum Years." *History of Education Quarterly* 26, no. 2 (1986): 155–79.

Wakelyn, Jon L. "Antebellum College Life and the Relations Between Fathers and Sons." In *The Web of Southern Relations: Women, Family, and Education*, edited by Walter J. Fraser, R. Frank Saunders Jr., and Jon L. Wakelyn, 107–26. University of Georgia Press, 1985.

Warbasse, Elizabeth Bowles. *The Changing Legal Rights of Married Women, 1800–1861*. Garland, 1987.

Ward, H. Trawick, and R. P. Stephen Davis Jr. *Indian Communities on the North Carolina Piedmont, A.D. 1000–1700*. Research Laboratories of Anthropology, University of North Carolina, 1993.

Weithoff, William E. *The Insolent Slave*. University of South Carolina Press, 2002.

Welter, Barbara. "Female Complaints: Medical Views of American Women (1790–1865)." In *Dimity Convictions: The American Woman in the Nineteenth Century*, edited by Barbara Welter, 57–70. Ohio University Press, 1976.

West, Emily. *Chains of Love: Slave Couples in Antebellum South Carolina*. University of Illinois Press, 2004.

———. *In Family or Freedom: People of Color in the Antebellum South*. University of Kentucky Press, 2012.

White, Barbara McGhee. *Somebody Knows My Name: Marriages of Freed People in North Carolina County by County*. 2 Vols. Iberion, 1995.

White, Deborah Gray. *Ar'n't I a Woman?: Female Slaves in the Plantation South*. W. W. Norton, 1985.

White, Luise. *Speaking with Vampires: Rumor and History in Colonial Africa*. University of California Press, 2000.

Williamson, Walter P. "The Bingham School." In *Our Living and Our Dead*, vol. 2, 371–72. The Society, 1875.

Wood, Alice Davis. *Dr. Francis Stribling and Moral Medicine: Curing the Insane at Virginia's Western State Hospital, 1836–1874*. GalileoGranniny, 2004.

Wood, Ann Douglas. "'The Fashionable Diseases': Women's Complaints and Their Treatment in Nineteenth-Century America." *Journal of Interdisciplinary History* 4, no. 1 (1973): 25–52.

Wood, Peter H. *"When the Roll Is Called Up Yonder": Black History in Hillsborough, North Carolina*. [Hillsborough, N.C.]: P. P., 2005.

Wyatt-Brown, Bertram. *Southern Honor: Ethics and Behavior in the Old South*. Oxford University Press, 1982.

Yanuck, Julius. "Thomas Ruffin and North Carolina Slave Law." *Journal of Southern History* 21, no. 4 (1995): 456–75.

Zwelling, Shomer S. *Quest for a Cure: The Public Hospital in Williamsburg, Virginia, 1773–1885*. Colonial Williamsburg Foundation, 1985.

INDEX

abroad marriage, 25, 98
African Methodist Episcopalian Church (AME), 119–20
Agnes (Aggy), 95, 97
Alfred, 89
Allison, James, 48
Almeda Schoolhouse, 90
Anderson, James, 117
Anderson, Jean Bradley, 11
Anderson, Tommy, 104
Anderson, Walker, 64
Anderson, William E., 42, 64
Andrews, Joseph, 19
Ann, 100, 101
"Appeal to the Colored Citizens of the World," 22
apprenticeship, 40–42, 48, 50, 52, 58, 64
Ashe, Sarah Ann, 72–73
Aunt Feriby, 101

Bacon, Nathaniel, 1
Baker, Susan Esther, 20, 166n24
Baptists, 117
Barringer, Paul, 89
Battle, Kemp Plummer, 33
Beecher, Eunice White Bullard, 66–67
Behind the Scenes, 94, 97–98
Benton, Samuel, 50
Berlin, Ira, 40
Berry, Job, 114–21, 151–52
Berry, John, 117
Berry, Rebecca Nash, 116, 117, 187n102
Berry, Richard, 116
Beverly, Heywood, 118
Bingham, Robert (son of William James), 88
Bingham, William, 82–83

Bingham, William (son of William James), 88
Bingham, William James (son of William): background of, 83–84; disciplinary regimen of, 82, 85–88, 95, 148; insanity of, 89, 123–25, 150; mentioned, 153
Bingham School, 65, 82, 83, 84, 87, 89
Bishop, George, 117
Boles, John, 43
Bowers, William G., 130
brain fever, 131
Bridges, James, 102, 104
Bridget, 108–109, 151
Brown, Henry N., 118
Buchan, William, 124
Burgwin, George W. B., 114–15, 116
Burgwin, Nathaniel Hill, 90, 115
Burke, Mary [Polly], 65
Burnside, 109
Burwell, Anna Robertson (Nannie), 30, 90, 178n15
Burwell, Fanny, 71
Burwell, John Bott, 69, 80, 82, 90, 143, 177–78n15
Burwell, Margaret Anna: description of, 70; gossip and, 66–67, 72, 73, 149, 150, 151; relationship with Elizabeth Hobbs Keckly, 94–98; relationship with Hannah, 101–4; relationship with Mary Ann, 98–101; role as schoolmistress, 63–64, 65–66, 67–68, 70–73, 77, 78, 80; mentioned, 11, 108
Burwell, Mary Susan (Molly), 67, 73, 90, 177–78n15
Burwell, Robert: as enslaver 94, 99, 103, 148; personality of 69–70; relationship with Elizabeth Keckly, 95, 97, 98; role

Burwell, Robert (*continued*)
    as Presbyterian pastor, 66, 133; role as schoolmaster, 68, 72, 75, 76, 80, 142, 150
Burwell School: administration of, 68–69, 70–73; community support of, 68; curriculum of, 74–75, 179n52; discipline in 80–81; reputation of, 89; students in, 63, 67–68, 128, 137; student life in, 73–78; mentioned, 11, 65, 151

cabinet making, 41–42
Cain, William, 115
Caldwell, Tod R., 120
Caldwell Institute, 65, 72, 76, 81–82, 89–90
Cameron, Anne (Nancy), 68, 133, 135, 136, 192n60
Cameron, Duncan, 7, 15, 133, 136, 189n6
Cameron, Mildred, 193n73
Cameron, Paul, 109, 110–11, 113
Cameron, Slit, 38
Cameron, William, 133, 136, 137
Caroline, 110
Carrington, Bettie, 75, 80
Caudle, Green, 38
Chambers, Benjamin, 106
Charlotte Female Academy (Queen's University of Charlotte), 80, 100, 104
Chavers, Lee, 52, 175n59
Chaves, Evans, 49
Chavis, Eliza, 68, 102
Chavis, William, 170n6
Chavois, Cuoni, 38
Chesnut, Mary Boykin, 39
Chilton, Mark, 11
Churton Street, 9, 154
Claiborne, James, 181n94
Coit, Elizabeth, 78
Colonial Inn, 9, 154
Cook, John H., 51–52
Compromise of 1850, 52
Copeland, Delilah. *See* Evans, Delilah
Copeland, Eli, 172n37
Copeland, John, 46, 172n37, 173n42
Copeland, John Jr., 53–54
Copeland, William, 172n37
corporal punishment. *See* Discipline

Cowen, Caroline, 67–68
Crabtree, Henry, 58, 176n79
Crain, Thomas D., 29
Credit, 29–30, 48–50
Croom, Alexander, 86–87
Crow, Anna Robertson. *See* Burwell, Anna Robertson
Curtis, Moses Ashley, 43–45, 68, 182n106
Cutler, Helen R., 67

Day, Reuben, 24, 25, 26
Day, Thomas, 41, 42, 47
DeRossett, Armand, 44
disability studies, 189n8
discipline: of the enslaved, 15, 19, 44, 94–95, 105; of students, 80–82, 83, 85–89
Domestic Medicine, 124
Dudley, Edward Bishop, 43
Dunaway, Stewart, 11

Easley, Mary, 78
Eastern Lunatic Asylum (Williamsburg, VA), 194n98
Eidenier, Betty, 11
Emancipation Proclamation, 112
Engstrom, Mary Claire, 10–11, 190n30
Eno Cotton Mill, 154
Eno River, 1, 153, 154
Episcopalians, 43
Evans, Delilah, 39, 40, 45–46, 47
Evans, Fanny, 39–40, 41, 42, 173n26
Evans, Henrietta Leary, 47, 52, 172n36
Evans, Henry: birth of, 39; business of, 42, 47–50, 173n45; education of, 40, 41–42, 172n23; Episcopal Church membership, 43, 45; move to Ohio, 50–52; political activities of, 53–54, 175n67; mentioned, 37, 151
Evans, Jane, 39, 40, 52
Evans, Julia, 47, 52
Evans, Lizzy, 47, 52
Evans, Matthew, 47, 52
Evans, Sarah, 47, 52
Evans, Sarah Jane Leary, 51, 52
Evans, Wilson Bruce, 39, 40, 47, 51, 52, 53–54, 173n44

Faddis, Thomas Jefferson, 29
Faucette, Lindsay, 112, 114
Faucette, Margaret, 114
Faucette, William, 114
Field Order no. 15, 113
Fisher, Edward C., 139
Fitzgerald, Robert, 33, 118, 188n114
Flower Place plantation, 31, 165n8
Franklin, John Hope, 40
Freedman's Bureau, 112, 153
Freedman's school, 117–18
Freeland, Patsy, 100
Freeman, Henry, 38
Freeman, Patsy, 52
Friend, Craig, 4
Friends Freedmen's Association, 118
From Dawn to Daylight, 66–67
Fugitive Slave Act, 52
furniture making, 41–42

Garland, Anne, 117
Garrett, Mary, 80
Garrison, William Lloyd, 23
George (Kirkland, son of Elizabeth Keckly), 97, 117, 151, 183–84n10
Glass, Lizzie, 78, 180n65
Glymph, Thavolia, 19
gossip, 4–7, 21–22, 147–52, 163–64n8, 164n10
Graebner, Brooks, 11
Graham, William, 47
Grant, Ulysses S., 120
Great Indian Trading Path, 1
Great Rebellion of 1805, 82
Green, William Mercer, 20, 43, 68, 80–81, 115, 126
Greensboro Female College, 90

Hamilton, J. G. de Roulhac, 10
Hannah, 101–4, 108, 151, 184n37
Harriet. *See* Smith, Harriet
Harris, B. V., 118
Harry, 57
Heartt, Dennis, 68
Hedricks, Christopher, 4
Herbert, Mary Lighton, 67

Hermitage plantation, 107, 108
Hillsborough, NC: Civil War and, 111–12, 152–53; description of, 1, 7, 9–10, 17, 123, 148, 149, 154–55; education in, 63–65; Free Blacks in, 37–39, 50–51, 60–61; ordinances of, 50; post–Civil War in, 153–54; slave rebellion in, 22–23, 108–9, 123
Hillsborough Academy, 65, 82–83, 84–85, 86–87, 89, 115, 164n17
Hillsborough Female Academy, 20, 30, 65, 80–81, 89, 179n52
Hillsborough Presbyterian Church, 22
Historic Hillsborough Commission, 11
historical sources, 10–13
Hobbs, Elizabeth. *See* Keckly, Elizabeth "Lizzie" Hobbs
Hodge, Hugh Lenox, 127, 128–29, 130, 137, 193n73
Hofstra, Warren, 4
Holden, William W., 120
Hooper, William, 106–7
Howerton, Thomas, 68
Hunt, Thomas, 104, 185n44
Huske, Bell Norwood. *See* Norwood, Annabella

insane asylums, 127, 133–34, 140, 142–43, 194n98
insanity, 124, 125
Ives, Levi Silliman, 45, 115

Jackson, James, 50, 174n55
Jackson, Nancy, 52
Jackson, Samuel, 129
Jacobs, Harriet, 93
Jane, 101
James Mayho v. James H. Whitson and Abner Peace, 58–60
Jeffreys, Uriah, 41
Jeffrys, Serena, 52
Jesse, 110
Johnston, Joseph E., 112
Jones, Allen, 46, 173n41, 173n42
Jones, Bernie, 59
Jones, Cadwallader, 61

Jones, Delia. *See* Smith, Delia Jones
Jones, Francis, 17, 18, 28, 165n8
Jones, Mary Cameron, 72, 179n43
Jones, Pride, 56, 179n43
Jones, Thomas P., 19
Jones Grove plantation, 31, 165n8
Jottings from Life, 67
Julia, 103

Keckley, James, 97
Keckly, Elizabeth "Lizzie" Hobbs: author of *Behind the Scenes*, 97–98; enslavement of, 94–97, 177n6; gossip and, 95, 97, 151; name of, 117, 183n4; son George, 97, 183n10; mentioned, 104, 108, 131
Kell, William, 24
Kerr, Annie, 74
Kinzer, Robert, 7
Kirby, Ned, 33
Kirkland, Alexander McKenzie, 95–96, 123–24, 131–32, 136, 183n10
Kirkland, Anna Cameron, 65, 130–37, 138–43, 144, 150
Kirkland, Anne, 104
Kirkland, John, 51–52
Kirkland, John U., 115
Kirkland, Phebe, 126–27, 128, 130, 150
Kirkland, Robert, 131
Kirkland, William, 7, 43, 104, 126, 131
Kollock, Sarah, 67, 90, 180n71
Ku Klux Klan, 120

Lane, John, 47, 173n42
Lane, Lunsford, 46
Latimer, C. M., 139
Lawson John, 2
Leary, Henrietta. *See* Evans, Henrietta Leary
Leary, Lewis Sheridan, 54
Leary, Matthew, 47, 173n43
Leary, Sarah Jane. *See* Evans, Sarah Jane Leary
Lebsock, Suzanne, 39
Liberator, The, 23
Lincoln, Mary Todd, 97
Long, Mary Alves, 142–43, 164n23
Long, Osmund F., 100, 139

Lucy, 101
Lyon, John F., 48

McCollum, Levi, 176n79
McKethan, Alfred M., 51–52
McLester, Maggie, 127, 189n13
McLester, Nelson, 127, 189n13
Mallett Family (Chapel Hill), 32
Mallett Family (Fayetteville), 32, 33
Mangum, William P., 17
Margaret Lane Cemetery, 60–61, 155
Married women's property rights, 70, 178n34
Martin, Henry, 38
Martin, Percy Ann, 171n14
Marshall, Joseph, 41, 172n22
Mary Ann, 98–101, 104, 108, 109, 151
Mayo, Anderson, 37, 54, 56–58, 151, 175n71
Mayo, Catherine, 56, 57, 176n77
Mayo, James (Jim), 37, 56, 58–60, 151
Mayo, Jesse Tatum, 56, 57–58, 175n71
Mayo, Melinda, 48, 174n50
Mayo, Richard, 38
Mayo, Simmons, 48, 174n50
Mayo, Umstead, 68
Mayo, William, 48, 174n50
Mebane, Giles, 83
Methodists, 43
Mickle, Andrew, 115
midwives, 25
Milteer, Warren, 37
Minnis, John R., 50
Minor, Julia, 68
Mitchell, 98, 99
Mitchell, Adaline, 48, 151, 174n51
Mitchell, Edith, 52
Mitchell, John B., 48
Mitchell, Mary, 174n51
Mitchell, William, 48, 52
Moore, Sarah S., 115, 187n101
Moore, Stephen, 115
moral treatment, 127–28
Morphis, Henry, 33
Morris, Janie, 11
Murphey, Archibald, 104, 105, 107, 108, 121

Murphy, Mary B., 73, 76, 177n1
Murphy, Susan, 73, 76, 78
Murray, Pauli, 24, 26, 27, 28, 31–32

Nash, Ann Strudwick, 68–69
Nash, M. G., 130, 190n30
Nash, Rebecca. *See* Berry, Rebecca Nash
Nash-Kollock School, 90
Nat Turner Rebellion, 46, 108, 148
New Voyage to Carolina, 2
New York State Lunatic Asylum (Utica), 142
North Carolina Hospital for the Insane (Raleigh), 89, 90, 124, 139, 143
North Carolina Medical Association, 90
Norwood, Annabella (Anna): attended Burwell School, 67; as an enslaver, 110, 116; insanity of, 137–38, 150; relationship with Rebecca Ruffin, 109, 113
Norwood, Annabella (Bell), 64, 75, 76, 90, 137–38
Norwood, John Wall: after the Civil War, 113, 114, 153; as a debt collector, 29; as an enslaver, 109, 110, 116; mentioned, 137
Norwood, Joseph, 115
Norwood, Robina, 29, 110, 137
Norwood, Walter A., 165n6
Norwood, William, 63, 78–79, 105, 109
November, 106–107, 185n37

Oaklands. *See* Price Creek plantation
Oberlin, 47, 52, 53–54
Oberlin College, 118
Oberlin-Wellington Rescue, 53–54
Occaneechi, 1–3, 155, 163n1
Old King Street Tavern, 9
"Old Slave Cemetery," 60–61, 155
Orange County, NC, 3, 148
opiates, 125, 134, 136, 137, 138
Owsley, Frank, 164n23
overseers, 104–105, 108

Page, Walter Hines, 89, 90, 153–54
Palmer, James M., 50, 176n79
Palmer, Mary, 100

Patsy, 18
Peace, Abner, 58–60
Peace Institute (William Peace University), 80, 142
Pearce, Mary, 75
personal liberty laws, 53
Pettigrew, Charles, 22
Pettigrew, Ebenezer, 85–86
Pettigrew, James Johnston, 85–86, 87
Pettigrew, William, 85
Phillip, 102, 103
Polke, Henry, 119, 120
Pompey, 57, 58
Poplar Hill plantation, 105, 137
Porter, Issac, 112, 186n79
Pratt, Moses S., 41
Presbyterians, 43
Price, John, 53
Price Creek (Oaklands) plantation, 28, 29, 30, 31, 32, 33, 165n8
psychiatry, 144

Raleigh Regulators, 46
rape, 26–27
Reeves, Fred, 57
Reid, David Settle, 51
Reiss, Benjamin, 142
reputation, 6–7, 149–51
Revels, Susan, 41
Rice, Elizabeth, 129
Robertson, Lucy Henderson Owen, 90
romantic friendships, 20, 167n28
Ruffin, Anne, 109
Ruffin, Catharine, 15, 131
Ruffin, Jesse: enslavement of, 104–7, 109, 110–11; gossip and, 151–52; post-Civil War life of, 112–14, 117
Ruffin, Julia, 109
Ruffin, Margaret, 109
Ruffin, Nancy, 109
Ruffin, Peter Brown, 61
Ruffin, Rebecca (Beccy), 105–7, 109–10, 112, 113, 137
Ruffin, Thomas: after the Civil War, 113–114; background of, 104; as an enslaver,

Ruffin, Thomas (*continued*)
106–108, 148; gossip and, 105, 121, 150, 152; judicial decisions of, 41, 183n5; mentioned, 7, 15, 109, 153
rumor, 5–7, 147–52
Rutman, Anita C., 3, 4
Rutman, Darrett, 3, 4

Sallie, 110
Sally, 59
Schwartz, Marie Jenkins, 100
sex education, 125–26
Sherman, William T., 112, 113
silk production, 55–56
slave catchers, 53–54
slave rebellions, 22–23, 108. *See also* Nat Turner Rebellion
slavery in Hillsborough, 18
slavery in Orange County, 18
small towns, 3–4, 147
Smith, Annette, 31, 32, 33
Smith, Baily, 46
Smith, Cornelia, 27, 29, 31, 32, 33, 188n114
Smith, Delia Jones: background of, 17–18; church membership of, 165n8; death of, 31; property of, 29; relationship with Harriet, 24, 26; as subject of gossip, 18, 149; mentioned, 34
Smith, Emma, 28, 31, 32, 33
Smith, Frank: birth of, 168n48; in Civil War, 32; death of, 33; description of, 25; gossip about, 28, 34, 152; property of, 29, 31; relationship with Harriet, 26, 27–28; mentioned 57
Smith, Harriet: background of, 24–25; children of, 27, 28, 31, 32–33; death of, 32; gossip about, 24, 26, 34, 152; rape of, 26–28; sale of, 24, 29; mentioned, 98
Smith, James Strudwick: background of, 15–18, 20, 165n6; bankruptcy of, 28–30, 128; birth of, 165n3; death of, 31; medical practice of, 25, 126–27; relationship with Harriet, 24–25, 26; mentioned, 57
Smith, Julius, 25, 26, 29, 31
Smith, Laura, 31, 32, 33
Smith, Lou, 73

Smith, Mary Ruffin: birth of, 165n2; background of, 15, 18; death of, 33, 170n91; description of, 18, 20; gossip about, 15, 21, 23–24, 31–32, 34–35, 148, 149–50; property of, 18, 29, 31, 32, 169n77; relationship with Harriet, 24, 26, 27, 31, 152; relationship with Maria Spear, 15, 20–21, 30, 31, 32–34; mentioned, 79
Smith, Sid: birth of, 168n48; death of, 32; description of, 25–26; gossip about 26, 28, 32, 34, 152; property of, 31; relationship with Harriet, 26–27
Society of Friends (Philadelphia), 117, 188n111
South Carolina Lunatic Asylum (Columbia), 142
Southern Historical Collection, 10–11
Spear, Maria, 17, 32, 65; background of 19–20, 166n23, 166n24; relationship with Mary Ruffin Smith, 15, 20–21, 30, 31, 32–34
Spear, Mary Ann, 20, 166n23
St. Matthew's Episcopal Church, 43, 47, 115, 116, 174n46
Stagville plantation, 109
State v. Anderson Mayo, a free negro, 57–58
State v. Mann, 183n5
"Study of an Old Southern Borough," 154
Stribling, Francis T., 134, 137
Strudwick, Edmund: accomplishments of, 90; relationship with John Knox Witherspoon, 128; treatment of Alexander Kirkland, 131; treatment of Mary Witherspooon, 128; treatment of Phebe Kirkland, 126, 127; mentioned, 57, 100, 115, 165n6
Strudwick, Manuel, 58
Strudwick, Mary Susan. *See* Burwell, Mary Susan
Strudwick, William F., 15, 28, 165n3
Swain, David, 47

Tatum, Absolum, 59–60
Tatum, Sally, 56
Taylor, James, 165n3
Thirteenth Amendment, 112

Thompson, William, 47
Tillinghast, John, 90
Tillinghast, William, 137
Tolbert, Lisa, 4
Toole, Grey, 33
Turner, Israel, 139
Turner, Josiah, Sr., 29–30
Turner, Sophia, 144
Turner, Thomas H., 165n6
Turrentine, James, 29–30, 57
Tusculum plantation, 55, 64, 128, 130

Underground railroad, 54
University of North Carolina, 82

Valentine, James, 38
Valentine, Mornell, 38
Vampill, Rudolph, 77, 180n65
Vasseur, Charlotte, 68
Von Daacke, Kirt, 38

Waddell, De Bernier, 120–21
Waddell, Francis, 115
Waddell, Haynes, 78–79, 180n75
Waddell, Hugh, 115, 116, 120, 129
Waddell, Mary, 65, 78–79
Waddell, Susan, 129, 193n73
Wadesborough Female Academy, 19
Walker, David, 22
Walker, Mag, 75
Walker, Mary, 164n15
Warrenton Female Academy, 19
Watkins, Lizzie, 80
Webb, Henry Young, 165n6

Webb, James: business activities of, 7, 15, 51, 165n6; medical practice of, 126, 127; relationship with James Strudwick Smith, 17; support for education, 64, 65
Webb, James Jr., 57
Webb, Mary, 65, 67
Webb, Sawney (William Robert), 87, 90
Webb, Susan A., 90
Webb, Thomas, 51, 110, 174n51
Webb, William, 165n6
Webb School at Bell Buckle, 90
West, Emily, 171n14
Western State Hospital for the Insane (Staunton, VA), 133, 134, 138
White, Deborah Gray, 27
Whitson, William H., 58–60
Wiethoff, William, 108
William, 100
Williams, S. B., 119–20
Wilson, Alexander, 72, 76, 81–82, 90
Wilson, John, 39–40, 41, 42, 171n15, 172n28, 176n74
Witherspoon, John Knox: attempts at silk production, 55–56; background of, 54–55, 64; daughter's illness, 128–30; death of, 130; involvement in Jesse Tatum Mayo's murder, 56–58; as a schoolmaster, 64–65; mentioned, 44
Witherspoon, Mary, 128–30, 150, 193n73
Witherspoon, Susan Kollock, 128–30
Wood, Peter H., 11

www.ingramcontent.com/pod-product-compliance
Lightning Source LLC
Chambersburg PA
CBHW020814230426
43666CB00007B/1007